INSPIRED

'My life is not a big life; in fact, nowadays it is a very ordinary, though privileged one. But it wasn't always so.' – **Herman Mashaba**

INSPIRED

Remarkable South Africans share their stories

JENNIFER LINDSEY-RENTON

MACMILLAN

First published in 2014 by Pan Macmillan South Africa
Private Bag X19
Northlands
Johannesburg
2116

www.panmacmillan.co.za

ISBN 978-1-77010-380-1
e-Book ISBN 978-1-77010-381-8

Editing by Sean Fraser
Proofreading by Jane Bowman
Design and typesetting by Karen Lilje, Hybrid Creative
Cover design by K4
Cover image from iStock

Printed and bound by Creda

Gordon Institute of Business Science
University of Pretoria

Published in association with the
Gordon Institute of Business Science (GIBS)

CONTENTS

CONTENTS

FOREWORD

The stories of people who rise from adversity into prominent positions of leadership must be told, and importantly, must be told well. A nation like ours must know of the pathways; must recognise that leadership is neither a birth defect nor the result of a lottery of birth. The more stories we tell, the easier it will be for successive generations to identify with individuals from similar circumstances. This identification is an almost necessary condition to wage a new struggle for excellence, and by implication, against mediocrity.

This anthology of stories of those among us who inspire is helpful for a number of reasons. Its richness is a consequence, in part, of its diversity. It also invites the reader to appreciate the similarities, rather than focus on the distinguishing features. We see in each of the stories the desire to excel, and this compilation allows us to understand that this desire to excel is not the same as the ruthless pursuit to 'stop at nothing', or to 'step or stomp on anybody in our path'.

All of the individuals here excel almost as a consequence of their caring. None of them has reached his or her position by either obsequiousness, or by suffering fools. Each of the stories is of courage because this is an essential ingredient of each individual who inspires. The best examples of courage you will find here are of the soft variants – the ability to apologise for error, or the aptitude to persuade others of the need to change course.

The stories about the most effective leaders are those of people who lead as a consequence of their desire for excellence, rather than the desire for leadership in order to wield power.

I want to thank the Gordon Institute of Business Science and Jennifer Lindsey-Renton for writing this compilation of inspiring life stories and, more importantly, I want to thank the subjects of these stories for the inspiration that their lives provide to the rest of us.

This book should assist in the conscious development of the next leadership cadre.

Trevor Manuel
August 2014

INTRODUCTION

RIGHT TIME, RIGHT PLACE, RIGHT LEADERS

NICK BINEDELL

Countries in transition – which might describe most of the world and particularly post-apartheid South Africa – can be divided broadly into those with a plan or strategy for success and, to be frank, those that are just flailing around. To my mind, the key differentiator of successful countries in transition comes down to a potent mix of institutions and leadership.

Institutions, as we now all know, play a vital role in the transformation of societies, as they grapple with the comprehensive set of both global and local challenges. These challenges range from socio-economic and political issues to ethnic, racial and religious questions; technological impacts; and the challenges and stresses of the increased urbanisation of populations – on individuals, resources and infrastructure. What we see are varying degrees of success around the world in how to achieve this transition in a conflict-minimal way.

Certainly, all change involves friction and all change has the potential to become conflicted. We know, too, that for societies to move swiftly into new verdant pastures, strong but adaptive institutions are necessary.

On the other hand, those institutions, and society in general, need to be inspired, led and managed by strong leaders; leaders who are able to knit together a narrative – a rich fabric, if you will – that reflects the time we are in and the work they need to do to fashion an agenda, develop a strategy, create a coherent story and vision, and lead an organisation that is lively, energetic, innovative and imaginative. To achieve this, personal qualities are absolutely critical.

Unpacking what those qualities are can be a complex web, and yet as academics and business people we constantly seek to make sense of the multifaceted nature of leadership. In the fourth quarter 2013 issue of the Gordon Institute of Business Science's *Acumen* magazine, one of our professors, Karl Hofmeyr, and Chris van Melle Kamp from leadership consulting firm Spencer Stuart, unveiled a collaborative research project they had undertaken into the subject. Based on discussions with 32 South African CEOs, their research shone the light on issues such as the evolution of leaders versus those who only 'got into their groove' once they found the company or industry fit that worked for them.

Of course themes such as having a clear strategy and taking advantage of opportunities came up, as did the importance of people. As one CEO told the researchers: 'A leader's job is 90 per cent people. Your job is to get results through them.' Naturally that raises all sorts of areas for discussion, ranging from 'soft skills' and EQ, to simply recruiting the right people for the job.

In the South African context, a leader's place within the broader society was also firmly brought home. As the research showed, 'Social investment, black economic empowerment and the broader transformation imperative all demand close attention and play out in countless ways that would be bewildering – and deeply frustrating – for chief executives in other settings. South African business leaders have to contend with a set of issues that their peers in other markets do not, and they must possess a number of other attributes to match,' including issues relating to transformation, diversity, motivation, hope, ethics and integrity. The modern-day parlance for this is sustainability, which is as much about good and ethical leadership as it is about the institutions that support society.

So the link between good leaders and good institutions is indeed a profoundly important one as we enter the long race of the twenty-first century. And it's why we need to increasingly highlight our accomplishments; those marriages between leadership and institutional success that show us the way forward and how it can be done.

This book reflects the stories of a group of extraordinary South Africans who have played or are playing a role in cajoling, inspiring, provoking and challenging us to do better; to do better than our history, to be better than we are doing now, and to rise to the expectations that younger generations – which will inevitably follow – are willing us to do.

I remember a conversation from some years ago when I made the point that South Africa must achieve consensus across generations, especially in light of our income inequalities, or we will face enormous social and political pressures. This makes connecting people across generations vitally important, which is why at GIBS we engage with schoolchildren – the leaders of tomorrow – as much as we do, to draw them into these conversations early on and, most critically, to listen to what they have to say.

As today's leaders, we need to be in touch with the aspirations and fears of the next generation. This is not a chore; it is exciting and energising to tap into the ideas of these dynamic and forward-thinking youngsters. Inevitably, one way or another, they are going to lead, so let's work with them now rather than later.

Yet in spite of this realisation, not a day or week goes by on our busy campus where one doesn't have a sense that there is so much more latent potential to do better. This is being driven by the urgent demands of those who remain disenfranchised, or who are from another generation and are looking at the leaders of today and wondering whether this generation of leaders is sufficiently values-driven, visionary and energetic to get the job done.

The stories captured in this volume are a small part of the type of conversation, the type of example and the type of drive that this nation needs to be a successful country in transition.

Even with the best will in the world, it is impossible to distinguish between the life experience of a Herman Mashaba, a Carrol Boyes, a Michael Jordaan or a Sizwe Nxasana, nor can one overstate the leadership qualities of a man such as Gary Kirsten, who played out his profession under the public microscope. Each of these individuals contributes to the rich tapestry that is South Africa's collective history and each one brings lessons of leadership, tenacity, vision and social influences to bear on this book and its stories.

Ask each of these leaders what differentiates them from the pack and you'll get myriad responses. For a man such as Terence Nombembe, South Africa's previous auditor-general, it boiled down to drive, focus and patience. As he says: 'I take my patience as an amazing strength in the kind of environment we live in, because if you're not patient you are going to lose people and become disconnected from reality.'

For Ferial Haffajee, indomitable editor of *City Press*, it boils down to curiosity and a constant drive to push the boundaries; even when you doubt yourself. I love the element of her story when she discusses the importance of testing your personal and professional limits: 'I usually feel like I have possessed, evaluated and made my decision, but of course every Sunday I wonder if I used the right words and I remake the paper in my head constantly. But I've learned as a journalist that you need to push boundaries. We've been taken to court many, many times for uncovering things and that just comes with the turf. I've had to apologise a couple of times … I grew up in a place where bullying was pretty common so I have grown to hate it; I don't take kindly to people trying to push me around.'

Something these leaders do have in common is a desire to serve, to make a difference, to give back. Businesswoman Wendy Luhabe highlights this beautifully when she says: 'My observation is that leaders who are driven by their ego tend to default a lot more than leaders who are driven by purpose. It requires consciousness to make sure that how you lead and how you make an impact on the world is always premised on what your purpose is in the world. All leaders need vision to fight against the moral degeneration we see everywhere in society.'

Many of the leaders highlighted in these pages are friends of GIBS; they know our campus and our students well and we've been privileged to host them at functions, forums and conferences over the years. The uniqueness of their stories and the individuality of their approaches to leadership never cease to amaze and this continues to reinforce the fact that no leader can copy another.

But, after years of examining my own leadership style and that of others, I can confidently say that all leaders essentially learn to lead in two different and equally important ways. The first is they have to find their own rhythm and come to terms with their own values; they have to understand their own style and the contribution they can make. At the same time, that style and approach have to find fertile ground at the right place and at the right time.

Smart leaders understand that. They know that they have to understand place – where they are, where their country is, and where the world around them is positioned – in order to resonate with the practical realities of what lies ahead of them. This grounding is vital. If leadership is naïve and gets too disconnected from reality, then extraordinarily dangerous experiments are conducted. Similarly, if leadership is too focused on the now, or indeed on the past, then there is insufficient dynamism and it does not bring enough vitality and enthusiasm to the challenge. So these two dimensions of the individual, and the time and place they are in, have to fit together in an authentic way.

But the great thing about leadership – and you only have to look to the likes of Winston Churchill, our own Nelson Mandela, Mahatma Gandhi and Mother Teresa as examples – is that it ultimately boils down to connections. Joining with people, then taking them forward. Harvard University's Marty Linsky, who is an extraordinary leader himself, once said to me: 'All leaders must disappoint their followers at a rate their followers can handle.' So it's about being ahead of the game.

South Africa is in the early decades of this game; of our long march to success. Although 20 years of democracy have been celebrated, it is only when we can look back after 100 years that we might have a sense of whether the leaders we have now, and in the next 10 or 20 years, were in fact right for the challenges they faced. Right now that remains an open question because, in so many ways, South Africa has not closed ranks and created unity. We have not found our true purpose or our true place in the world.

I hope the readers of this book are encouraged and challenged by these stories and that the voices in these chapters whisper in their ear the need to act swiftly and make a difference.

Nick Binedell

August 2014

Having started his professional life in sales and general management within the Barlow Rand Group, **PROFESSOR NICK BINEDELL** changed focus 20 years ago to concentrate on the area of business education, bringing his personal insights, experience and business acumen to bear on the way South African leaders are equipped to compete in the dynamic world of global business. This passion for business education led him to found the Gordon Institute of Business Science (GIBS) in 2000.

TURNING FORM INTO FUNCTION

CARROL BOYES

SPLICING GENES

Such is her talent that one might imagine that Carrol Boyes' fascination with art began before she could walk and talk, yet it was only when she was nine years old that her love affair began. 'I was completely intrigued by the fact that people could draw a likeness of a person or animal, and from that moment I was hooked. I didn't study art at school, though, because at the end of Standard 7 we had to choose between Maths and Art, and if you wanted to go to university you had to do Maths. Art was just something I was passionate about and every evening and weekend I would draw and paint instead of doing my homework!'

Born in Cape Town in November 1954, at a young age Boyes moved with her family to a farm outside Pretoria where she attended an all-girls' school from Grade 1 right up to matric. Her mother gave up her own part-time work to look after Boyes and her two brothers when the family moved to Pretoria, while her father was a doctor and a farmer. Her dad, says Boyes, was the 'practical one' in the family who loved to fix things, while her mother's side of the family had a strong artistic streak in them. 'My maternal grandfather and his brothers were very creative and used to paint, so I think the combination of those two sides of my DNA landed me where I am today. On the practical side, it's not just the products I make that are functional, but I also really enjoy the manufacturing, the factory and getting involved in new ways of producing items.' Her father also taught her the value of hard work – a trait that she holds dear to this day.

Education was a 'non-negotiable' in the Boyes family. 'We were brought up in an environment where it was just expected of us that we were going to go to university to study. Expectations of women were different then than they are now, but from that perspective my brothers and I didn't have different criteria – it was taken for granted that we would all go to university and have a career.' Upon leaving school, Boyes enrolled at the University of Pretoria for a Fine Arts degree, initially planning to major in the History of Art and Drawing. Her plans took a turn in second year, however, when she became 'completely hooked and passionate about sculpture and sculpting', making this her major.

CASTLES IN THE AIR

It quickly became Boyes' dream to be a sculptor, so after graduating she got a job as a waitress during the day and at night she worked on her art. 'I had had quite a sheltered upbringing and barely survived that first year; I realised pretty quickly that this was not going to pay the bills.' At that, Boyes packed up and moved back to Cape Town, where she got a job teaching art to primary-school learners and English to high-school pupils at schools in Retreat and then Hout Bay. At the same time she did her teaching diploma by correspondence through Unisa, completing that in 1980. It was a time of great unrest in the country, which Boyes found harrowing. 'In the time I worked with those children I probably learned more myself than I ever taught them because I came from a completely non-politicised household. I saw the injustices that they and their families lived with every day. Those were the years that I really grew up.'

During her 11 years teaching every spare moment was spent sculpting, but it was only when she turned 35 that lightning struck. 'I suddenly had this idea that I should put my sculpture and something that is practical together. I believed that this was a way to be able to fulfil my creative desires but still be able to earn a living. When we eat our breakfast the spoon we touch should touch us, as well as be a quality piece that lasts a lifetime. I started making sculptural candlesticks and then moved to sculptural spoons, knives and forks. I was suddenly able to pay the bills – and that was all the impetus I needed.'

FOLLOW THE YELLOW-BRICK ROAD

In 1989, Boyes decided to take a leap of faith, and having paid off her debts and built up a nest egg to last her six months, she left her teaching position. 'There was a feeling of optimism and hope in the country and I felt it was time for me to do something new and different as well. When I decided to give up teaching to start my own business, my father was horrified! He insisted that artists don't have the ability to put food on the table and it took quite a number of years to convince him that this was a business that was sustainable.' Looking back, Boyes laughs at her naïvety that she thought a business could get off the ground in six months. 'I've subsequently learned that a lot of businesses take two years or more to turn a profit, but I didn't have that luxury. I don't know what I would have done if it hadn't worked in the first six months. I think one has to be a little bit crazy and take some risks to make it work, but I couldn't live with the regret if I hadn't taken the chance.' In fact, Boyes' lack of business experience and training meant that she did not even have a business plan when she started out.

For the first seven years Boyes struggled with the idea that this could work and kept wondering when the bubble would burst. When she had applied for an overdraft at the outset she was told that she would only be granted a loan if her father stood surety for her – an idea that appalled her in her mid-thirties. So her decision to rather go it alone forced her to be conservative with her finances – something she is grateful for in hindsight. She would never have dreamed in those early days that before long she would have distributors and agents in 31 countries, employ over 500 people and have a range of over 1 500 products. 'In the beginning most things were a challenge, but I think my lack of confidence was one of the things I struggled with the most. I didn't believe in myself enough to make the choices that had vision, because I think I was wondering if I was doing the right thing and if it would last. I think if I had had more confidence in myself then I might have made better choices.' Her choices stood her in good stead, however, with the business growing by more than 100 per cent every year for the first six years. She attributes part of her success to making a decision early on to create a high-end product line, from marketing and positioning to pricing. 'I didn't want to compete with manufacturers at the low end of the market as it was too crowded and so many were doing it very well. I decided to only use the best materials and to create beautiful things that could be seen, felt, touched and used.'

Boyes has always taken inspiration from the human body, but is also in tune with the world around her. 'I look at life and things that pass me by – shapes, colours, just anything we look at every day. I can get inspiration from the strangest places, so it can be a hanger or a lamp post – just about anywhere. But the human body is still first and foremost my inspiration.'

Boyes also finds inspiration from Pablo Picasso. If she could, he would be the first person she would invite to dinner (with Richard Branson, the late Steve Jobs and Aung San Suu Kyi making up the rest of the guest list). 'Picasso was a huge talent. I love the way he lived a passionate, wonderful life and I love that he was creative right until the last night of his life. He was 91 when he died and when they found him the next morning he had been drawing before he went to sleep. I'd like to think that I'll be able to look back and have lived a fulfilled life like that.'

Learning on the job was a key aspect of Boyes' early career as a sculptor. 'You learn as you need to. If I suddenly needed to know how to fill in a UIF form or go to the bank for an overdraft, I would learn as the need arose. That's how I learned about business. I also read as much as I possibly could over the years. I'll never be an accountant, but I have basic logic and 2 + 2 needs to make 4 in my mind! But I know what works and what doesn't.' She also had to learn how to physically make her creations, taking what she knew about making jewellery but extrapolating that to a much bigger product. This required mastering very different equipment to what she was used to and she found all the naysayers extremely frustrating. 'I couldn't stand it when people used to tell me that because it hadn't been done before that it couldn't be done. I was determined to prove them wrong.'

After six months working alone in her home studio, Boyes was finding it a lonely process so moved into a shared studio with other artists. Another six months saw her move back into her own studio however, because by that time she could afford to hire someone to help her with the polishing and cleaning. 'Things were really growing at that point after the first year, and very soon it became three and then four people, and grew exponentially after that. It was strange, because I never planned to build an empire or create a huge organisation. I would have been quite happy being an artist and just paying my bills every month!' By the time Boyes and her employees had moved into every room in the house, including the hallway, she knew it was time to move to bigger premises. 'My partner was very kind and generous but it really did become impossible.'

As with many entrepreneurs, Boyes' initial growth was due in large part to a mixture of luck and a network. 'At the studio I worked at I met the daughter of an interior designer who had a small shop in Long Street. She suggested that I bring some of my sculptures down to the store to see if they would sell. I was very fortunate in that everything sold relatively quickly, and as the shop was considered to be 'hot and happening' in the interior world, I was extremely lucky to become one of their stable of artists. I really was in the right place at the right time, and I cannot emphasise enough how important word-of-mouth is for any business looking to grow.' This first growth spurt brought with it a burst of publicity and things really started taking off.

But the growth she experienced brought with it its own set of headaches, particularly when it came to finances and human resources. 'It's a constant battle trying to balance growth with debt. And then you have the growth in employee numbers as well – I find being responsible for employees extremely stressful.'

One of the best pieces of advice Boyes ever received was from Stanley Lewis, founder of the Foschini Group, who told her that having a business that looked like an inverted pyramid – with everything resting on her shoulders – was not sustainable. This meant finding people whom she thought were passionate about the business, as well as sharing her own passion. 'I think it's very important to be passionate about what you do. If you're going to inspire your people to follow you to the sun and stars, they need to feel your passion; they're not going to break boundaries and follow you there otherwise. They need to embrace your dream and your vision.'

Many of the people who started out with Boyes remain with the company to this day, but as the business has grown Boyes has made sure that her employees have too. 'We started off with people who could not speak English or Afrikaans, so the first thing we had to learn was how to communicate. Then some people wanted to learn to read and write, or drive, so that was the next step. Now we focus on developing different skills, but they're all equally important when it comes to empowering people.'

GROWTH AND DEVELOPMENT

By 1992 the business had 12 employees and had grown so big that her family were drafted in. With the head office based in Cape Town, Boyes built a manufacturing plant on her father and brothers' farm in Limpopo. She took on a general manager and a management team, which allowed her to focus on the areas she was more passionate about – although she still made time to visit the factory at least every other month. The large numbers of unemployed people in the area who had huge talent in wood sculpting also resulted in her hiring over 200 employees from the area. She later bought several premises in Cape Town, which are used for the factory and for operations, and her range grew to include various materials, including pewter, aluminium, stainless steel, zinc, wood, leather, glass and resin.

Boyes also began to look at exporting when South Africans in Australia, the UK and America began taking her products over and the demand spread. 'These

South African expats then started setting up businesses to sell my designs and they would ask to become agents for the brand.' This led to her decision to open her own retail store at the V&A Waterfront in Cape Town because she had a vision of how she wanted her products to be displayed and marketed, and strict guidelines were put in place regarding how the brand should be presented to customers. She did not realise at first just how difficult it would be to compete in other countries, regardless of whether they spoke the same language. 'Exporting really takes all your patience and resilience, not to mention finances!' Having learned about the different markets and worked out how things need to be done, her art is now found in countries ranging from Algeria to Zimbabwe and 29 others in-between.

In 1996, Boyes felt as if she had been 'stabbed in the heart' when she discovered that people had started to copy her work, but had to learn to 'deal with it'. In fact she now believes that it encouraged her to be even better. 'To be the best you have to constantly challenge yourself to produce new and exciting designs, never allowing yourself to become complacent.' As a first-mover, she was aware that she had a competitive edge over others, which she believes accounts in large part for her longevity and success.

GIVING BACK

Part of Boyes' passion for her art lies in developing talent in others, which is what led her to create a mentoring programme in 2003. This sees her bringing in young people from across the country to work alongside her, with the view that they can slowly but surely take over the creative reins of the company. 'There are many great people who can do the "business" side of the business much better than me, so I'm not worried about that. And my stepdaughters have a very good handle on the way the brand should be taken forward, so I nurture the creative side and am confident that everything is in place to take the company into the future.'

Boyes has no plans to completely leave the business anytime soon, but sees her role as being increasingly focused on the creative side. Being accustomed to being the final decision-maker, it has taken her 25 years to achieve the confidence to believe that hers is a sustainable business that 'doesn't all have to revolve around me. The business is my baby, but I want to take a back seat as far as the nitty-gritty running of the company is concerned. I want to be involved in the product development and the creative side, but still have feedback from the people on the ground here and get direction from the company as to what we need to focus on from a creative perspective. I don't see myself stopping creating. It's what I love.' Her intention is to continue focusing on the overseas market and opening more dedicated stores, while nurturing new talent and coming up with fresh designs.

The biggest challenge Boyes has faced, apart from a lack of self-confidence, has been to not take the business too much to heart. 'My work comes from my soul, so I take everything personally. It's not like I'm growing an orange and if it's less than perfect then that's okay; when it comes to one's creations, you are always trying to explore new things, you're putting your heart and soul and your mind on the line, and any little hiccup in the whole process can make one go on a bit of a wobbly.' Criticism is another area where Boyes has had to learn to toughen up, discovering along the way that sometimes she makes good products and sometimes she doesn't. 'If something is not going to work I have to accept that and get on and do something new. On those days when I get out on the wrong side of the bed, I still get shaken and feel hurt by criticism, but I am a million times better than I used to be. I never stop questioning myself and searching my soul, though. Every morning I wake up, I have to believe that today is the day that I'll make that perfect item that will be the best of my career!'

Stress is inevitable in any business, and Carrol Boyes (Pty) Ltd is no different. Boyes admits to having woken up many times in the middle of the night feeling as if 'somebody is standing on my chest', because she worries about making the right business decisions. She believes, however, that if she sticks to her values and is honourable and fair in her dealings, the decisions she makes will ultimately be the right ones.

When it comes to creative decisions, her approach is somewhat different, however. 'If I've got a creative problem I can't resolve or a creative decision to make, I go to bed and somewhere between fast asleep and waking, when your conscious and subconscious get sort of mixed-up, I find a lot of solutions come to me.' One thing that does keep her up at night is her concern that she won't get to make all the things that are in her head before it's time to go.

Boyes measures her success in a different way to most other businesses – by the way in which she has touched other people's lives. 'If I have brought joy to my customers' lives – if they picked up a spoon at the dining-room table and have laughed at the sculpture on them, then I have succeeded in what I wanted to do. Art is not just for galleries.' This aspiration can be seen in the brand and culture of the company, which has been carefully nurtured over the past 25 years. By combining a mixture of structure with creativity, Boyes believes she can get the best out of her staff, who enjoy having fun and exploring their creative souls while at work. Richard Branson is someone Boyes looks to emulate in part. She loves his passion and 'quirkiness', as well as his ability to have fun at work, all the while building a sustainable business empire. She was also a devotee of Steve Jobs, who, like her, was passionate about design as well as creating an excellent product.

In trying to balance work and fun, Boyes has come to recognise that one of her flaws is in not saying 'no'. 'I don't want to make somebody lose their spirit or their passion about something, so I tend to give them the opportunity and credit to do something, even when I know it's not going to work.' On the other hand, Boyes sometimes needs someone to tell her 'no', as she has been known to get carried away and take on too much, rather than letting the experts in her team do what they do best.

Being proudly South African is something that Boyes strives for – both in her business and personally. 'I love the fact that South Africans around the world can pick up a pair of salad servers and there is a thin thread of connection to home. I'm a South African first and foremost. I love to travel and see what's happening in the rest of the world and with other artists and in design, but while travelling feeds my soul I can't imagine living anywhere else except here; it's the country I love.'

As Boyes has moved to focus on the creative side of her business, her time has freed up to allow her to apply herself to another passion – the empowerment of women. She does this largely through a business taken under their wing – Monkey Biz – which, among other things, enables women to earn a living from home through beadwork. 'The decisions I make in the business very much revolve around making sure that women have a good opportunity; a good chance of a good life.' She realises that these opportunities are hard to come by for many South Africans, which is why she advises the women she works with to soak up every bit of knowledge they can and throw their heart and soul into something. She has learned from experience that it takes hard work to be really good at something and to build a business, but 'if you really want to excel at what you do, understand that you have to put in the extra hours. If you believe in something, just be stubborn – dig in your heels and believe that you can do it.'

Looking back over her career she wonders if it is because she is a woman that she has been so cautious. 'I struggled to trust what was happening, so I would employ just two extra people when we really needed 10. I think women are more careful and more guarded than men. I see it with my brothers; they are far surer of themselves than I am, and readily take chances.' Despite this, there is no denying that Boyes took a huge risk when she decided to go out on her own. She has also received validation from external sources, as evidenced by the awards she has accumulated over the years. These include the TUKS Alumni Board's Laureate Award in 2004 and South Africa's Most Influential Woman in Business and Government Award in 2008.

And when all is said and done, what would Boyes have written on her tombstone?

'She made them smile!'

CARROL BOYES has taken her rightful place among the few artists who have truly turned form into function. Her iconic creations grace homes across the world, with her business generating opportunities for hundreds of women around South Africa. Having started her enterprise from a small room in Cape Town, Boyes has played a key role in every function of the company, learning as she went and empowering others along the way.

NOURISH THE BODY, NOURISH THE SOUL

ROBBIE BROZIN

THE PRODIGAL SON

The Brozin family have entrepreneurship in their blood, and the apple did not fall far from the tree when it came to Robbie Brozin. Born in Middelburg in what is now Mpumalanga, when he was 12 Brozin and his three siblings moved with their parents to Johannesburg, where he attended King David High School. The family was very close and very traditional, spending every Friday evening together – a tradition that Brozin has encouraged with his own family.

'My mom's an old-fashioned kind of housewife. She fetched us from school and made sandwiches, played bridge and stayed at home with us. For both my parents education was totally non-negotiable; it wasn't even a question. Although my father and my grandfather were always entrepreneurs – my dad in furniture, retail and car dealerships, and my grandfather also in furniture – they were well-educated. I have always looked up to my father and my grandfather; they are like beacons to me. My grandfather came from Lithuania and built a business, while my father ran a business and always did things exceptionally well. He ran eight Comrades Marathons and has always been an incredible inspiration to me. I wish I had his wisdom; he has the ability to look at both sides of the story and approach the solution with wisdom. When he had problems with his business thanks to the rand getting a hammering, he was always calm and the way he handled it was incredible; he always dealt fairly and honestly with people. I look back now and at times things must have been desperate, but my dad was always calm. I'm much more emotional than him; in fact, he joined me at Nando's and was like my wicketkeeper; he can look at things in such detail. He emigrated to Israel five years ago but he still keeps an eye on the business!

'My wife's family are also strong on education and have a long history in the medical field, so she really works with our kids. One of my sons is a doctor, the other is an actuary and my daughter is studying to be an occupational therapist. It's a very highly intellectual family which my kids get from my wife's side of the family! It's funny, though, you've got to have a basic education and have gone to university, but does one need to be a CA or have an MBA? They don't guarantee you success; when you cross over into a Nando's-type environment, things like an MBA fall away. Emotional intelligence is much more important to me. I'd put up my business partner, Fernando, who has a technical education, up against an MBA when it came to a negotiation any day! I've worked with some people with no interpersonal skills and we've just chucked them out. I've taught my sons all about interpersonal skills, and I learned my biggest lessons from Kingsley Holgate!'

When the family moved to Johannesburg, Brozin Senior established a business called Teltron, a Sanyo agency. The younger Brozin did not immediately join the family business, however, deciding instead to do his two years' army service when he left school. 'Most of my mates emigrated to get out of the army, but I just wanted to get it over with. I was so naïve; it was crazy! I'll never forget – we had a selection process and most of the Jewish guys ended up becoming chefs, which was considered a cushy post. One of my mates had said to me, "Whatever you do, try to get into the kosher section on the chefs' side," so during selection I went and stood in that line but the sergeant took one look at me and said there was no way I was going to be a slap (chef), so I ended up in the regular army. I wonder sometimes how different life would have been if I'd gone into the chef section; maybe I would have had more food experience? I instinctively liked the food side, though.'

After completing his national service, Brozin went on to study for a BCom at Wits – where he would meet his future wife, Lee – following which he started studying to be a chartered accountant. 'I failed very badly! I just couldn't do accounts and tax.' He did two years of articles at Pricewaterhouse, but hated it. 'I just wasn't good at it; it was a nightmare!' Throughout his studies Brozin was also selling anything and everything he could get his hands on. 'After the army, I linked up with a friend of mine and we used to sell clothes from our car boots. We got over-runs and end-of-season runs from the Pierre Cardin factory and we were always trading. We also used to keep books for the local traders and supply some of them. It was crazy but we built up quite a little business, which gave us pocket money so we never had to ask our parents for money. It gave us a real trading mentality.'

At the time Brozin was still living at home, but moved out and married Lee when he finished his articles, choosing to go into his father's business. 'There was a lot of enticement to go and live overseas and do all kinds of stuff, but it never spoke to me – I just didn't want to do that. But I hated working for my dad for two reasons; the first was that I got special treatment because I was the boss' son, and the second was that it was a horrible business. You were caught between the Japanese on the one hand and Pick n Pay on the other; you're the meat in the sandwich. The Japanese are telling you what to pay in yen and Pick n Pay is saying this is what you can sell it for in rands, and you're lucky if you can squeeze a little margin in-between that.'

Because so many in Brozin's family, including his father, were lawyers or accountants by profession, it was a 'big decision' not to become an accountant himself. 'I think it was an important decision because I never had a safety net; it's not like if things didn't work out I had something to fall back on.'

So it was that Brozin decided to leave his father's business, which he did on the first of April 1987, just nine days before his first son was born. 'My wife was absolutely vicious at me! She had been teaching at Eden College but had stopped when she fell pregnant, and I had nothing but trading and selling to bring money into the house. I went off and bought and sold and did a few odd deals and stuff like that. I had the full blessing of my father, though. I had always wanted to work for myself and at that stage I got it in my head that I had to create a brand if I was to be master of my own destiny. I always tell young would-be entrepreneurs that it's very rare that you actually do work for yourself. You might think you're working for yourself, but you're always going to have partners like the bank, an investor, your wife or clients. There are always going to be people telling you what to do! But if you have a product that is yours, you can be master of that product's destiny. The product is almost your freedom to express yourself. I instinctively decided that that was really what I wanted. I wasn't a margin or a commission guy; I was always embarrassed to go back and ask for my commission.'

After eight months of buying, selling and surviving, Brozin was having lunch with his friend Fernando Duarte, who worked at Teltron. They were eating at a Portuguese chicken restaurant where they would meet once or twice a week, and Brozin turned to Fernando and suggested that they buy the restaurant and 'conquer the world'. 'It was spicy and I think the world craves a bit of spice; it was healthier than fried food and it had a heritage – which helps if you want to go global. I have always travelled from a young age and I love it; I love exploring and going out and seeing.'

Since leaving his father's business, Brozin had tried a mail-order business selling South African products abroad, but it was difficult not only from a logistics point of view, but also because he had no passion for someone else's product. 'You've got to believe in the product, so when we bought Chicken Land with a loan from my dad, I thought it was just going to be a sideline because I was still busy with all my other little bits and pieces. I thought I would just put Fernando in there and then go on a Monday morning and collect a little brown paper bag of cash and it would just grow. We were only 26 and we were naïve to the endth degree!'

CHANGING LIVES – ONE CHICKEN AT A TIME

The pair bought two-thirds of the business and eventually bought the previous owner out, but as Fernando was more technically inclined they decided to open another business fixing TVs and video machines in addition to running the restaurant. 'We were busy with a whole lot of stuff, so we decided that I would do the food stuff, which I really enjoyed. I can't really explain it, but I enjoy everything about the food industry. I say to people who join us that if you can't satisfy your needs in the restaurant business then you're tired of life. There's something in there for everybody, from store design to retail development, legal, leases, creativity, product design, food design, science, manufacturing. We're not just running a restaurant, we're running a brand. From very early on we took a view that we're going to be in the brand business and we're going to be in the people business. We wanted to create a new culture when it came to running a business. Our core purpose is about having fun, making money, changing the way people think about chicken and changing people's lives one chicken at a time.'

As the business started growing in South Africa, Fernando rejoined Nandos and the pair began to look at foreign expansion, but not all of it was well thought out and strategic. 'When we moved into Bangladesh, that was part of my youthful exuberance and non-strategic kind of thought! We grew without much strategy in the early days. We were in Pakistan, for example, then Dubai and Bangladesh approached us. It just made sense at the time to open up in that particular area. We almost kept away from America at that time because we saw ourselves as specialists at third-world markets, but then when London really started kicking we realised that we could crack first-world markets as well, so we have restaurants on the East Coast of the States now. Normally you've got to have 50 or 60 restaurants in an area in the US if you want to establish your brand, but in DC – with just 12 or 14 restaurants – people are already talking about us. So Friday is Botswana Day in one of our restaurants and the Zimbabweans come on a Thursday afternoon; you can't believe how many people from different communities think it's home!'

In 2011 Brozin stepped out of the business from his role as Group CEO. While remaining a shareholder, he is not involved in the day-to-day running of the enterprise, focusing rather on the purpose of the business. 'To maintain a strong culture in a world where our business is getting bigger and bigger, we've got to think smaller and smaller. If we start just thinking about pure numbers and the sheer size of the company, we can forget where we came from. Our turnover is significant but if we don't worry about the small detail we can lose what makes us unique. I think what has really made us special is the fact that we came from Rosettenville, on the wrong side of the tracks, and we had a little bit of edginess. We haven't become just another big corporate, but now we have professional management running the business. I see myself as a wartime general; if you're a peacetime general you don't know what it's like to be a wartime general. If you're a peacetime general you have more time for strategy, for sitting and planning, but in wartime the bullets are flying and hitting you. So today I'm back where I was at the beginning: looking at the brand, at the people. If I look back 25 years we did some basic stuff that is still relevant today, but it won't be if we don't make it relevant. There're things like having fun, our basic vision and the fact that we're a values-based organisation. We say there are five values that we really have to embody – pride, passion, courage, integrity and family. We don't put them on the wall, but we like to hug the group with them. I hate it when you walk into an organisation and their values are on the wall and they say they believe in them but they don't live them.

'Life isn't a dress rehearsal, you know, you're living to have fun. And at the same time there's a responsibility to make money, because for me money is what sustains you; it's pure capitalism. At times we had a lot of fun and made no money and there were times when we made a lot of money and had no fun; my job is to balance both. The detail is important, so when we have a board meeting, where is it going to be? How do we have them? Are there fruit and sweets on the table?

Whenever we travel we try to bring in sweets from all over the world. We dress in jeans and takkies. That is the kind of style that we want to have.'

Making the change away from the CEO position was very difficult for Brozin. 'Your ego takes a massive knock. When you're the CEO, all the decisions stop with you and everyone wants an answer and they come to you. We've always been decentralised, but ultimately the buck stops with you. So you get the good and the bad – the cash flow responsibilities and the magnificent Olympics tickets! And suddenly they both fall away; the telephone stops ringing and when you go into a meeting everyone goes quiet. You've got to respect the new CEO and not undermine him; he'll do certain things that you don't like and there are certain things that he'll do much better than you. You know, you've got to get over that. Nando's is not a dynastical business – I'm not going to hand it over to my kids – so it's got to be professionally run but with a vision and a value system that can sustain beyond any individual. Choosing a new CEO was difficult because we needed someone who got the values but also had the ability to make some structural changes; the business needed adult supervision because I'm not terribly detail-oriented and I hate rules! The business is much more process-oriented now and I'm focusing now on building a nice cultural connection to have the best of both worlds.'

HEART AND SOUL

Brozin now spends 50 per cent of his time on the Nando's side, together with Robby Enthoven, with the two of them looking at the broad strategy of where the business is going in the next decade, and 50 per cent of his time doing humanitarian work and embedding this into the Nando's culture. 'To me success is when the business no longer needs its founders. We're not there yet because Nando's still needs guidance on the culture, but when we get the balance of process and culture really embedded together, then we'll be there. We're really focusing on leadership development internally; to get people to really understand the fabric of the brand and all the good stuff I think the business must stand for.'

One of the projects Brozin is working on is a new Nando's headquarters, which is 'really going to talk to the soul of our brand. At the moment it's in quite a dodgy neighbourhood and it's a bit higgledy-piggledy because we added on here and added on there, but when we looked at the cost of fixing it was fairly substantial capex, especially for that neighbourhood, so we had a choice to either move to a leafy suburb like Rivonia or Rosebank or stay and be part of the rejuvenation of the city. I came up with a plan and showed it to Robby and he said we needed to go even bigger, and that we needed to make a statement that tied into the soul of the brand, so we're doing something spectacular. It's going to be an oasis in that neighbourhood and will hopefully help regentrify the area; it's in large part thanks to the amazing perspective of the Enthovens and Robby's eye for detail.'

Enthoven's father, Dick Enthoven, is someone else who has inspired Brozin along the way. 'Dick invested with us when we had about three restaurants; I think it was a sense of madness but we've been partners for 25 years now! We don't have any agreement; it's always been a values-based kind of relationship. He and my dad are very different kinds of people – my dad is about costs and Dick is about value, so the combination of those two have been fantastic.'

Dick Enthoven is very involved in the art world and started an art programme with Nando's, which is something Brozin has become heavily involved in. 'We look at our art programme and see how we can change our artists' lives. We're not just transacting, we're trying to make artists famous. We created an entry-level programme called the Creative Block, which is a 6x6 block where artists can express themselves and we have a curator from Spier Architectural Arts, Jeanetta Blignaut, for that. Then those who survive the block build or paint bigger pieces for us, then we think about how we can really change their lives from there. We've dedicated 300 square metres for art in our new headquarters so our walls will be like one big art gallery where artists can also paint. We're planning to link up with galleries in Berlin, Amsterdam, London and Savannah to negotiate residencies for artists who have come through our programme. In this way we're slowly building a sustainable model where we're building a lovely collection because our soul tells us to do it.

'Art has done so much for me and I want to share that with other people. I had no clue about art, but it opened my world to creativity and gave me another dimension. Whether you're a cleaner, in admin or the CEO at Nando's, everyone will get a chance to meet the artists and see the beautiful work they're doing. We're probably one of the biggest art buyers in South Africa. We've won so many awards from Business Arts South Africa but for me it's not about the awards. I hate being nominated for them; in fact, I reject most nominations and the ones I can't I feel uncomfortable accepting, because it feels like you're at the top and the only way is down!'

Brozin's other passion is working with Kingsley Holgate on the eradication of malaria. 'I enjoy working with Kingsley immensely. The way he treats people, his humility – he just connects at all levels. I think my biggest asset is my ability to connect with people at any level. I can talk to a king and I can talk to a beggar, so the two of us work together really well.

'The work we're doing is fascinating and I'm completely obsessed! My mates look at me like I'm 100 per cent mad but we're not doing it for the accolades. We were nominated by the UN for an award for our work so I took him to New York and it was like taking Crocodile Dundee to New York – we had such fun! We also met some incredible people like Brian Brink from Anglo American, and Steve Knowles, a brilliant guy who was running the AngloGold Ashanti programme in Ghana. His programme mixes nets with spraying and larvaciding and a whole range of other things, so while everyone else is confused about what to do and battling with politics and personal interests, we thought that his programme made a lot of sense and started implementing it in Mozambique. He reduced the incidence of malaria from 80 per cent to below 5 per cent, which is what we're trying to replicate.

'In fact, Brian saw what we were doing at Nando's, creating bracelets and pyjamas to raise money and a bunch of other things, and he really liked how creative we were being, so introduced us to the Permanent Secretary of the Ministry of Health in Mozambique, Dr Marcellino Lucas, who asked for our help. We've impacted about 30 000 people now in just the three months we've been spraying – both through eradicating malaria and job creation. We believe in the importance of engaging with Mozambique in part because it is Nando's heritage, but also because we want to make a difference there. We believe we can inspire leadership and creativity through the work that is being done by, for and through Africans. But we're only tackling one region of 40 along the border so there's a lot to be done, and the South African government is not prepared for malaria if it gets to us.

'I love the challenge – it's almost like starting Nando's again! And companies are really benefitting. Other corporates have joined us because it's just good business. Malaria affects a company's P & L in terms of costs like training and recruiting, as well as lost income. Just think of all the extra airtime and Cokes that can be bought if the population is alive and well!'

Brozin laughs at the thought of retiring, and loves nothing more than being inspired by something that he in turn can inspire others about. Failure, on the other hand, is something that scares him. 'I fail all day every day, but while I may fail in the battle, I don't fail in the war. Failure for me would be when we give up on malaria or on Nando's. I don't mind failing on the small things as long as we learn from it, and you have to forgive yourself and others. I won't forgive if something is done maliciously, but I reward failure if something's been done for the right reasons and you've accepted that you've failed.

'We have closed countries, we've closed restaurants. Looking back, I've done such silly stuff it's criminal! When I handed my baby over to the new CEO I was sometimes embarrassed at the things we'd done, but it was my journey. You know the song, "You Raise Me Up"? That song makes me think of my dad and Dick – they never said, "I told you so" when I failed; they told me to get back up and give it another go. It's amazing when you surround yourself with optimistic people who are there to lift you up when you need it. In life you get people who suck your blood and people who inspire you, and I'm fortunate that I've had realistic inspiration in my life. Sometimes, you know, you feel uncertain or unconfident; your mind at 3am can play funny tricks on you and you think everything is negative, but then some people are just able to give you some perspective.'

Brozin is not one who is quick to anger, but he is concerned about the state of the country at present. 'I think the pity of South Africa is that we have come to believe that instant gratification and quick money are the way forward. Young people need to realise that it takes 15 years to become an effective "overnight success". The other problem is that I think South Africans are world class but we underestimate and undervalue ourselves. Just look at GIBS; to me it's world class and Nick is a world-class thinker. And I'm not just blowing smoke! They have frontier thinking and the people who are coming through there are looking for solutions. I tell people that nothing is impossible, but you've got to take things step by step; the journey is part of the reward. Money is not the reward at the end of the day; money will come, but if the money is the reward for you you'll never be happy. Sometimes when you have no money you come up with a better solution. I believe in fate 100 per cent. I believe that God puts you in a place where he knows you are there to make a difference to somebody you might not even know. So don't sit there and be depressed and bitch and moan; get over it and look for why you're there!

'I look back at the most random things that have ended up happening, like my plane was delayed on the way to Hong Kong and I sat in the airport and spoke to a guy who has ended up being one of our suppliers there! In South Africa you have to be optimistic. You look at all the problems we have with the government and unemployment and there just doesn't seem to be a solution, but we will come through it. We should all be about job creation but there are no incentives to hire people. Prices for everything are going up, we've got Aids and single parents and values are going out the window, but yet you see magnificence every day here. My sense of South Africa is that whenever we have a problem we've got to go to the brink before we sort it out. Why do we have to fuck this place up before we fix it? Let's start building now with what we have instead of breaking it first. But there's also opportunity in having to fix things. We have spirit here unlike anything you'll see in Europe or America, and people are willing to help and participate when we talk to them about things like malaria. Most South Africans have a spirit of sharing and philanthropy and doing. Now what we need is the government to do its part – even 50 per cent would be nice!'

Brozin's passion for doing things for the right reason resonates with his choice of epitaph: 'Here lies a mensch.' 'For me everything is about being a mensch – a person of integrity and honour. You can make money, but if you're doing it or giving it away for your own personal benefit or pride or whatever, you're not doing it with humanity.'

An energetic and enthusiastic entrepreneur, **ROBBIE BROZIN** made a name for himself as the driving force behind the phenomenal success of Nando's. With restaurants in 24 countries, Brozin has now chosen to take a back seat on the day-to-day business issues to focus on a subject he is equally passionate about – eradicating malaria. Working with the UN and Kingsley Holgate, Brozin has helped to save the lives of thousands of children by providing them with much-needed assistance in the fight against the disease.

THE STAR WITNESS

EDWIN CAMERON

FROM HUMBLE BEGINNINGS

Edwin Cameron was born in Pretoria on 15 February 1953, to Kenneth and Salomé Cameron, at a time when their lives were in a state of disintegration. His father had been a volunteer in the South African army during the Second World War, but after being wounded and held as a prisoner of war, he had returned home an alcoholic who was unable to hold down a job. Growing up with an unstable father and a mother who only had a Standard 6 and was not able to care for her children, Cameron learned from an early age that the only way he would be able to escape the daily grind of poverty would be to educate himself out of it.

The difficult circumstances of Cameron's youth saw one of his sisters being given away for adoption and his mother and father divorce twice, with the second separation causing an irrevocable fracture in the unhappy family unit. At the age of seven, Cameron was sent with his remaining sisters, Laura and Jean, to the Presbyterian Children's Home in Queenstown in the Eastern Cape.

Laura was the first positive role model for Cameron, being a protector and comfort for both her younger brother and sister, providing them with love and stability in an insecure and unpredictable world. It was during their first holiday from the home when they were staying at their aunt's house in Pretoria that Laura was killed when a van knocked her off her bike. One of Cameron's most compelling memories of that dreadful time was seeing his father at Laura's funeral accompanied by two guards, having been given a day's reprieve from his prison sentence for car theft.

Upon their return to school, Cameron and Jean grew even closer, with his sister replacing Laura as a mother figure and role model. Cameron immersed himself in his schoolbooks. 'I turned to excelling at school. Intellectual achievement pointed away from the unbearable.'

Cameron acknowledges the time he spent in Queenstown as having left him with an 'intense, central, motivating awareness. There were many poor, deprived children in South Africa. Many intelligent, ambitious children, willing to work and strive. Many who yearned for escape, release, transcendence from constricting material circumstance and poverty.' What made Cameron different from most, however, was the colour of his skin. When his mother was able to take care of the children after almost five years in the children's home, they proceeded to lead a transient life in various towns and cities around the country.

Cameron's circumstances finally took a turn for the better in 1967, when his mother managed to secure him a place at Pretoria Boys' High School – a highly regarded government school that changed the course of his life. As Cameron walked through the gates of the school – his eighth in as many years – he felt 'nearly suffocated with apprehension and excitement. I craved all the elegant learning the school seemed to offer, and all the opportunities beyond that. I could hardly believe that all this had become available to me.'

The school transformed Cameron's life. 'What I learned there – perhaps even more importantly, those I met there – gave me access to rich opportunities.' One person who in particular made a dramatic impact on the young Cameron was the headmaster, who was 'an extraordinary man, a man of liberal instincts both personally and politically, and a very fine man, who took young people, intellectual pursuit and development issues seriously'.

Cameron's hard work was rewarded when he secured a scholarship from Anglo American to study law, English, Latin and Greek at Stellenbosch. The completion of a BA Law and an Honours degree in Latin, both cum laude, while lecturing in Latin and Classical Studies, led to his entry into the hallowed halls of Oxford University as a Rhodes Scholar. Three years later, Cameron returned to South Africa with a BA in Jurisprudence with first-class Honours, the Jurisprudence prize, BCL with first-class Honours and the Vinerian Scholarship.

SETTING A PRECEDENT

Cameron went on to earn an LLB from Unisa, receiving the medal for best law graduate, and joined the Johannesburg Bar in 1983. The inequities of the apartheid system had long concerned Cameron, which is why just two years into his legal career he abandoned a promising career as a commercial lawyer, determined to 'fight injustice in the courts and offer legal advice and support to organisations and individuals resisting apartheid'. That year was also a tumultuous one for Cameron for another reason. Before the age of 30 he had finally come to terms with his sexuality, leading to the dissolution of his marriage. In 1986, Cameron began working as a public-interest lawyer at the University of the Witwatersrand's Centre for Applied Legal Studies (CALS). He soon found himself embroiled in what he considered to be an 'outrageous curvature of the laws of logic and fairness', when he objected to the death penalties imposed on six Sharpeville residents for murder. After the six lost their appeal, Cameron spoke out against the government's refusal to commute their sentences. His activism included the penning of scholarly articles, speaking to foreign media and writing an opinion piece in the *Sunday Times*, which was then picked up by newspapers in London. A battle ensued, with the Chief Justice demanding that the Johannesburg Bar Council take disciplinary procedures against Cameron. Fortunately, enough of the Council members refused to apply any punitive measures – but still few of his fellow lawyers were courageous enough to point out any shortcomings of apartheid judges.

This was not the first time Cameron had invoked the wrath of the judiciary, however, with the Minister of Justice the previous year having released an official statement describing Cameron as a 'lesser known officer of the court', whose criticism of the judiciary was 'distasteful and improper'.

A prosecution witness who recanted his testimony in the case of the Sharpeville Six was all Cameron needed to throw himself into a renewed effort to reopen the case; the day before they were due to be hanged, they were granted a reprieve to appeal for a new trial. Despite Sydney Kentridge, a prominent South African lawyer on the London Bar, flying home to take on their case, the Six lost their appeal, but their sentence was commuted and they were taken off death row. Cameron believes that this was in large part due to the international furore that had developed about the Six, which forced the apartheid government's hand.

During his time at CALS, Cameron also began to focus on HIV/Aids, drafting the Charter of Rights on Aids and HIV, co-founding the Aids Consortium, and founding and being the first director of the Aids Law Project. In addition, he helped to secure the express inclusion of sexual orientation in the South African Constitution.

JUDGEMENT DAY

What felt like Cameron's own death sentence was handed to him on 19 December 1986, when his doctor at the time phoned without warning to tell him that he had sent a sample of his blood for testing, which had come back as HIV-positive. 'The shock was double,' remembers Cameron. 'Apart from the blow of learning that I was infected, most immediately I felt as though I had experienced a stunning bereavement – the impending loss of my own life. I was 33, building my career. In many ways I was just starting my life, and Aids was incurable. Death would assuredly overtake me within a year or two.'

Looking back, Cameron wondered if his doctor had assumed Cameron's knowledge of his HIV test, given that Cameron had confided in him his sexual activity post his divorce, but he remains firmly of the belief that 'without proper support, including counselling, an unpresaged HIV-positive test result is almost always damagingly counterproductive. I had had no preparation for anything so instantly and brutally terminal.'

But life continued regardless of Cameron's inner turmoil. The country moved in and out of a state of emergency, and forced removals, conscientious objectors and the creation of 'homelands' kept the Wits Human Rights Centre inundated. In 1988 Cameron was among a group of lawyers who met senior figures in exile to discuss constitutional transition, which was followed up by a second meeting early the next year. That year also saw Cameron advising the National Union of Mineworkers on HIV/Aids, as well as helping to draft and negotiate the first comprehensive Aids agreement with the Chamber of Mines.

During that time Cameron spoke of his status to only two people – to his family and friends he said nothing. Apart from the fear he felt, shame also kept him from reaching out to loved ones. 'I was tainted, soiled, polluted. My blood and body were fouled with the most conspicuously vile infection known to recent human history. Widespread and much-publicised revulsion to Aids – and fear of those with HIV – didn't help to combat these feelings.' Worldwide condemnation of those suffering from Aids, and in particular those denied their basic human rights by the apartheid government in South Africa, led Cameron to becoming even more involved in Aids policy and litigation. Yet despite working so closely with colleagues who were committed to justice, fairness and non-discrimination, as well as clients with whom he developed strong bonds, Cameron denied himself consolation by not being able to publicly state his own HIV status.

Life took a dramatic turn for all South Africans in 1994 when Nelson Mandela became President of a democratic South Africa. Cameron, in particular, was affected when he was named by Mandela as an Acting High Court judge in October to chair a commission into the arms deal.

On 1 January 1995 Cameron's dream of becoming a High Court judge was realised. Prior to his appointment, he had met with the head of the Constitutional

Court, Justice Arthur Chaskalson. They discussed the fact that Cameron was living with HIV, yet Chaskalson believed that given his good health, it did not warrant becoming a public issue.

While Cameron had been open about being gay, for many years he and his sister kept their time in the home a secret; they felt 'ashamed, soiled, disadvantaged'. It was not until 1996 when Cameron was invited to speak at the Johannesburg Guild Cottage, a children's home and treatment centre for abused children, that he first spoke out about his own experiences. This was just the cathartic experience he needed to accept the circumstances of his childhood, and for the first time, a weight was lifted from his shoulders.

Spring of 1997 seemed to smile down on Cameron. The love of a supportive family, a new love affair and his job as a High Court judge had conspired to lull him into a false sense of security about his health and wellbeing. The contentment was not to last, however, when the moment that had been hovering over Cameron for 12 years finally dawned.

As a judge in the Johannesburg High Court, Cameron presided over one of the busiest courts in the country. Given his background as a human rights lawyer, he was under no illusions when he joined the High Court that he was facing a steep learning curve, but he was determined to master the complex contractual and company-law problems and insolvencies he dealt with every day. And he was not about to let HIV get in the way.

Cameron vividly remembers the day when he could no longer deceive himself that his HIV had progressed to Aids. It was a cool day in October 1997 when he was unable to finish climbing the two flights of stairs from the judges' common room to his chambers – a climb he had done every working day for almost three years. 'Each step seemed an insuperable effort,' he remembers. 'My energy seemed to have drained from my legs. I was exhausted and although I was perspiring, my mouth was dry. I didn't feel pain – just overwhelming weariness.

'I had been determined to keep up. Every judge in Johannesburg works under remorseless pressure. I didn't want to let anyone down. But even more, I didn't want to admit to myself – couldn't afford to admit to myself, still less to colleagues – that I was desperately ill.' A highly intelligent man and a deep thinker, Cameron's solution to the crisis he faced was out of character. Instead of facing up to the truth and seeking help from his doctor, his response was 'to stretch my working hours, to cut out alcohol and late evenings to conserve energy, to bury myself in books and files so that I could stay abreast. To stop work would be to admit defeat. And admitting defeat meant death.'

As he stood in the stairwell with his head pressed against the cool wall, Cameron's mind raced. With his workload intensifying, his thoughts had been occupied with his cases, yet he knew that the time had come when he could no longer ignore the obvious.

That evening he went to see his doctor, who confirmed what Cameron already knew. One of the more harrowing symptoms Cameron exhibited was thrush in his oesophagus, making it difficult for him to swallow. While he had been steadily losing weight, Cameron's physical stature was such that this was not as noticeable on him as it may have been on others; however, he had now reached the stage where his body was no longer able to absorb food. Then he faced even more distressing news; he had contracted PCP – pneumocystis pneumonia.

Cameron had managed to keep the virus at bay for 12 years, and in so doing had bought himself enough time to be among the first in South Africa to access the life-saving antiretroviral (ARV) drugs that had been developed by Dr David Ho the previous year. Remarkable stories had begun circulating about this new 'miracle' treatment, which saw the number of Aids deaths declining rapidly in the West. There was, however, a caveat. The drugs were not only inordinately expensive, but it was then thought they were also only successful in approximately 70 per cent of cases. Cameron was in a fortunate position because he could afford the treatment, but was terrified that it would fail. Few facts were known about ARVs at that time, and Cameron would wake in terror in the early hours of the morning only to lie awake wondering if his end was near.

Cameron declined Jean's offers of support, believing that 'to accept sympathy and support meant acknowledging weakness and dependency'. In the interim his workload continued unabated, which included daily drives out to

Vereeniging for six weeks for an out-of-town session of the High Court. He had been put on a daily dose of antibiotics in an attempt to eradicate the PCP, but just 10 days into his Vereeniging circuit, a visit to the doctor revealed that the medication had not worked. A stronger dose, with bed rest, was required; Cameron, however, refused to consider the latter. The drugs wrought havoc on his body, causing what was left of his appetite to recede, reviving the thrush and triggering a rash on his torso and face.

Despite taking an antifungal medicine, the price of which put it beyond the reach of the average South African, Cameron was devastated when the thrush continued to spread. 'This was one of my worst moments – I often think my worst. It felt like a defining moment, inviting despair. Fungal spores grow on dead bodies … the treatment hadn't beaten the PCP. The thrush was back. I was feeling ghastly. Was my body shutting down for death?'

In typical Cameron fashion, the judge refused to let the disease get the better of him. The previous year had seen him take on leadership of a committee that advised the South African Law Commission on Aids. With the commission's tacit approval, the committee undertook to submit watertight draft legislation to the commission, which in turn would present it to Parliament. As Cameron juggled his work, the pressures of the committee and his own battle with Aids, he came to realise that the effort of hiding his illness while being a 'highly visible and respected Aids policy advocate' was no longer tenable. 'In simple practical terms, it just seemed to divert too much energy. Secrecy is all too often a worrying and time-consuming and energy-sapping business. And it was just unnecessarily exhausting.'

Cameron did not have to wait too long for the committee's hard work to pay off, however. In early 1998, the commission approved their recommendations for outlawing pre-employment HIV testing. The recommendation went to Parliament and, within the year, the law had changed. This lifted a weight off Cameron's chest and, given the continuing onslaught of the thrush and PCP, he decided at last to arrange to take time off to rest and hopefully recuperate. His nervousness at phoning the Judge-President to ask for time off was replaced by relief when he was granted leave with no questions asked. At last he realised that he could chance relying on others for help; with every person he approached, 'their responses touched me and moved me and reassured me'.

Finally the PCP began to retreat and Cameron's doctor outlined the ARV options available at the time. 'I had been scared right out of further ambivalence or uncertainty. If there was a chance that the treatment would fail me, there was twice as much chance that it would succeed.' After telling his family and some close friends, Cameron began his treatment on 13 November 1997. The cost of the drugs was almost prohibitive – Cameron knew that he was extremely fortunate to be one of the few HIV-positive people in South Africa to be able to afford the medication. Yet, at one third of his after-tax monthly income, and given that Cameron shared his monthly salary with others, he would not be able to afford the drugs for long. The medical insurance for judges amounted to a paltry R800 a year for Aids – covering just a fifth of a month's worth of his ARV's.

Cameron knew that other judges and Members of Parliament were getting up to R10 000 a year for chronic medications, yet despite repeated pleas to a judicial colleague who represented the medical interests of his fellow judges, the inequitable situation remained. Upon his return to court after 10 days' leave, Cameron had had enough. He began by writing to his colleague who was, after over a year, yet to deliver on any of his promises to rectify the inequalities in the medical-aid system. Cameron suggested to him that should he 'not be willing to take immediate action to end the irrational discrimination against Aids, he should resign from the medical scheme's board'. He followed up by writing to Judge-President Friedman, who Cameron believed was a 'wise and humane man', and who had been the person who had appointed his colleague to the insurance scheme's board. To Cameron's surprise both immediately reacted positively, and in the new year, persons living with Aids were granted the same coverage as all those suffering from chronic conditions.

In this time Cameron had been taking his medication, and side effects such as nausea and painful, sensitive teeth could not detract from the realisation that his energy was being restored. 'Life forces were coursing through my body. Illness was yielding to a nearly novel feeling – renewed and joyful wellbeing.'

That December, just six weeks after not being able to climb two flights of stairs at work, Cameron took his sister, Jean, and her family to Cape Town for what had become an annual ritual. Part of that ritual was climbing to the summit of Table Mountain. As Cameron and his family crested the mountain, he made himself a promise. Going forward he would work tirelessly to break down the barriers that limited the vast majority of persons living with Aids in South Africa from accessing the life-saving drugs that had brought such joy back into his life.

Along with his work at the courts, Cameron also took on the role of Chair of the governing Council of Wits – a role he held for 10 years – and co-founded the Wits Law School Endowment Appeal. He also began to speak publicly about the need to make ARVs more widely available; for the pharmaceutical companies to relinquish their grasp on their intellectual property; and for the government to face the challenge head on. Yet he continued to do so without stating that he was living with HIV himself. Talk had spread during the worst of his illness and he knew that it was only a matter of time before it was common knowledge; increasingly, friends and colleagues were showing concern for his welfare and a journalist approached him directly about his HIV status. Besides this, he began to accept that if he started speaking as someone living with Aids, 'I would do so with greater moral force, more unchecked energy, and better clarity about what had to be done'.

ON THE FRONTLINES

In December 1998, the stigma of Aids reared its ugly head in the stoning and stabbing to death of Gugu Dlamini. Just three weeks previously, Dlamini, a sex worker, had spoken on a Zulu radio station about her HIV-positive status. Her attackers came from her neighbourhood, accusing her of shaming her community. Despite charges being filed, her murderers were never brought to account due to a lack of evidence.

Dlamini's bravery was an inspiration to Cameron, who resolved to publically announce that he was living with HIV. He had all the privileges of a wealthy white South African, which Dlamini did not, yet she had showed courage where he had not. 'I have seen time and time again how people have made a difference to my life, so I have a sense of the difference that I could conceivably or potentially make in other people's lives. We're all the victims of our spirits and feelings and you can construct a world in your mind that is a negative world, but you can also change it.' His decision was also influenced by the recent death of another Aids activist, Simon Nkoli, as well as the strength and integrity shown by Zackie Achmat, who not only came out with his HIV status, but also set up the Treatment Action Campaign shortly thereafter.

The decision on how to announce his status without it becoming sensationalist was made when Cameron found himself a candidate for a newly vacant position at the Constitutional Court. Prior to his public interview for the post, Cameron met again with Justice Chaskalson, and the senior judge broached the idea to Cameron that he make known his HIV-positive status at the upcoming interview. 'There is nothing to be ashamed about,' he said. 'Many people have HIV. And the time has surely come for someone in public life to begin speaking out. The commission offers you an appropriate and dignified environment to do so.'

Cameron knew that Chaskalson was right, yet he still worried about what his family, their friends, his friends and his colleagues would say. 'The inevitably sensational aspect of the event appalled and frightened me,' he says, yet he spoke to his family who strongly supported his decision. He then spoke to close friends and colleagues who were not yet aware of his status, and on the weekend before the commission he met his mother, Sally, who was then 78, to tell her what was about to take place. She had long supported her son in his career and had held his Aids activism in high regard, and upon hearing the news, she quietly said, 'I thought as much, my boy.' Despite her concern about the implications of his announcement, she went on to wear a red Aids ribbon in solidarity until her death two years later.

When the commission convened in Cape Town the following week, two friends travelled with him and sat right behind him during the proceedings. For Cameron, it was a lesson about 'the tangibility, the felt proximity, the physiological closeness, that friendship and support can bring'. Having previously made an unsuccessful bid to the Constitutional Court, Cameron knew what to expect, yet this appearance carried a great deal more significance. In a carefully constructed statement, Cameron discussed the fact that while he was legally and ethically entitled to remain silent about his status, he was in a unique situation in that he had a secure job, supportive family and friends, and the means to access treatment. These factors, he said, were a privilege not afforded to many South Africans, which was a situation that needed to be reversed. He closed his statement by explaining that, 'my hope is that my decision to speak today may contribute to a greater climate of openness and caring, and to the prospect of proper medical treatment, for all South Africans living with HIV or Aids'.

The stunned silence in the room was broken by one and then many questions, with Cameron stressing that he was making a statement because 'I am not dying of Aids. I am living with Aids'. After all this time, the relief was indescribable. While the commission recommended Cameron for the position, it was given to another High Court judge, Sandile Ngcobo, yet Cameron believed that 'events have their own timeliness, their own rightness, their own roundness'. The support he received from the public and media was overwhelming; 'The news was carried on the front page of almost every national newspaper, and on the main national television news. I think that my statement struck a "right note" in the national life at the time. People had at last become concerned about HIV. People were, I think, waiting for someone to come forward, someone with a public profile, and say, "Yes, I have Aids", and that was my role.'

Yet in some quarters the stigma remained. Cameron had thought that others in similar positions of authority would also come forward, yet none did. This was not helped by then-President Thabo Mbeki's Aids denialism. Six months into his presidency, in October 1999, and for three years after that, Mbeki maintained that Aids was attributable to social and behavioural factors, as opposed to a virus. Cameron went so far as to take Mbeki to task at the XII International Conference on HIV/Aids in Durban in 2000, saying, 'To my regret, I cannot believe that President Mbeki's speech at the official opening of this conference last night has done enough to counter these adverse conditions. I personally yearned for an unequivocal assertion from our President that HIV is a virally specific condition that is sexually transmitted, which if uncontained precipitates debility and death, but for which antiretroviral treatments now exist that can effectively and affordably be applied. To my grief, his speech was bereft of this.'

Despite his criticism of the President, however, Mbeki accepted the recommendation of the Judicial Service Commission that Cameron be appointed to the Supreme Court of Appeal in October that year.

As a killer, Aids surpassed the previous most destructive epidemic – the great plague of the twelfth century – in 2002, by which time it had taken the lives of over 25 million people. Yet at that time there seemed little hope of impeding the virus, as intellectual property rights prevented cheaper generics – which would have saved millions of lives – from being made. This meant that governments and businesses needed to address a question of the most enormous importance. Were they prepared to let people die simply because they were too poor to afford the medicine that could save them? The rank immorality of the notion that tens of millions of poor people should be denied access to available medications because of limitations on the use of human knowledge had to be pronounced: and the opposition to the immorality had to prevail.

The following three years saw little progress being made, despite the creation of an Aids advisory panel by Mbeki. Cameron met with world leaders to discuss the impact of Aids, gave speeches around the globe and won numerous prestigious awards, yet thousands of poor South Africans were still dying unnecessarily. Despite this activism and his workload he was also determined to encourage young people to not be a victim of their circumstances. By becoming patron of Sparrow's Nest hospice, the Community Aids Response, the Soweto HIV/Aids Counsellors' Association and the Big Shoes Foundation, he felt he was able to guide young South Africans who may have felt disenfranchised. 'There are people who are real victims of accident or fate and there are people who are totally disempowered by external circumstances, but one has to have the right cast of mind, and start organising – a club or a group, for instance. It is vital to realise your own power to improve your own circumstances and to improve the world around you.'

Cameron's continued attempts to draw attention to the plight of South Africans living with HIV and Aids occasionally drew the ire of politicians and the media, yet he was determined to 'challenge the authority and respectability' of those denialists who 'repeatedly boasted that they had secured the ear of President Mbeki'.

When it came, in August 2003, the government's commitment to treatment was unexpected but very welcome. By the time the first treatment sites offering ARVs to poor patients was opened in April 2004, an estimated one in five South African adults had HIV or Aids.

Cameron continues to use every platform available to him to speak out on issues close to his heart, and his elevation to the Constitutional Court on 1 January 2009 further cemented his position as a leader in his field.

'I speak – I must speak: my life forces me to speak – with sombre passion – about this. I nearly became one of the dead. After a poverty-ridden childhood, my white skin earned me passage into a relatively affluent South African adulthood. I did not party or take drugs or have multiple exposures to the seminal deposits of innumerable sexual partners. I led the generally cautious life of a hard-working lawyer. Yet I fell ill from Aids. It was transmitted to me in a single, incautious episode of unprotected receptive sexual intercourse during Easter 1985. It is only because of medical microbiology and its antiretroviral interventions that I am living today. To live is to know. It is to feel the joy of life's forces coursing through one's veins. To survive Aids is to feel the joy of escape, and the elation of continued life. It is also to bear the duty to speak, and the responsibility to bear witness.'

And as for his tombstone? Cameron hopes it will declare, 'He died happy.'

EDWIN CAMERON is living proof of how passion and determination can make a positive impact on the lives of others. Born into an impoverished and broken family, Cameron succeeded against all odds to reach the pinnacle of the legal profession in South Africa, becoming a Constitutional Court judge in 2009. Yet Cameron's success is all the more remarkable given his willingness to discuss his HIV-positive status. An engaging and candid man, Cameron has given hope to thousands of South Africans battling the disease.

SLOW AND STEADY WINS THE RACE

BOBBY GODSELL

GRASS ROOTS

Bobby Godsell was born into a peripatetic family. His father, Cyril Godsell, was born in England but emigrated with his family to Canada in the 1930s before returning to England as a young adult, while his mother, Winifred was born in South Africa but moved with her parents back to their home country, England, as a child. The couple met in England where they were married and had two children, before moving to South Africa where they had a further two children. 'My parents left Britain in 1947 and told us that they had lived there through two world wars and one great recession, and they wanted to go somewhere where they could raise their young family with better prospects and a more peaceful environment. Although that is an exaggeration as my mother was born in 1918, the same year as Nelson Mandela.'

Godsell was born in Boksburg in 1952 but he too moved at a young age. While in Canada his father had left school in Standard 8, working as a postman before becoming a specialist boilermaker. As an artisan, Godsell Senior got a job in Durban in 1955, helping to build a refinery for SAPREF, a joint venture between Shell SA Refining and BP Southern Africa. His mother was a bookkeeper who, never having been to university, worked her entire life. 'Neither of my parents earned a degree; I come from a genuine working-class background. Throughout my childhood we lived in rented accommodation and for most of the time we didn't have a car. I enjoy reminding Cyril [Ramaphosa] that, as his father was a warrant officer in the South African Police, he came from a far more bourgeois background than me!'

The young Godsell attended Brighton Beach Primary School, which he remembers well thanks to the events of 21 March 1960. 'I was in Standard 3 at the time of the Sharpeville massacre, which coincided with the end of the Mau Mau rebellion in Kenya. A very large group of angry black South Africans marched from Cato Manor, near Westville, towards Durban in protest, so my all-white government primary school stopped classes and each of us was interrogated to find out if our mothers were at home. Mine wasn't, so I had to stay at school and the memory of that stays with me; the rumour was that the domestic workers might slit the throats of the children at home! It's important to remember these things because we talk about this legacy of apartheid; often it's used as an excuse for terrible performance now, but there is a psychological legacy that is very deep among white and black South Africans.'

Godsell had been aware of the political and social situation in the country prior to this incident, however. 'I wrote an essay in Standard 1 about the Chinese invading South Africa. I lived on the Bluff and in my essay the whites were trying to get onto ships and the Organisation of African Unity was coming down from the north. I was interested in politics from a very early age and I was obviously quite a precocious – and I am sure very irritating – child!'

Godsell is a cricket fan who remembers, as a child, going to Kingsmead and 'thinking about where the moon was and what that had done to the tide and what it had done to the pitch. Some peculiarities! I also remember we had a whaling station on the Bluff and I once went and saw a whale being cut up. It was a very interesting event!'

Although Godsell once considered becoming a Methodist minister, his passion for politics saw him joining the youth movement of the Progressive Party in 1967 when he was just 15 and a student at Grosvenor Boys' High – a school he remembers with fondness and with which he still maintains contact. 'The Progressive Party was a breakaway from the Union Party; I joined at a very interesting time as the following year the government passed the Improper Interference Act – how Orwellian! This particular law said that a political party couldn't consist of members of more than one race group. The Progressive Party, while predominantly white, did have quite a few coloured and black members, including some coloured representatives in Parliament. So both the Progressive Party and the Liberal Party were faced with a dilemma – should they accept the new law and kick out their non-white members, or should they disband? The Liberal Party chose to disband but the Progressive Party decided to accept the law and continue as an all-white party.

'The youth movement was predominantly Indian, most of whom were communists, so I was making friends across the colour line as well as across the lines of ideology. The youth movement was absolutely opposed to carrying on as an all-white party. Life in South Africa really forced ambiguities and moral compromises on people. And it still does, of course.'

Godsell credits his parents for his open and tolerant outlook on life. 'What was marvellous was that my parents supported me in doing this, as did my school. In my matric year I won a competition that the Progressive Party ran in which young people had to write an essay about what you wanted South Africa to look like in 10 years' time. At the school's prize-giving this was acknowledged, which was an incredibly brave thing to do.'

Both of Godsell's parents were interested in politics, with his mother following her son's lead and joining the Progressive Party, ultimately becoming their regional secretary. 'My parents were completely supportive; their values were entirely congruent with mine. I brought black friends home and they'd join us for dinner or they slept over. My parents were very interested in ideas; they always encouraged us to read and think. My father was in and out of work and there were times when it was difficult to put food on the table, but we were always welcome to bring a friend home for supper – the meal would just be stretched a little. It was a basic quality of valuing people and being interested in other people. At university my three best friends were a Jewish South African, a Greek South African and an Afrikaans South African, and I loved taking them home because my parents would engage with them in a curious way.'

Godsell's mother came from a wealthy family and when she completed high school she attended a secretarial finishing school, so when it came time for her children to go to university she was very supportive. Godsell's father, however, 'took a lot of persuasion'. Coming from a family in which no one had a tertiary education, initially the elder Godsell could not understand why his oldest son should continue studying instead of going out to work. Fortunately, by the time Godsell matriculated both his brother and sister had been through university, so his father was more amenable to the idea.

Godsell believes that while South Africa has 'many things to be worried about in terms of education', the country must have one of the highest 'first-generation-at-university' penetration rates of any country in the world. 'We have a dramatic increase in black South Africans going to university, but there are still issues when a kid is 18 or 19 and is expected to support their family. For poor families, in particular, it is an issue. In fact, I think that a lot of black kids who have bursaries send some money home.'

Before he could go to university, however, Godsell was obliged to do military service, a duty he carried out 'briefly and rather ineffectually as part of the commando system'. He then obtained a bank loan and a bursary from Baker's Limited to pay for university. 'The bursary was the magnificent sum of R300 a year, which about covered my fees, and once a year I had to report to the personnel manager of Baker's and show him my exam results. I think that was as valuable as the R300!'

Godsell's initial plan was to do articles in the day and study law at night, but by securing a bursary he could study full-time. A hurdle in the form of Latin presented itself however, as he struggled with the language which was a prerequisite for law. As he loved sociology and philosophy he decided to follow that route, completing a BA with those subjects as his majors. Although he had initially planned to undertake an Honours year (he would later earn a Masters in Liberal Ethics through UCT), a letter he wrote to his friend, Alex Boraine, changed the course of his life. 'Alex was an employment practice consultant at Anglo American, and with the impertinence of a 21-year-old I wrote to him and told him that he needed an assistant and that I was available!'

In 1974 Godsell's career with the company, which would last 35 years, began. For the first five years Godsell would tell people that he worked for Boraine and not Anglo American; he loved the work but did not love the company. 'It was a big capitalist organisation that employed cheap black labour to dig the gold mines that built the South African economy.'

Working his way up the ranks, Godsell became an Executive Director of Anglo American in 1991 and CEO of the gold and uranium division in 1995. During that decade he also became President of the Chamber of Mines, remaining in the position for seven years until 1999. Godsell became CEO of AngloGold in April 1998, two years later adding co-Chair of the Millennium Labour Council and the following year Chairman of the World Gold Council to his résumé. Under Godsell's leadership, AngloGold merged with the Ashanti Goldfields Corporation in 2004, creating AngloGold Ashanti. Godsell retired as CEO in 2007, yet despite him and his marketing director being accused of excessive hedging, upon his retirement the then Chairman of AngloGold Ashanti, Russell Edey, commented that 'Bobby Godsell is a visionary who has done much to shape the destiny of both the South African labour relations landscape and that of AngloGold Ashanti'. Godsell remained in his role as non-executive director of Anglo American corporation, a position he had held since 1991.

Godsell's intention was to become more involved in civil society, and together with Dr James Motlatsi he published a book in 2008 entitled *Do It! Every South African's guide to making a difference*. He also chaired the board of St Augustine's university and Business Leadership South Africa, while sitting on the boards of the IDC and Polymetal International. His retirement was short-lived, however, as he took on the role of Non-Executive Chairman of Eskom that year. A media storm erupted the following year when Eskom underwent power shortages and posted record losses, which led to the CEO, Jacob Maroga, tendering his resignation verbally but then recanting. The ensuing boardroom struggle saw Godsell resign and Maroga being fired. Despite accusations of racism, Godsell was supported by both the National Union of Mineworkers as well as the ANC. Godsell had long enjoyed a constructive relationship with the unions, dating back to his involvement in forming Anglo American's employment practice policies. His role in the mining charter as well as his strong relationship with Cyril Ramaphosa, were also critical in bringing together different sides.

A STAKE IN THE GROUND

The following year Godsell was appointed to the National Planning Commission (NPC) by President Jacob Zuma, the aim of which was to create a National Development Plan (NDP). According to Godsell, the NDP has 'given a framework for South Africans to think of the future'.

In his years at Anglo American Godsell learned a great deal about people and leadership. 'I certainly reject the concept of the heroic leader. It is a rather male concept; the man on the shining horse. It's the Napoleonic concept that the American business culture has given strong emphasis to. I would define leaders as people who are able to persuade other people to do what they want. It's a very simple definition but I think that there are just two basic human impulses: one is individual accountability and the other is collective. Ultimately we must all make decisions and choices and must take responsibility for what we do, but most of the things that we achieve in life we do collectively. For me the concept of leadership is the ability that leaders have to get a group to focus on a common objective and work cooperatively. In my time as CEO of AngloGold Ashanti, not all of my executive colleagues were leaders, because persuading others to do what you want them to do is difficult.'

Godsell believes that leaders are often put into their positions because of their school tie, their culture or their skin colour. He often wonders why so many leaders, in business and in politics, are unwilling to admit that they make mistakes. 'For 12 years I ran a large company and it was a big responsibility. In particular there were two things that determined the fate or fortune of the company: the one was the dollar price of gold and the other was the rand/dollar exchange rate. I could do nothing about those two things so, as a team, we had to make guesses. We had a 12-month budget, a three-year plan and a five-year plan, all of which made assumptions. Sometimes we got it right and sometimes we got it wrong, but leaders pay a terrible price when they can't admit to making mistakes; there is a danger of making the same mistake again and again.

'If you admit your mistake, you are firstly acknowledging that you are human, secondly you look for collective wisdom from other people, and thirdly you are less likely to repeat your mistake. Dealing with the good decisions is easy, it's when the merger goes badly, the business is in trouble, the mine is late or you over-budgeted – that's the time when you learn the lessons.'

Godsell measures his success according to two barometers. The first is whether or not he leaves an institution in better shape than he found it, while the second is if he can look at himself in the mirror and be satisfied that he has retained his integrity. 'I would describe myself as a 51 per cent CEO – in other words, I hope that I got just slightly more judgement calls right than wrong; slightly more senior appointments right than wrong. I am happy that I achieved this at my time at AngloGold. You know, if you shaft people in order to get one rung up, unfortunately you do things to yourself.'

Godsell believes that for 95 per cent of the time during his tenure as CEO, decision-making at AngloGold was collective, but there was also 5 per cent when the evidence was not clear and the team was divided. 'There is a moment for all leaders when you have to make the decision and it is up to you. What's critical is that you make the decision – even if it's the wrong one – because often the worst thing is to do nothing. When we tried to buy Normandy and failed; now if I had the time to do it over I would have done the deal very differently. I made a bunch of mistakes. The top guy is left to make the lonely decision sometimes.'

Something that Godsell believes he did well in his 12 years as CEO was firing people. 'At certain intervals I had to sit down with senior people and tell them that both of us knew it wasn't working. I tried to fire someone without destroying their self-esteem and without allocating blame in a God sense. Nobody enjoys being fired, but I've kept contact with most of the people I've fired because I tried to do it with integrity.'

When it comes to character, Godsell believes that the most important question one needs to ask is if you like and respect yourself. His concern is that people see leaders as heroes with none of the doubts or temptations to which ordinary humans succumb, when in reality everybody has various roles – as an employee, parent, husband, citizen, friend – and they need to have integrity in every role they play.

Godsell has 'overwhelmingly' found his most challenging role to be that of a parent, with the second most challenging being a husband. He describes his wife, Gillian, as 'smarter and more successful than me. I respect her very deeply.' He considers himself blessed. 'Gillian and I have been married for 39 years and we have a wonderful partnership but things are never secure – you can't be complacent. She's changing, I'm changing. Our daughters are now grown up but, in a way they are now as demanding as they were when they were two, but there is less we can do about it now. We are developing adult/adult relationships with our children, and it is very difficult and a constant effort! But it is having integrity in those relationships that matters to me; it is much more important than whether I was a great CEO.'

Godsell is concerned with how people can learn to live in a post-apartheid South Africa without being apologetic, as well as being non-racial and interacting with people across race and gender barriers. This is in part why he took on his current role in the NPC. 'As a citizen, the NPC is the most exciting thing I have done. I was attracted to the NPC because we have spent 20 years – which is not all that long – trying to first identify the wounds of 300 years of race-based conquest and conflict. So we had 300 bad years in the office, and they were really bad years, and 20 years identifying our wounds and starting to lick them.

'And that process isn't finished. It won't be finished in my lifetime, probably not even in the lifetime of my children. But the wonderful thing about the NPC is that it's saying, "Let's also look forward. Let's be honest about the past, but let's look forward and say where would we like South Africa to be in 2030."' It was an incredible privilege, he says, to serve with 25 other South Africans in trying to answer those questions, and enter a dialogue with society about those questions.

'We are a robust, argumentative society, which is a huge strength. I used to get "Is South Africa going to make it?" all the time in London. I could never understand what this question meant. What are your fears? Is it a coup d'état? Look at Egypt – can you see that happening in South Africa? No, actually I can't. We are robust and we are a nation of dialogue; it's a family that has big family arguments all the time but hasn't yet divorced.

'I think for most adult South Africans their identity is very significantly informed by their race. This coincides, of course, with class; if you are white you probably grew up in a suburb, you're kind of upper working class or middle class, you have been either to a good government school or a private school. But on the other hand there is a new reality emerging: my three daughters all have friendship groups that significantly and deeply cross the race barrier. I would say that, for them, gender issues are probably more compelling and more urgent than race issues. And I find that exciting and terrifying because there's a whole bunch of stuff I don't understand, and the legacy of patriarchy is a deep one. But it's a kind of new agenda. You know what is true is that we need a new vocabulary, maybe even a new language. I think, unfortunately, gender is still a big and oppressive issue.'

In terms of politics, Godsell's concern is that the two largest parties in South Africa 'articulate non-racialism but their very architecture is race-dominated. I really look forward to the political party that is about class issues, about gender issues and about how we should implement the NDP. I mean, the delightful thing about the NDP is that all the major parties, particularly the ANC and the DA, have endorsed it. So there is an agenda and a vision, and the debate should be "How do we get there?"'

Godsell's contribution to civil society developed further in 2013, when together with the founder member of NUM and his co-author, Dr James Motlatsi, the pair launched the Citizens' Charter. The two also work together as Patrons of the National Education Collaboration Trust, and aim through the Charter to encourage South African citizens to 'commit to the values of active citizenship and to engage in some personal action to realise these values'. To move this forward the Charter has created resource groups in the fields of education, health, environmental sustainability, youth and employment, and crime prevention, as well as regional steering groups to help 'promote and sustain active citizenship throughout the length and breadth of our beautiful country'.

As for his epitaph, Godsell hasn't 'the slightest interest!'

'I am not going to orchestrate my funeral, I will be happily somewhere else, so I am very delighted to leave that to whoever – and anything or nothing. Tombstones are for the survivors, as are funerals. So they should do whatever makes them happy.'

Best known for his many years at the helm of AngloGold and AngloGold Ashanti, **BOBBY GODSELL** came from a working-class background in Durban and worked his way up through the ranks of the mining conglomerate. Never one to shy away from hard work and speaking his mind, Godsell has also played a key role in promoting the importance of civil society in South Africa, with the aim of creating a better country for all who live here.

FREEDOM LIES IN BEING BOLD

FERIAL HAFFAJEE

TURNING ADVERSITY INTO ADVANTAGE

With each of her parents, Ahmed and Ayesha, hailing from families with eight children, it was drilled into Ferial Haffajee from an early age that education would be her best way out of hardship as well as the apartheid system. 'My mom dropped out of school – tragically, I think, because she could have gone so much further than she did, and my father was lucky enough to have matriculated and attend one year of Medicine at university before he too was forced to drop out due to a lack of money. My parents were both among the older children in their families so there was an expectation that they would leave school and begin working to fill the family pot. You know, my parents' life stories have always, and continue to, inspire me. By working their way up from being a seamstress and a dispatcher to having office jobs, they made a lot out of a life that really didn't give them very much.'

Haffajee was a *laat lammetjie*, with two older brothers who now live in Cape Town and Durban. The children grew up in Bosmont, 'a coloured area kind of halfway between Johannesburg and Soweto'. Haffajee attended Chris Jan Botha School, explaining that 'like all schools in our area, it was named after an apartheid bureaucrat so I have no idea who he was. It was a good school, though, with capable teachers and a great principal. It was very political and had a reputation like some of the schools on the Cape Flats for really drilling its pupils very well and turning out many graduates. I was lucky to go there.'

Haffajee matriculated from Chris Jan Botha and was accepted into Wits in 1985, but had a different view to her mother when it came to a choice of what to study. 'I always knew I wanted to be a journalist, but my mother, like most mothers of her generation, thought that if she was going to slog hard to send a kid to university then it better be for them to become something like a lawyer or an accountant. What I really wanted to do was become a trainee at *The Weekly Mail*, which had started up the same year out of the ashes of the *Rand Daily Mail*.'

In order to pay her way Haffajee took on numerous and diverse jobs, from working at her aunty's butchery and being a sales assistant at Scott's and Woolworths, to helping at the clothing factory where her father worked, among others. 'I just basically took any job I could find and I am very, very happy now that I did, because the sheer mundaneness, or that kind of menial work, made me work really hard because I knew that that was not what I wanted to do with my life.'

Haffajee initially studied for a BA with Law with a view to attaining an LLB, but then decided to follow her 'head, heart and ambitions' and changed course to study African Literature Honours instead. 'For me African literature was the only thing that bore any resemblance to my life, and I wanted to know more about the system and more about my country. After I completed my BA I started my Honours while I also worked at the Centre for Applied Legal Studies at Wits, but then in the same year I was accepted into *The Weekly Mail* training project so I left university for that opportunity.'

I HAVE A DREAM

Haffajee's passion for journalism and literature helped her to 'understand why our lives and our country was like it was. I saw literature as the narrative of my life; it gave me meaning. But journalism was really my way of extending my work as a young activist. I read stories by journalists who had helped to change the country and had done amazing work, and I wanted to be like them. My teachers and fellow journalists were always a source of inspiration to me; there has always been a hand to pull you up if you showed you were keen, which has been wonderful.'

Although the Haffajees were not overt political activists they were extremely politically aware; her brothers were very inspired at university by revolutionaries such as Che Guevara, as well as the music of The Beatles and Jimi Hendrix. 'They were also influenced by Steve Biko – one of my brothers studied with him. Every holiday they would bring all that knowledge, all that music, all that culture back home with them. I guess it was a very natural influence for me – plus my high school was fiercely political so we were right in the middle of the boycotts, including the boycott of the Tricameral Parliament, so it was always going to be in my blood as well.'

Haffajee's parents were conservative and would have preferred that their children kept their heads down and concentrated on their studies, but Haffajee was 'never going to be that kid!' For Haffajee and her peers, university was 'sometimes lectures and mostly being part of the uprising of the time'. Haffajee was arrested a few times, but these were just short detentions arising from her activism on campus and work in the community.

The Weekly Mail was a very liberal newspaper, with a founding stance of 'campaigning journalism'. 'We had lawyers on call all the time. Irwin Manoim was one of the founders and he developed the infamous model of blacking out; we would be banned and then he would black out the text and publish like that.'

Haffajee started as an intern but moved across to the labour beat as soon as she could because that was where her passion lay. 'My heart belonged to the union and it played a big role in my life. I then moved across to politics and arts and everything in-between. I loved all the desks but I was deeply political and almost immediately began doing investigations and political reporting. By that time my parents were resigned to me being a bit of a maverick rebel kid, but by the time I officially became a journalist the winds of change were coming. We did cover the last of the violence between the ANC and the IFP, as well as the third force, though.'

BREAKING THE MOULD

After three years Haffajee moved to the SABC in 1991 because she wanted to learn about broadcast journalism, and then moved on to join the *Financial Mail* in 1994 to learn about business. During her time at the *Financial Mail*, Haffajee won the Sanlam Award for Excellence in Financial Journalism in 2001 and moved her way up the ranks to become the managing editor in 2002, before going back in 2004 to *The Weekly Mail* as editor of what is now the *Mail & Guardian*. Haffajee was just 36 at the time and was the first woman to be named editor of a major national newspaper in South Africa. She also became the boss of her partner at the time, Paul Stober, as he was one of the deputy editors. '*The Weekly Mail/Mail & Guardian* always answered a need for the kind of journalism I enjoyed, so that is why I went back.'

During her five years as editor of the *Mail & Guardian*, Haffajee was awarded the Top Woman in Media Award by MTN and *The Media* Magazine, yet her role was not without controversy, with Haffajee being threatened for republishing a controversial cartoon depicting the Prophet Mohammed. By 2009 Haffajee felt that it was time to do something different. 'The marvellous offer of the position of editor at *City Press* came up and, without arrogance, by then I could edit the *M&G* with my eyes closed. It had become my world and I got it and I got the people and the readers, so *City Press* was a marvellous challenge.'

Given that Haffajee has been editor of *City Press* for five years, the obvious question is 'What next?' Because she feels that she has more work to do at *City Press* there is no rush for her to make a decision, but she thinks that she will in all likelihood do something online or in the digital media space. 'I feel my life is definitely a work in progress, especially with the rapid change in not only the world, but in my world. I feel like journalism is in an evolutionary/revolutionary time; it's very exciting but also fundamentally challenging. There is so much to learn every day. I feel like I'm caught behind if I don't know the latest things.

'Just take this year, with all that has happened. The thing is that the stories are being told everywhere. So the Oscar story, for example, is live on Twitter, live in the courtroom, live on TV, live on radio, so you've got to think, "Okay, how am I going to take the long view and transfer meaning or great news?" It can be pretty nerve-racking at times but very, very challenging. I'd like to stay in an established media project as opposed to starting something new. I'm quite innovative from inside an organisation – I enjoy being an "intrapreneur". Wherever I've worked I've started new projects that have had long lives and made quite a bit of money for the organisations concerned, like the *Financial Mail's Little Black Book* and the *Mail & Guardian's* "100 Young South Africans you must take to lunch". I enjoy highlighting new talent and introducing different groups to each other who may not otherwise have met.'

Haffajee is passionate about South Africa, which is why despite having had many opportunities to work overseas, she has remained in the country. 'I would love to do an Al-Jazeera and I love New York and many places in the world, but I have strong family ties and I love my city and my country, so it hasn't crossed my mind to leave.'

THE PRINCIPLE OF THE MATTER

'Certain journalists, such as Anton Harber, the founding editor of *The Weekly Mail*, have been important personal mentors for Haffajee. 'Anton is a constant inspiration to me. Charlotte Bouwer has also been a mentor, as well as the former *Weekly Mail* assistant editor, Barbara Ludman, who taught me how to write'. These days, however, Haffajee is finding herself increasingly inspired by younger journalists, some of whom she has met through her current and previous roles as a board member of the International Women's Media Foundation, the World Editors' Forum, the International Press Institute and the Inter Press Service. The characteristics that Haffajee looks for in people are the ability to create value and to be visionary. 'I have come to a point in my life where I appreciate people like Nelson Mandela who really just had the absolute capacity to see beyond the obvious. There's a whole lot of business people and union leaders – not now, but in the past – who I think played fundamentally important roles in our country. Look at how the organised working class has managed to improve their lives. I think our political leadership kind of lacks it at the moment, but I don't think South Africa as a whole lacks visionaries and inspiring people.'

When it comes to leadership, Haffajee believes that every leader needs to be curious and have an ability to listen. While she admits to sometimes not being a very good listener herself, she hopes to make up for that with 'oodles of curiosity'. When putting the paper to bed Haffajee has the last word, so she finds herself constantly testing limits and occasionally second-guessing herself. 'I usually feel like I have possessed, evaluated and made my decision, but of course every Sunday I wonder if I used the right words and I remake the paper in my head constantly. But I've learned, as a journalist, that you need to push boundaries. We've been taken to court many, many times for uncovering things, but that just comes with the turf and I've had to apologise a couple of times.

'Take *The Spear*, for example. When the Goodman Gallery displayed a painting depicting President Jacob Zuma with his genitals exposed which the ANC objected to, I had to decide whether or not we should publish a copy of the painting. I sometimes find that is part of the making of a new society; you are finding the edges. I grew up in a place where bullying was pretty common so I have grown to hate it; I don't take kindly to people trying to push me around. Sometimes I have given in to pressure, for example when I took the image of *The Spear* down from our website because I was scared and I was trying to do the right thing. In my experience, I've found it's better to stand up to that kind of bullying political pressure, though.'

Haffajee is concerned at what she sees as South African leaders being cowed by many things, which she attributes to a lack of bravery or the ability to lead and make a decision. She gives an example of Jacob Zuma and the broader ANC, whose lack of leadership she believes hobbles the country. She also sees this in the business sector. 'I think business leaders in this country need to learn to speak out and say their say, because we are not without inspiring, innovative and brilliant leadership. I don't know what has happened in the last, maybe 10 years; it seems like the business sector and the labour sector feel like they have a lesser stake in South Africa, but that isn't our founding story at all. Of course there have been some instances where people have put their heads up and said things only to get them lopped off. Zwelinzima Vavi, Michael Jordaan and Reuel Khosa are some of the line-up of skulls, so maybe that's part of the reason people keep their heads down. But I don't think that is right for a young country in the making.'

When it comes to politics, Haffajee wonders if things are going to go through a tough patch given the slide in ANC numbers in the 2014 elections as well as the growth of the EFF. 'I think we're going to be pulled in radical directions with the EFF in Parliament, and if a genuine workers' party starts out of whatever NUMSA is planning, I think we're going to head into pretty tough but maybe hopeful seas, because it's true that the fruits of freedom haven't gone to enough people. I was very upset by the violence during the march by the Democratic Alliance to Albert Luthuli House. I disliked the lack of tolerance shown and the fact that people were armed. I also disliked that, with the ANC's long history of leadership, no one managed to do the right thing and let the march continue. That is part of what we do in South Africa, we march. The violence related to the protest movements should not be ignored. My country not being all it could be makes me very stressed.'

Something else that causes Haffajee stress is the inability to walk freely at night as she does in cities like London and Addis Ababa. 'In many parts of our continent people have freedoms that we don't. We need to take precautions against crime and the high rates of rape and gender violence in our society instead of being able to enjoy freedom as women to move around.'

As far as her own leadership style is concerned, Haffajee thinks that she has been influenced by her upbringing and growing up in political and other organisations. 'I think we have quite a flat and consultative set-up here, but I've also learned in my role that you have to be able, at some point, to stop the consultation and make a decision. I am fairly exacting and demanding; some people like it and some don't.'

Despite all her years in the business, Haffajee still loves journalism and what it means for South Africa. 'I love finding out things and, in the end, I like sculpting and crafting what I hope are beautiful pieces. Sometimes they are not, but I feel incredibly lucky to do something I love and be paid for it, because I recognise that that is not the lot of most people.'

Something that Haffajee is becoming increasingly interested in is the economy. 'I know that it is nerdish, but I really want to know why we are unable to get more young people into the economy. I'm also still curious about the human mind; what makes us tick? And as I get older I'm curious about longevity and health, although there are some yoga poses that have me completely flummoxed!'

Haffajee's admits to many flaws, which 'get pointed out a lot on Twitter!' Among these she counts impetuousness and being demanding. 'I am constantly reminded that I can pay attention to the "softer" stuff – to what makes humans human – and to spend more time talking to all parts of my colleagues, rather than just to their journalistic minds. I do think that I can be empathetic, but it's a constant work in progress!'

Haffajee is fascinated with Twitter because it has taught her brevity and a whole new way of communicating. 'I'm interested in being part of that community, but it can be pretty vicious. It's important to learn which of the feedback to ignore and to understand when you are picking up an important trend. I'm getting better at it; I've learned how to make agile use of the Block button and when to engage a real trend about our coverage. I've learned to care less about what people think as I have gotten older, but I'm also not the sort of person who can say I don't care at all. I care what important people think of me and I enjoy their feedback, so if they tell me that I messed up on something, I'll listen and try to fix it.'

Learning through trying is something Haffajee believes has stood her in good stead during her two decades as a journalist. 'I have built up good technical skills and I'm not shy to learn things; I mostly learn through reading and trying things. I'm also part of the African Leadership Initiative, which is a lovely programme at the Aspen Institute. They put you through a two-year, part-time programme, which has five modules. You really learn about the great philosophers and thinkers; from the classic through to the present. That is having a massive impact in helping me to discern my values and try to live by them.'

These values are framed around the idea of what makes a good society and what makes a good citizen. Haffajee strongly believes that success is not just about lots of things or lots of money, but about a larger impact that people who become leaders leave behind. Haffajee measures her success by her legacy as well as how much she gives. 'It's not just about giving money because journalists are never going to be rich, but rather about giving time – particularly to young people. I try to ensure that I'm giving away 10 per cent of what I earn, as well as helping kids and being a mentor. Those are important things to me.'

Haffajee learned some lessons about mentorship from a social worker friend who stayed with her, as well as from the young people in her office and students who she more formally mentors. In addition, she also sits on the board of Gender Links and tries to find time to work with a project called Men on the Side of the Street, because that was a cause her father was passionate about. Despite this, or perhaps because of it, Haffajee believes that she does not have a good work/life balance, something she is trying to rectify by making time to read, practise yoga and go to gym. She has also made a concerted effort over the last two years to see the people she loves who were forced to take a back seat during her rise to the top. This new philosophy is the basis for how she hopes to look back upon her life: 'What a ride! That was fun.'

Even as a child, **FERIAL HAFFAJEE** was never one to shy away from a challenge, which is why at just 36 years old she found herself as the first female editor of a major South African newspaper, the *Mail & Guardian*. Having heeded her parents' advice that education would be the key to her success, Haffajee studied and worked her way to the top, from where she engages both her detractors and her defenders.

NOTHING VENTURED, NOTHING GAINED

MICHAEL JORDAAN

NO ORDINARY LIFE

Michael Jordaan considers his upbringing to have been a 'typical, suburban, middle-class one', which in the South African context was 'probably a relatively privileged upbringing'. Born and raised in Pretoria, Jordaan's family was Afrikaans-speaking and he attended Menlo Park Primary, spending holidays with his paternal grandparents on their farm in the Banghoek Valley outside Stellenbosch. Following his parents' divorce while he was in primary school, Jordaan lived with his mother, but his trips to Stellenbosch continued and he developed a strong bond with his German grandmother, Hedwig.

Jordaan credits his parents and grandparents with instilling in him a strong set of values, describing his father as 'the most polite person you will ever meet', his mother as 'such a soft person, really focused on the humanity in people', and his grandmother as 'very, very loving person'. Having come to South Africa from Germany just before the Second World War, when 'life was already very tough', his grandmother introduced the concept of saving to him, amassing her

1c and 2c pieces for him to deposit in the local Stellenbosch Distriksbank every holiday. 'I would go to the bank and hand the coins over the counter where they would write up something like, "R2,32 deposited" in my savings book.' But these were not the only transactions that Jordaan was involved in, as he grew up fascinated with finance, financial markets and banking in general. Although he admits to having 'a very, very bad idea of what it was all about fully', he liked the idea of the stock market and wanted to understand the mechanics of it. 'One thing always led to another with me. I bought and sold things, so for example I would make sandwiches and sell them on the beach while we were on holiday in Plettenberg Bay; and then I bought rabbits with my profit and fed them with waste from our local grocery shop and sold them to the pet shop. I was always hustling with my pocket money and eventually saved up enough to buy myself a horse! I then went on to sell the horse so that I could buy a share in the bank I had been depositing the money from my grandmother into. I think I bought and sold some gold coins in-between as well; I was always hustling!

'I was lucky that the shares in the bank went up; it could have gone either way, but because it went up I think my love for the markets was validated. It's all these little experiences you have in your youth that add up. For me it was a savings culture, discipline and a little bit of luck.'

When it came to high school, Jordaan's mother sent him to Paul Roos Gymnasium in Stellenbosch where he lived in a hostel annexed to the school, spending his precious Sunday afternoons with his grandmother on the farm as his grandfather passed away shortly after Jordaan's move to the Western Cape. 'I had been there often on holiday so it was a great place for me. In fact it's the same farm where I live now with my family; many years later in 2006 I purchased it back after my father had sold it. It was always very special for me.'

Education was important to the family, with both his grandparents earning doctorates and both his parents having Masters degrees. 'I come from a family where hard work – and particularly academic hard work – was highly prized, so after school it was a natural step for me to go on to university.' Jordaan attended Stellenbosch University where he attained a BCom, and it was at university that he really came into his own. 'At school I was very shy and introverted – I used to read a book a day and didn't make friends easily, but when I got to university everything changed. It was an easy transition for me because I'd been living in Stellenbosch – I just swapped my school uniform for civilian clothes. I believe I became an individual when I reached university because of the absence of very strict authority and uniforms and so on. I felt that suddenly the pressure was on me to perform; it wasn't the school system where you learn things by rote or if you didn't do the right thing someone would give you a caning. Now it was up to me and I loved the freedom; I could make of it what I wanted. I also loved the people. Suddenly I had free spirits all around me; people with differing ideas and on different sides of the ideological spectrum; there were lots of debates at the local pub! I wasn't a great student and I was often at the copying machine, but luckily I was good at achieving under pressure! I loved varsity and I wish I hadn't passed everything so quickly because I think one should stay there as long as possible!'

Jordaan began his academic career by studying a BCom Law, but in his second year he realised that as much as he appreciated law and thought it a wonderful dogma, it was very limited to South Africa. 'You can become a lawyer but you can't practise anywhere else and I found that I loved economics and the international aspect of it, so I took some extra subjects in my third year so that I could complete my BCom Law degree as well as do my Honours in Economics.'

When Jordaan finished his Honours year in 1989 conscription was still in force, which meant that he had to complete his military service. 'I went to the navy and, at the time, I thought I was very lucky because they'd just shortened it from two years to one year, but I look back now and think of all the wonderful things I could have done with an extra year in my youth. I would probably have travelled the world and who knows what would have happened then!'

In the beginning Jordaan did not enjoy his time at the navy, having become used to the freedom and flexibility of university life. 'Initially we did basic training where they try to break you down and build you up; you're always running and being shouted at and you don't sleep a lot. But after three months I was selected for an officers' course, which was actually a lot better and a lot more civil! There are some nice traditions in the navy, and we learned everything from sailing and tying ropes to behaving like an officer and learning how to march with a sword. I never really did anything with the training that I got, which shows what a waste it was. For everyone.'

A STRANGER IN A STRANGE LAND

His time in the navy saw Jordaan awarded the SAS *Simonsberg* trophy for Best Officer on Course, but upon his discharge he wanted to gain some international experience in banking, so he applied for a management trainee programme through Deutsche Bank. 'The bank at the time let some foreigners into the programme so I was very fortunate to be part of the 10 to 20 per cent they let in. They took us through all the different departments of a typical commercial bank and my first assignment, where I spent three months, was as a teller. I stood behind the counter and dealt with basic, basic queries and counted money. I think that stood me in incredibly good stead; today you see people who are catapulted into middle- or senior-management levels after having studied and I sometimes think that if I ask those people how many zeroes there are in a billion they won't know! It sounds like a terribly incremental way of approaching it, but I do think there is value in it. I'm not saying you necessarily need to spend ages working in the mailroom to understand how a corporation works, but it's very useful to understand the detail of how things fit together.'

Jordaan lasted two years in Germany before looking out of the window of his little flat in Frankfurt one morning and deciding that it was time to return home. 'I could imagine a normal, good life there and I had a girlfriend at the time, but I just didn't feel fulfilled. I think that is something that happens to a lot of South Africans; you start feeling like a number when you're abroad. And it's not only friends and family that you have back home, but somehow also a desire to achieve something and to make things better at home. I wrote a little note to the bank, which I gave to them the next day, and within a few weeks I found myself on a plane back to SA.'

HOME, SWEET HOME

Says Jordaan, 'I actually kissed the earth when we landed at OR Tambo! People looked at me very strangely! It was a terrible time in South Africa; Chris Hani had just been shot and it was probably the closest we've ever come to a revolution so people thought I was crazy to come back, but I've been very happy here. I'm one of those people who encourages other South Africans who are living abroad to come home and make it better.'

While working in Germany, Jordaan had managed to complete his Masters degree in Economics through Stellenbosch University, so upon returning he began his PhD through his alma mater, with his dissertation being on Banking Supervision. He was six months into the dissertation when he saw an advert in the newspaper for a position at Rand Merchant Bank (RMB). 'The advert read: "Archie and Ben were professional golfers and keen rivals. One day during a game they had each scored 30 when Ben hit a bad shot. Archie immediately added 10 to his own score. Archie then hit a good shot and he had won the game. Why?"

'So I sent in my application even though I didn't really know very much about RMB; their ad seemed an interesting way to recruit. I had to go for a few interviews, but three months later I got the job. I had been there a year and had worked in two different departments before Paul Harris approached me and said he was looking for an assistant. He told me that I would get a better overview of the bank with him than if I was working in one department, so I was lucky that he noticed me. Incidentally, it's something I always did later in my career when I was CEO – I looked for promising youngsters and had them work with me for a year as an assistant.

'I love finance and the abstractedness of it. I love the fact that it touches nearly everything in society; it has an impact on politics, markets, economic events, growth rates, different industries and so on. I really think anyone in banking is in an incredibly fortunate position where you seem to feel everything that happens around you. So, broadly, I loved what I was doing, and then at FirstRand I found a culture that I could really relate to. The bank was suitably strategically tight in the sense that you couldn't just go out there and do things that weren't part of the strategy, but it was very operationally loose; it wasn't as if you had a boss that you had to report to at the end of every day – it was really up to you to go get the results you wanted. I think that had a lot to do with the fact that it was founded by entrepreneurs who were still very much involved in the business. I was just lucky, I think, that I could work very hard and get some results, and that I got them in an environment that really suited me. If I was put into a bank that was far stricter or more hierarchical or more stiff, I doubt whether I would have done half as well as I did in this particular environment.'

Jordaan moved up through the ranks at FirstRand, holding consecutive CEO positions at Origin; FNB Home Loans, where he was instrumental in bringing about a R400 million profit turnaround; and eBucks, which he launched in 2000. From there he moved in 2002 to lead FNB's Customer Solutions Division, and two years later became CEO of FNB when he was just 36 years old.

'On the whole I really enjoyed my time as CEO, although in every single job there are things you don't like. I would love, for example, my own meetings; when I was with my team and we were discussing business, that was great – but there were certain meetings when you felt we were just sitting around a boardroom table and not getting the job done. To use a sporting analogy, I wanted to be the captain more than the coach – I wanted to be part of the game – so when I felt that the pace wasn't quick enough or we weren't getting on with things, that would be frustrating.'

During his time as CEO, Jordaan was nominated as a World Economic Forum Global Leader, as well as the CNBC Africa Business Leader of the Year for Southern Africa, and during his tenure FNB was nominated the most innovative bank in the world, thanks in large part to the annual innovation competition, the FNB Innovators Programme, which Jordaan launched in 2004.

Jordaan's time at FNB was not all plain sailing, however, with one of the most controversial incidents of his tenure – the flighting of TV adverts in which schoolchildren read out their hopes for the country – taking place while he was away on holiday. 'I think there were 33 000 people working for FNB across many countries but if things went wrong the buck needed to stop somewhere. I really believe that, as part of a leadership philosophy, when things go well you don't take the praise but give it to the people who really made it happen. But when things go wrong, don't be shy to go out there and say, "Listen, I am accountable." Those times aren't fun, but those are the things you have to do if you're a proper leader.

'When the controversy around the advertising campaign with the school children happened I was on leave and there was a huge amount of misinformation around it. The objections weren't around the adverts but the online clips, which were withdrawn when only about 40 people around the world had seen them. So it was just a massive, massive misunderstanding … fortunately it had no business effect, despite the fact that it was in the newspapers for quite a long time. I would have been very worried if it had harmed the business in some way, but luckily it didn't. It was just a very delicate management situation. You know, I love the banking bit, but not the spinning that sometimes comes with being a CEO.'

One aspect of being a CEO that Jordaan enjoyed was working with so many people. 'I love it when you give people a challenge and they succeed. I love it particularly when they succeed beyond what they themselves thought that they could do. I really think that that is the best part of being in a privileged position as a leader; you surround yourself with people who are better than you. First of all, you have to have the confidence to do that, and then you need to be able to set them free. I think as much as I love the technical side of financial services – and I really do – the real kick is out of the people and when they do well.'

BACK TO HIS ROOTS

For the last six years of his tenure as CEO of FNB, Jordaan commuted between Johannesburg and Stellenbosch, where his wife and three daughters lived full-time. One of the reasons for his departure from the bank was that he wanted to spend more time with his family, but he also believes that a CEO should not stay in that position for more than 10 years. His latest venture has been opening a private investment firm, MonteGray Capital, the office of which sits on the site of the bank he used to visit in the holidays with his grandmother's cents.

'There are just two of us at MonteGray and I obviously do miss some of the adrenalin that you get every day being in the big seat, but I like the fact that I can be informal now. We're investing in disruptive technologies, so I have lots of exposure to people who come and pitch new ideas, which means I don't find any lack of intellectual stimulation. Some of the ideas are crazy – I think there are a lot of crazy people out there! – but every now and then you just get so excited by people and their inherent optimism. I really want to help young entrepreneurs who have great ideas and great execution capabilities to build up businesses that in five or ten years' time could be a challenge to big business. I truly think that big corporates are only going to survive if they're innovative enough and use technology.

'I also have a lot of friends here, so for me it has been a very happy trade-off. I'm lucky that I have been able to make a big switch in my life now, because I think the world is going to change so much in the next few years that young people are going to have to get ready to pursue many careers and lifelong learning if they're going to keep up. If you look at technology, for instance, I think that small companies with highly competent people will only need modest start-up capital to use open-source technologies to take on large institutions.'

While Jordaan has no plans to study further, he remains a voracious reader. 'The funny thing about any topic is that the more you know something the more you realise how little you know about it. So, for instance, I live on a wine farm, we have a wine brand and I'm the Chairman of Wines of South Africa, but the more I learn about wine the more I feel like an amateur!' When he's not in his office or reading, Jordaan finds time to fit in helping to run the farm; acting as Chairman of Mxit; director of Compuscan, Angelhub, the JSE and Invenfin; and managing the family's wine and champagne bar in Stellenbosch. He credits many people with his success, as he finds he is inspired by different people every day. 'You know, sometimes you just meet somebody and they have a great attitude and energy and you joke and laugh, and I find that inspiring. I'm just broadly inspired by people who have the right attitude about life.'

Jordaan considers himself 'such an ordinary person' and does not enjoy being the focus of attention. 'I don't have a big ego, but I think that's important for leaders. I think leadership is just an amplification of one's personal values and character – in other words, the way that you live. Character, for me, is if you are generally respectful of other people, you are trustworthy, you have humility and you don't mind if people tell you that you're wrong. We all have to continually work on our characters because we all make mistakes.'

A common theme running throughout Jordaan's life is innovation, although he describes himself as more of an 'intrapreneur' than entrepreneur. 'I love talking about and implementing new ideas, but ideas are worthless if you don't execute them. I think that the pendulum has swung for me – I started out at a young age as an entrepreneur and then moved into intrapreneurial positions in the bank, but now I'm back starting my own business again. I have a healthy disrespect for authority, so this – combined with wanting to understand how technology can change our lives for the better and how it can enable businesses to better serve their clients – means that running my own business at this stage is really where I want to be. I've always been a geek, but a playful one; so I was never a really good coder or a really good hardware maker, but I loved "toys". Any new gadget or gizmo or technological widget was always fascinating to me. I loved to take things apart and would never quite know how to put them back together again! That's why I've always loved Twitter – I see it as a novel way not only to talk to people but also to find out what's going on in the world without having to wait for conventional media to pick it up. There's a great conversation going on out there and I love the humour as well.'

Jordaan has no plans to take his business abroad and hopes that his children will always live in South Africa, despite acknowledging that the country is not all it could be. 'South Africans are sometimes unhappy because we could be doing so much better, and I am definitely of the school of thought that if we implemented some of our policies, like the National Development Plan, better, we could have a 5 per cent-plus growth rate. If we took education more seriously, we should have a million kids entering the schooling system in Grade 1 every year and having that same number of children writing and passing matric every year.

'But while it is clearly easy to talk about all the things that we should be doing better, at the same time I don't think we run the risk of becoming a failed state like some of the scenario analysts want us to believe. I think in many ways we have become an "ordinary" country, in the sense that we are somewhere between a developed country and a developing country. We have the benefit of being part of a continent that is fast-growing, so businesses are expanding out there. I'm basically optimistic about our country, but I'm an optimist who is saying that I do think we could do so much better. The fact that I am here, the fact that I am living in South Africa, when, like any other people we could be living abroad, says I am voting with my feet and I am here and I would like my kids to be here.

'As technology becomes more and more pervasive I think we need to be mindful of the context of the world we live in. If you travel the world you see that there are 193 other countries that we are competing with and there are great ideas that we could be getting from all of them. I think people should travel more, but not on expensive trips where they stay in first-class hotels; they need to get out there and converse as much as possible and understand what the world is about. I worry that we're a little insular and we need to be more competitive – particularly through education. We all know the country has major, major challenges in the field of education, and in the long-term a decent standard of education is what will make the economy grow. Education is also important because it helps us to understand each other better. Clearly, there is room for communication – not just between business and politics, but between people of all walks of life in South Africa.'

Apart from getting the best education possible, Jordaan believes that a key message for young people is that they need to look after themselves. 'I'm inherently lazy and I don't do enough exercise unless I make a conscious decision about it, but we really take our bodies for granted when we're young, and as you get older you begin to get issues with it. If you are fit and eat well, then you will sleep well, and if you sleep well then you will have a better quality of life and you will be able to achieve more and your enjoyment in life will just be so much more. Unfortunately, I'm not naturally the guy who gets up at 5am to go for a 20 kilometre run so I really have to be disciplined!'

Jordaan is also a strong believer in taking risks, which is something he is concerned that young people are afraid of. 'I grew up in an Afrikaans environment where we were never really told that risk is a good thing. Attributes like hard work and loyalty were considered good, but nobody would say that when you grow up you have to take chances in life. I'm not saying take wild, reckless chances, but reward is absolutely correlated with risk. This speaks not only to entrepreneurialism but to all disciplines, from academics to business to any endeavour that you choose.'

When it comes to his success, Jordaan measures it according to how happy he is. 'I think happiness is really important; it's probably the root of everything for many, many people. I've realised that many of the conventional things by which people measure success are not appropriate, and I certainly don't believe that materialistic success is what makes people happy. If you are basically grateful for the things around you – and for me it's for the friends I have and my relationships – then you'll be successful.'

This attitude towards success can be seen in Jordaan's choice of an epitaph: 'I'd hope my family and friends would say that I was a good husband, dad and friend.'

MICHAEL JORDAAN received many accolades during his illustrious career in banking, which included First National Bank being named the most innovative bank in the world during his tenure as CEO. Never one to sit back and enjoy the limelight, he turned back to his entrepreneurial roots in 2014 when he opened his own venture capital business, while also working with his wife to run their boutique wine farm and wine bar in his beloved Stellenbosch.

A TEAM PLAYER

GARY KIRSTEN

WORK HARD, PLAY HARD

Given the passion that Gary Kirsten's parents had for sport, it is little wonder that he ended up playing cricket for a living. 'I was born in Cape Town and grew up in a family that was very much involved in sport, so my parents exposed me to all different games from a very early age. My dad encouraged us to play as much sport as possible and it came naturally to us. We went to all the provincial matches when I was a youngster and developed a passion and a motivation to be involved in sport as much as possible. My mother also loved sport – we spent a lot of time at home talking about and being involved in sport in one way or another. My dad also encouraged me to get a good matric, but sport was the topic of conversation in the home and we lived for that.'

Cricket and rugby were the two sports Kirsten focused on most, although he also enjoyed tennis and played squash in the winter months. His father believed in team sports as he thought his sons would have more fun that way, but the boys could 'generally play anything'.

'At one point I was playing tennis quite seriously; I became more involved in cricket by chance really … I was also very much into my rugby but I was probably best at cricket, which made the decision a little easier. A lot of things fell into place at a later stage – by the time I left school I hadn't decided whether I wanted to play cricket professionally; I was still playing rugby as scrumhalf until I was 26.'

Kirsten's father was an engineer and his mother, while predominantly a stay-at-home mom, also took on a number of projects of her own. The house was a busy one, with three sons and a daughter from Kirsten Senior's first marriage and two sons from his marriage to Gary's mother. Following his parents' divorce when he was 16, Kirsten's mother went on to have a third son with her second husband. Kirsten's father passed away when he was just 18 and in matric at Rondebosch Boys' High School.

TWO ROADS DIVERGED IN A WOOD

Following matric Kirsten went to the University of Cape Town to study for a BA but threw in the towel after two years to find a job. 'I started working as a medical rep, which I did for two years, but throughout that time I continued playing cricket and rugby. By the time I was 22 I was playing club cricket and had played for the Western Province B team, and I was offered a contract for Western Province, which turned into a contract every year until I retired in 2004. I was never interested in playing for another province because my roots are firmly in Cape Town. I played for six months in Holland in 1992 and did a bit of other travelling with sport, but playing for a team that wasn't Western Province or South Africa was not on my agenda. In 1993 I was selected for the South African side and my first tour was of Australia – which was incredible. I would say one of the highlights of my playing career was batting in my first Test for my country, as I never thought I'd get to play a Test for the Proteas. Another highlight was scoring 275 against England in December 1999 when I was about to be dropped from the team (an innings that lasted over 14 hours – the second longest in Test history), and when I scored 76 in my final match for

South Africa against New Zealand before I retired. That match was really the culmination, for me, of 11 years spent playing 101 Tests and 185 ODIs for my country. These kinds of milestones showed that I'd been around the block and done my service for my team and my country.

'From a coaching perspective, winning the World Cup in 2011 is certainly a great memory, but I really enjoyed coaching India and SA in general; I was very privileged to spend time with those guys. My highlights from that time are less around the milestones I achieved and more around the journey I was on. Coaching is a different space altogether; you do it to try to add value to a group of people and the individuals in that group. I really look at my work in that way rather than the trophies that we gathered at the end of it all. Every individual I have come across – certainly in my experience as a player – needs someone to play for, and I wanted them to play for me. I wanted them to know that I had put so much time and energy and invested so much of myself into their games that they would play for me.'

Taking on the coaching roles for both countries presented different challenges for Kirsten, with many doubting his ability to gain the respect of the Indian team. 'I was very conscious of the brand of the Indian team on the subcontinent, but they were really known as individuals as opposed to a team. It was my responsibility to move their focus from themselves to the team because I believed that if they really made an effort to perform for the team they would also reach their individual goals. I love coaching a team because of the variety of individuals you get to work with and steer in the right direction.'

BOWLING A MAIDEN OVER

Kirsten met his wife, Deborah, in Cape Town in 1996 when he had been playing for the Proteas for three years and she was studying at UCT. 'I was on the road a lot but we got married in 1999 and had Joshua in 2003, James in 2007 and Joanna in 2011. Debs is really a mentor to me in many ways in terms of the values by which she lives her life. I wasn't a Christian when we first started dating, but Debs was open about her faith, and when I visited her family home and got a taste of a different way of life I was drawn to Christianity. Debs has non-negotiables in her life in the way she conducts herself on a day-to-day basis. I realised that I had been making questionable decisions and she was the catalyst for me to create a connection to God and a solid foundation on which to build my life.'

Relationships are extremely important to Kirsten, who believes that only when he has built relationships and connections can he influence people. 'I think everyone needs mentors who believe in you when at times you don't believe in yourself. My dad was an inspiration to me, as were Duncan Fletcher and Alan Solomons who coached me at university. They were both fantastic coaches and really drove my career forward. They played a very important part in my development in sport, in both rugby and cricket. I've also learned a lot from having been a player and listening to coaches and the impact they've had on me. Because of that it became part of my coaching philosophy that any information I give to my players must be of relevance to them.' When it comes to business mentors, Tim Southey is someone from whom Kirsten has learned a great deal, including how to conduct himself in a business and corporate environment.

As for cricket, 'There are too many people to mention who inspire me in cricket. I'm always looking for individuals who inspire me to be better at what I'm doing. I marvel at some of the quality individuals who are playing cricket now.'

HEART AND SOUL

Moving from being a player to a coach meant that Kirsten had to ensure that he was seen as a leader, and not as a friend. 'There are certain things you have to do and you need to act in a certain manner as a leader if you hope to inspire the people you are working with. As a coach, you can't be seen as one of the boys. I was clear with every player I coached that my role was to get the best out of them, which would require me to challenge them at some point, which I was not shy to do.

'Like any industry leader you have to be careful how you conduct yourself; you have to be careful how you behave in front of other people. I was very aware that if I was going to stand up and ask the team to do something in an intense, highly pressurised situation, my credibility was on the line.'

Kirsten believes in continually searching for wisdom: 'I try to learn something every day – something you can get out of the day to take forward into your life. We'd be naïve if we thought we'd reached the pinnacle of our lives. When I give talks or am chatting to young people I share my experiences with them, as well as my best thinking on how to make something special happen in whatever career they want to go into. There have to be certain non-negotiable fundamentals in place if you're to create some sustainability in your endeavours, which are applicable across all industries. If you're embarking on an endeavour that is high performing, that will push you to a new level, you need hard work, sacrifice and discipline. Everyone has their own definition of what these mean to them, but whatever it is, you need to understand what's required for you to embark on your journey and take your level of achievement to a new space.'

Kirsten does not believe that the generally accepted definition of 'work' accurately sums up what he does, which entails coaching an IPL team, the Delhi Daredevils, giving leadership talks around the country and India, and growing his cricket academy. 'I love my work. I get to travel, talk to business people about the parallels between sport and business, and engage with people around the game of cricket. My aim is to wake up every morning and give each day my best shot.'

Feedback is important to Kirsten – a concept he defines differently to criticism. 'I'm scared of the word "criticism"; feedback is more relevant to me. It's easy for people to criticise those in the public domain because there is no comeback from the words you use about someone; I don't think anyone likes criticism from an untrustworthy source, so I'll take any feedback from someone who is looking after my best interests and then embrace it, because that will make me a better human being. I think everyone needs to play to their strengths and work in the areas they're best at. You won't enjoy your work if you're not working to your strengths and you also won't be optimising your abilities. I continually try to understand how to optimise myself as a human being, so I enjoy waking up every morning and being able to add value to other people's lives through coaching interventions; I'm fulfilled by that.'

Wherever possible Kirsten tries to avoid conflict, because he does not believe that much can be achieved from it. 'Sometimes I think that in business there's a natural path towards conflict, but I like to believe that as human beings we can achieve things and make decisions without having to enter into conflict. I suspect my parents' divorce when I was 16 left some scars, but if there is communication across all levels then I think conflict can be avoided.'

Something that Kirsten acknowledges he needs to work on is his ability to focus on the operational details with which he sometimes struggles. 'I try to work with people who complement me in a coaching environment, because I know that I'm more of a big-picture thinker and I need someone to help me to operate and move decisions forward on a daily basis. I like to look at an occasion, event or group of people and move them forward to a long-term goal, which is important in sport because you need to have a strategy to get you to the end of a season.

'In cricket you're extrinsically measured by performance and results, but I certainly don't measure myself in that way. I know within my conscience and my greater thinking that I need to wake up every day and give 100 per cent value to any connections I have that day. I measure myself on the journey rather than the end and beginning point, which is the beginning and end of one's life. I'm scared to set my sights on winning trophies because that's not how I live my life. I aspire to take a group of people and motivate them in a certain direction. If I'm involved in a team and we have a tournament we'll set realistic goals, and whether we achieve them or not that's neither here nor there. It's important that I give full value to every day on the journey.

'So I don't have the remotest clue where I'll be in five years' time! In professional sport there's hardly any coach out there with a five-year plan for his career because teams and environments change so quickly. There aren't many Arsene Wengers and Alex Fergusons out there.'

When it comes to giving back, Kirsten is still trying to find a natural calling for a cause, but given his passion for the game of cricket he believes that the sport is a vehicle that can add huge value to people who are disadvantaged and starting life off on a back foot. 'In Africa there is tremendous opportunity to move into environments and people's lives and add value to them. I haven't come up with a concrete answer yet as to how to take that calling forward, but I have a feeling that Africa is the place where I want to try to make a difference. I've also had some fantastic experiences in India as well; it's really become a second home to me and there's great opportunity to add value there as well, because there are so many people who are limited in terms of their opportunities and chances.'

One of Kirsten's ventures, the Gary Kirsten Cricket Academy, was started in 2006 as a business. 'My passion is around coaching but there isn't longevity in team coaching, so I wanted to build a sustainable business in Cape Town where I live. I put the Academy on hold after two years because of my India and South Africa coaching roles, but I picked it up again at the beginning of 2014 and I'm in the process of redeveloping and redesigning it now. Essentially my vision is to develop an internationally recognised cricket academy that has a state-of-the-art facility to provide a variety of high-performance services for cricketers from around the world. We provide professional coaching for individuals, teams and coaches across all ages and levels, and we really strive to provide a cricketing experience that allows every person who steps onto the field to learn how to express themselves with flair and individuality, while seeing them grow into leaders in their own right.'

Between all his work and family commitments, Kirsten has also found time to return to university, studying for a BCom in Marketing through Unisa. "I really wanted to challenge myself and prove that I could get it, but I also think it's important to have a degree and achieve something academically. It's been useful for me while I've been setting up the Academy, but I've also learned a lot about business by listening. I'm fortunate that I get to spend a lot of time with people in different spaces and across different industries, and I'm always trying to see what I can learn and apply it to my own life.' Kirsten also enjoys reading, but admits to being a slow reader. 'I've been diligent in trying to understand performance across levels, so while I rarely finish a book, I'm often dipping in and out of four or five different books at the same time.'

Despite his love for India and for coaching, his first priority lies with his wife and young family, which is why he did not renew his two-year contract as coach of the Proteas in July 2013. His decision disappointed many South African cricket fans, who were ecstatic when the team went to the top of the ICC test rankings in 2012. 'In 2012 I was away from home for 250 days, which was no longer tenable. The beauty of coaching an IPL team is that I get to spend time in India, which I really enjoy, but it doesn't take me away from home as much as coaching an international team does. So it's pretty intense for eight weeks, but for the rest of the year I can spend time with my wife and kids. Perhaps when my children are older and if the circumstances were right I would coach another national team, but right now I'm happy with the decision I've made to sign with the Delhi Daredevils for three years.'

He also loves his home country, which he believes is in a crucial period. 'It's interesting times in South Africa. It's been 20 years of democracy and in many ways we could be regarded as a miracle country. There'll never not be issues, particularly the social issues that need to be dealt with, but we have a fairly stable environment and there is a consciousness about the unequal distribution of wealth, which people are trying to rectify. There is unpredictability, but there are also opportunities to do incredible things to help people.'

Kirsten has received accolades from many quarters, including from the Indian captain MS Dhoni, who described his coach as 'the best thing to happen to Indian cricket'. As a player, Kirsten was acknowledged by ESPN as someone with 'discipline, temperament and a penchant for hard work that established him at the top of the South African batting order', as well as having an 'ability to concentrate for long periods and a burning desire to score runs'. In terms of his personality, Kirsten was seen on the field as a player who was 'calm and level-headed, bringing a healthy degree of common sense to the art of batting', as well as someone on whom the team could depend 'in times of crisis'. Kirsten was also named *Wisden's* Cricketer of the Year in 2004.

Yet Kirsten is not one to believe in legacies. 'I think you go into spaces and give all of yourself while you're there. If, at the end of my time on earth, my kids think of me as their hero, that would be more than enough.'

Born into a sporting family, **GARY KIRSTEN'S** rise to the top of the cricketing profession could have been predicted from an early age. One of a few leading players to have successfully transitioned to a coaching role, Kirsten is known for his passion for the sport as well as his players. Having played 101 Tests for South Africa, Kirsten went on to lead the Indian cricket side to win the 2011 World Cup, and took the Proteas to the top of the ICC Test rankings in 2012.

CARPE DIEM

WENDY LUHABE

UNCOMPROMISE

Wendy Luhabe's family was forcibly removed to Daveyton from their home in the old Benoni location of what is now Actonville when she was just eight years old. Luhabe remembers a sense of loss; of moving from what was their home to a 'matchbox' house. The four Luhabe children were brought up extremely strictly, with their parents emphasising the importance of both values and education. 'My parents were real disciplinarians. We used to get beaten up if we told a lie or didn't do our chores. They wanted to bring us up with a proper value system.'

Luhabe's mother was a nursing sister while her father was a clerk, so both had attained a high level of education for black people of that era. Luhabe's mother, in particular, was a role model for the young woman, as she was 'ahead of her time in terms of not accepting what society defined women should or should not do; she was her own person. She was an inspiration because she kind of broke the mould of what the status quo for women was, and I think a lot of what I have become I took from her, because we are obviously influenced by what we see as we grow up. I didn't see her as a woman who conformed to what society expected of her at the expense of what was important to her.'

Luhabe was 'around 10' when her mother left the marriage and took her and her siblings to Cradock in the Eastern Cape, before she changed schools again to spend her last two years at a boarding school in Healdtown in Fort Beaufort. The children did, however, keep in contact with their father, spending every summer with him in Daveyton.

Marina Maponya was another inspiration for Luhabe, because she was a successful businesswoman in her own right, which was a rarity at the time. 'Her whole family was entrepreneurial, but it was unusual for a woman to have as high a profile as her husband [Richard Maponya]. She had her own identity and was one of the first black women, if not the first, to sit on corporate boards way back in the 1980s. Like my mother, for me Marina represented a woman who was doing things women had not done before. Here were these two role models who were finding their way in the world and doing the most with what they had.'

Initially Luhabe had only read about Maponya and admired her from afar, but later got the chance to meet her through various women's organisations. The reality lived up to Luhabe's expectations. 'She didn't give up her mothering, nurturing side; she was a businesswoman, but she never traded in her femininity. Sometimes women in business take on the characteristics of men, but she never did that. She was self-assured and comfortable with who she was. What's great about being a pioneer is that you have the opportunity to define how things are done, so you create a model that works for you.'

While Luhabe did not consciously choose to marry her business side with her feminine side, she believes that this was always something inherent in her. 'If Marina had been more masculine and more harsh as a person, I'm not sure I would have related to her. I think I was drawn to her because she reflected a model of a woman who was powerful and self-assured, who understood what role she could play and was prepared to play. She really embodied a combination of qualities that resonated with me.' Some of the qualities Luhabe admires in people are a sense of compassion as well as honesty, while 'two things that cause me stress are people who are late and people who don't honour their word. If you say you're going to do something, then you need to do it.'

Luhabe was always interested in the way the world works, which is why she found herself investigating the possibility of studying Social Sciences at Fort Hare University upon completing her matric. 'I really wanted to understand why society functions the way it does and to be an instrument for change. I did not specifically choose to study Social Science, it was what black women studied at university in the 70s if they weren't good at maths or science, which I wasn't. My plans were either to be a social worker or a psychologist, or both. I had no idea much beyond this. My choice had been influenced by a book my dad gave us to read as children called, *Your Erroneous Zones*, by Dr Wayne Dyer. The book explains how our thinking is shaped and how to change it to produce desired results.'

The South African landscape changed abruptly with the Soweto uprising in June 1976, however. Fort Hare experienced disruptions in 1976 and 1977, so in 1977 Luhabe left to go to the University of Lesotho, but because it did not offer a degree in Social Sciences she enrolled instead for a BCom. 'That decision, which really was the luck of the draw, turned out to be a crucial defining moment in my career and working life.'

Luhabe knew, however, that she was not cut out to be in the financial, accounting or auditing professions, so she decided to take up a career in marketing instead. 'I spent 10 years in marketing, eight of them with BMW South Africa, and not one of those were wasted. You can learn a lot about people in marketing, especially about the image they have of themselves. Marketing trends give us a lot of insight into the psyche of a nation.'

GOOD THINGS COME TO THOSE WHO WAIT

Getting a job in marketing was not plain sailing however; it took Luhabe a year to find a position she felt was right. 'I was living with my older sister and, after pounding the pavement for almost a year, taking the train from Daveyton to Johannesburg almost daily to look for employment, finding my first job was an unexpected surprise.' A university friend introduced her to Johan Rupert, who had recently bought Vanda Cosmetics, a direct-marketing business. 'Unlike most jobs that were offered previously, which I felt were more suitable for a matriculant and an insult to a university graduate with a BCom, this was an entry-level management job with a respectable salary, a Ford Escort as a company car and an expense account. I was so grateful to finally find a job that I shared my first salary with everyone in my family. I knew what I deserved and I was prepared to wait for it. I don't think it was about being stubborn, but about knowing what I was worth. I think that women often end up settling for less than they're worth, which I wasn't prepared to do.'

For Luhabe, this was the first time that she had to use English in any formal capacity. 'You can imagine the displacement I felt at finding myself in an unfamiliar working environment in which almost every practice was foreign, including the language and culture. White managers remain largely unaware of what their black counterparts have to deal with as they enter a working environment that espouses unfamiliar cultural practices.'

The job entailed accessing the black market for Vanda as well as recruiting salespeople, yet Luhabe did not have a driver's licence. She began by testing the products herself and then visiting the factory to see the production process, after which she visited distributors in Johannesburg. Next up was a visit to Port Elizabeth to meet other distributors there, giving Luhabe her first experience of flying on an aeroplane. One of the distributors in PE was too afraid to venture into the townships, so she offered Luhabe her car to do some workshops there, but Luhabe still did not have her own licence – nor had she ever held a workshop. The distributor gave Luhabe a 'crash course' in driving and within 36 hours Luhabe, having failed once, was the proud owner of a driver's licence. Passing her test was a significant achievement, as well as a 'valuable lesson in overcoming defeat when one fails'.

Her final task was to forge relationships with the team at the head office. 'Other than the cleaner and the tea lady, I was the only black person in the office. Before this I had never interacted with white people other than with my lecturers at university. This was a new learning experience.

'How we approach our first job is extremely important. Careful planning and proper orientation to the company were particularly helpful for me to understand what the business of a cosmetics company was. My first job taught me about the importance of values in one's relationships with others; about the management of resources, ideas, knowledge, people and relationships. It was in this job that I conceptualised and developed an educational approach to the development of new markets. I did not believe a company could be successful if it simply imposed its products on a market without educating the customers about the use and benefits of the products. My experience at Vanda gave me remarkable confidence, a very good foundation for my professional development and a sound launching pad to further myself, to remain ambitious and pursue my aspirations.'

An opportunity to work at BMW came about during a breakfast sponsored by the car company, at which Luhabe was fortunate to have the opportunity to talk to the then MD, Dr von Koerber. She did not, however, follow up on his job offer for another year and a half, but was pleased to find that a position in the marketing research division was still available should she want it. 'I felt this was a good place to start in order to acquire a good understanding and competence in marketing BMW's range of products. The division was headed by a woman and working for her was an inspiration and source of encouragement in a male-dominated environment.'

Two years later, Luhabe negotiated a transfer to BMW's headquarters in Munich for a few weeks in 1986, followed by almost three years at BMW North America in New Jersey. Her mother brought her son, Lumko, who had been living with his grandmother, to join her in the US where he attended school. 'There I was, in a new country, with a new culture and a new job. And as though all of these new challenges were not enough, I had a 12-year-old son who did not speak English to add to the excitement and adventure. My time overseas was the period when I grew the most emotionally, spiritually and intellectually. Both in Germany and the United States I worked with decent people who accepted me for who I was, who were helpful, who gave me due recognition, who did not marginalise me, patronise me or undermine my capabilities. The only criticism would be that they didn't utilise me fully.'

It was during her time in the US that Luhabe came to realise that her real passion lay in human resource development. 'I felt that so many people have potential that is never realised for a range of reasons, the most important being lack of opportunity and support, or not being able to find someone who believes in or sees their potential. To be acknowledged by others is the most affirming experience anyone can ask for. I wanted to facilitate that for black professionals; to see them, to believe in them, to use my own personal experiences to encourage them. As my confidence grew over the years, so did my courage. If you asked me what single quality I would want to pass on to future generations it would be courage. Courage to be themselves, to be unique, to dare, to succeed, to fail and to live. Courage offers us compassion, openness, unity, respect, appreciation, gratitude and empathy. These seven qualities are mandatory if we want to live fully, purposely and within our power.'

It never occurred to her that she would stay in America because she believed that South Africa was where she could make a contribution, and upon her return Luhabe began to think about starting her own business. It was three years before she left BMW, however, because she felt that given the opportunities BMW had provided her, she had an obligation to share some of her newly acquired knowledge with others at BMW South Africa. But being overlooked for a senior management position was the impetus Luhabe needed to hand in her resignation. 'Before leaving BMW I made two last attempts to make absolutely sure that there were no options I had overlooked, but neither of these materialised. The only choice I was left with was to start my own business. Sometimes naïvety can be a blessing.'

SEIZING THE GAP

Luhabe left BMW in 1991 with no clients, no office and no business plan. 'All I had was an idea, R20 000 I had fortuitously won in a competition from Office Mart, a BMW I had negotiated before leaving the company in exchange for human resources consulting services, a child in private school and a bond for a new apartment in Hillbrow. Throughout my life I have taken calculated risks, explored the unknown and been a companion of challenge, but nonetheless taken responsibility for all areas of my life.'

Luhabe's company, Bridging the Gap, was established in January 1992. By the end of the month the business had its first client – Sasol II in Secunda. Just days later, Luhabe secured her second client, with her role being to coordinate a professional development programme between black South African professionals in financial services and New York-based companies in the same sector. The first two programmes she designed were aimed at first-year university entrants and graduates looking for their first jobs in a corporate. 'I realised that even those people who are lucky enough to go to university often have absolutely no knowledge of the challenges beyond university and therefore do not apply their minds to choosing appropriate fields of study, while graduates often do not know how to market themselves, how to inform themselves and how to prepare for job interviews. The overall objective was to raise the level of confidence of all these intelligent and motivated black students who, had they lived in a normal society, could have claimed the world as their oyster.'

The programmes were offered at Fort Hare, the University of the North, the University of Zululand and Vista University, and were sponsored by Ericsson SA, Nestlé, Anglovaal and Southern Life, yet after just three years they were shut down due to lack of interest from the universities. 'This highlighted to me the great challenge that we face as a society, the helplessness and vicious cycle of self-defeat that overwhelms us.' Luhabe was not about to admit defeat, however, and devised a third programme for bursary students and new employees. 'The objective was to prepare them more effectively for their employment environment, teach them about performance objectives, to take responsibility for their jobs, make informed choices, invest in their personal growth and development and ensure that they did not become a liability to their employers or themselves. This programme was very successful in improving performance, integration and retention, and was particularly successful in cases where people found themselves in unsuitable jobs and had to find alternative employment that was more aligned to their career goals and aspirations.

'My motive was to inspire the students to believe in themselves and to place a value on their achievements despite the quality of our education system at the time. I wanted to convince them to recognise that what they had achieved was admirable and valuable. This was also an attempt to reverse the many years of discrimination, begging for opportunities, years of holding back, and of compromise just to have a job. People who have no work cannot live with dignity. Work occupies our time, our minds and inspires our creativity. It gives us an opportunity to add some value through our living, for our lives to have meaning.

'People must also take responsibility for managing their own careers, their relationships and the opportunities presented to them. When we take responsibility, make conscious choices and decisions, we reach desired outcomes. Taking responsibility and being accountable is hard work, but the returns will appear.'

Luhabe had studied Maslow's hierarchy of needs while at Fort Hare, which she then applied to her own life. 'Each stepping stone was clearly moving me closer and closer towards my present position in life. I understood that both relationships and opportunities are catalysts for our own personal growth and advancement through our life journey. The main obstacle I have faced during my career is that I can't do the same thing for too long. I need variation and adventure in my job. Because I learn quickly I was always underutilised; I was never sufficiently challenged, not with the work I did or the level of employment that I reached. Idleness is not something I am familiar with, and my attributes are clearly better suited towards an entrepreneurial environment. I enjoy managing my own time, deciding what I want to do, choosing who I work with and creating things; sadly you can't do any of those things if you work for a corporation.'

In 1993, a chance meeting with Nick Dennis, the then CEO of Imperial Cold Storage (ICS), led to Luhabe being invited to join the board as a non-executive director. 'At the age of 36 I knew nothing about being a director of a listed company. During the first year of my appointment I spent an hour prior to every board meeting going over the numbers with the financial director to make sure I could follow the discussions at the board meetings. I used to think of myself as an acorn waiting to become an oak tree.' Within three years Luhabe had been invited to join an additional five boards, with more offers coming later, yet she resigned from most of these when she turned 40 because she felt she was not able to add the value she hoped to, given that the businesses were 'too set in their ways'. She also believes that people should not be on boards indefinitely, and that the contribution of CEOs begins to diminish after 10 years. Some of the boards she has served on include Vodacom, the Industrial Development Corporation, Glenhove Fund Managers, the JSE, Tiger Brands, the Institute of Directors and Vendome SA.

The second company Luhabe was part of creating was Women Investment Portfolio Holdings (Wiphold), together with Tomatoe Serobe, Louisa Mojela and Nomhle Canca. 'We provided the seed capital of R500 000 to start and then we raised R25 million in the IPO in 1999. We followed that with a rights issue of R75 million. It really was the first women's company to facilitate the participation of women in the economy in a meaningful way. This intervention changed the economic landscape of South Africa when it inspired the participation of women as investors and encouraged them to take responsibility for their financial independence. Our first countrywide workshops to mobilise women were entitled "Beyond Labour and Consumption". If I had to choose a career highlight it would probably be Wiphold, because it had an impact on so many lives. I always describe it as having revolutionised the participation of women in the economy.'

In 1994 Luhabe married Mbhazima Shilowa, who went on to become the Premier of Gauteng in 1999, who also had a son from a previous relationship. Something she has strived to do in her parenting style is not to live her unfulfilled dreams through her children. 'It's something I see in society; parents tend to influence what their children do and don't really give them the freedom to decide what they want to do. Fortunately, my parents weren't like that. I try to instil the values in my children that my mother did with us, but I've adapted them for the times we live in. I'm not the kind of person who just takes something as it is and passes it along; I bring my own experience and my own observations of what I think is needed to equip them for the challenges of the time. I'm always observing what works and what is effective in society. My big interest in life is to understand how we can be more effective – as parents, as educators, and as business people.'

Luhabe's next venture was with Nku Nyembezi-Heita in Alliance Capital. The aim of the company was to facilitate the employment and development of black women, particularly in the pension fund management sector, as well as to improve the investment and fund-management skills of young black professionals. 'I knew nothing about asset management when I became involved in this venture, but Moss Leoka and Norman Bergel invited me and insisted that I consider the opportunity.'

Later still, Luhabe was invited to invest in Ogilvy & Mather, along with Graça Machel and Moss Mashishi. 'When I studied commerce little did I know that I would end up as an entrepreneur. What we achieve in life is the result of our own efforts, courage and ability. But it might not be possible to reach great heights were it not for generous sponsors and mentors. This is certainly true of my own experience. Johan Rupert gave me my first job, Dr Eberhard von Koerber gave me the opportunity of becoming the first black person to be employed in a junior management position at BMW South Africa, Nick Dennis gave me the opportunity to become a director of ICS, and Josephine de Lange, the Training Manager at Sasol II in Secunda, gave us our first contract at Bridging the Gap. Relationships are in many cases more important than one's competence. These relationships are often developed growing up, at school or at university, yet when a nation increases its prospects for shared experiences, the influence of stereotypes diminishes. We need to cultivate a legacy of discipline, hard work and accountability among young people; our country cannot afford managers who are not professional, not hard-working, and who rely on race and favourable patterns of discrimination to get their jobs and keep them employed.'

DEFINING MOMENTS

One gap in particular still worried Luhabe in 2002: the gap between the generation of black managers and professionals from each of the last three decades of the twentieth century. 'Any learning that was transferred from one generation to another was limited and often almost by accident. As far as I could tell, there wasn't any work that had captured these experiences and placed them in the public domain so that all South Africans could learn from them, grow from them, and develop more proactive solutions to workplace challenges.'

Luhabe set about writing a book, *Defining Moments*, with four objectives in mind: to tell the story of black managers and professionals between 1970 and 2000; to pass on the experiences of black executives working during those decades; to be deliberately provocative and cultivate a culture of debate; and to use the book to enhance prospects and commitment for successful mentorship. The funds raised from the book were put towards the Wendy Luhabe Foundation, which assists financially with the education of women.

Luhabe has received many awards over the years, but none particularly stand out for her because she considers all of them to be recognition of her contribution. 'All of them have been a privilege and I think to be recognised in your own lifetime is not something that happens for most people. Having said that, I don't care at all what people think of me!' One such 'privilege' was receiving a call from Hillary Clinton to join the International Council of Women Business Leaders in 2011, an initiative by the US State Department. Other recognitions have included an Award in Recognition of Championing Women Empowerment by the Black Management Forum, a Global Leader for Tomorrow by the World Economic Forum, Leadership in Practice from Unisa's Business Leadership School, and an Outstanding Young Person award from the Osaka Junior Chamber. Luhabe has also been a member of the Club of Rome, a Patron of the Duke of Edinburgh's International Award Foundation (the work for which saw her appointed Honorary Lieutenant of the Royal Victorian Order (LVO)), has rung the bell at the New York Stock

Exchange, served as Chairperson of the International Marketing Council and is an aspiring harpist.

On the education front, Luhabe studied for her Management Advanced Programme at Wits Business School and has been awarded honorary doctorates in Commerce by the University of Stellenbosch as well as Fort Hare. She was also inaugurated as the Chancellor of the University of Johannesburg in 2006, is on the supervisory board of the IMD business school in Switzerland, and sits on the International Advisory Board of Essec Business School in France. One of her projects to promote education among disadvantaged students was as a member of the founding board of the Patrons for Student Sponsorship Programme, which has helped over 500 students to access private school education. Luhabe is also a Patron of Junior Achievement South Africa.

Luhabe believes in constantly learning, which she does through conversations with people. 'I really enjoy the relationships I have built with business schools both at home and abroad, as I am constantly exposed to different generations of people and ideas. You discover what people are thinking about, what the cutting edge of management is, what all the elements of business are. I learn a lot from that.'

With all the decisions that Luhabe has made in her life, she has always given them careful thought before making them and then moving on. 'One of my favourite sayings is *Carpe Diem* – Seize the Day. When I have made a decision I know it's the correct decision, and if it's not the correct decision, then it's done; I don't agonise over it. I rely very much on divine inspiration about decisions I should make so I communicate very much with God to guide me in my decision-making.'

Making decisions with integrity is extremely important to Luhabe, who is concerned at the number of leaders she believes are driven by their egos rather than a purpose. 'My observation is that leaders who are driven by their ego tend to default a lot more than leaders who are driven by purpose. It requires consciousness to make sure that how you lead and how you make an impact on the world is always premised on what your purpose is in the world. All leaders need vision to fight against the moral degeneration we see everywhere in society.'

As a leader, Luhabe tries to work with others in a collaborative style. 'I believe very much in the collective and I like to tap into people. My approach has always been to recognise that the people who are sitting at the table have something to contribute; I have a responsibility to make sure that their contribution is brought into how an organisation is run. I have not experienced that on boards that I was not a chair of and it may be a quality that women have and not men. I want everyone to participate in the decision-making and everyone's contribution should be valued. When someone lets me down I don't shout, I just let them know that I'm disappointed and that I had higher expectations of them. I don't suffer fools gladly!

'I also wonder about the theory that, as human beings, we only tap into 5 per cent of our potential. My curiosity is about why we can't tap into more; what stops us? What would the world be like if we were able to tap into all of our potential?'

Luhabe measures her success by the impact she makes on people's lives. 'My passion is about impacting positively on people's lives and using my experience to help people see what's possible for their own lives. Each generation accumulates its own experiences and unless we find a way for those to be passed on to future generations, what happens is that every generation has to start from scratch. Mentorship needs to be intergenerational to grow a body of knowledge.'

Luhabe's purpose is all-important to her. 'I want to leave the world a better place by having empowered people and helping them. I would like my tombstone to say, "I lived my purpose." I'm a strong believer that each generation should leave the world a better place for the next generation. If each one of us took the time to find out what our purpose is, and lived our purpose, then the world would definitely be a much better place for the next generation. There is an expression that the richest place in any nation is the graveside, because it is full of dreams that were never realised, potential that was never fulfilled, and purposes that were never lived.'

WENDY LUHABE has a strong belief in living her purpose, which is to leave the world a better place for future generations. An entrepreneur, social entrepreneur, businesswoman, wife, mother and harpist, she has spent years 'bridging the gap' between women and the economy, and measures her success by the impact she has had on people's lives.

FROM ADVERSITY COMES STRENGTH

KABELO MABALANE

NATURAL-BORN TALENT

Kabelo Mabalane was 'born, bred and buttered' in Diepkloof, Soweto, in December 1976. The eldest of three children, his mother was a teacher and his father an insurance broker for Liberty Life. Both parents held education in high esteem, so when the young Mabalane decided to go into the music business his father was not a happy man. 'You know, your mom loves you and she'll love you regardless, but my dad … as much as he loved me, he was distraught!'

Kabelo's mother taught English and History at Progress High School in Pimville and was also the school librarian, but she had a passion for music. 'It was education, education, education in my house; my mom was always studying and doing a course here and a course there, but my theory of why I ended up in the music business is because my parents were most happy when they had friends over and they would play music on their old record player.'

Kabelo's family home was a political one, particularly on his mother's side. His uncle was arrested in 1986 and spent time on Robben Island, while his mother was very outspoken against the apartheid regime. Kabelo often found himself playing the role of diplomat, and still does when the topic of politics comes up at the dinner table. 'For my mother, it's important that we understand where her generation came from and how difficult life was for them. And she's right; it informs how you deal with things going forward because my generation mustn't forget. There must be a healing process and you can't just yank people out of where they come from. I think it'll take another 50 years before we no longer need to focus on the past.'

Kabelo's formal education began in 1983 when he started Grade 1 at Mayfair Convent, a private primary school, where he stayed for seven years before starting high school at Sacred Heart College in Observatory, Johannesburg. He only spent one year at Sacred Heart, however, before moving to St Stithians in Sandton where he repeated Standard 6. The apartheid structures were beginning to fall apart at that time but there were still very few black children at the school, so Kabelo remembers being something of a 'novelty'. Fortunately no animosity was shown towards him, and it was not until the following year when the government called a referendum to let white voters decide if they should continue dismantling apartheid that Kabelo remembers there being any 'drama'.

'There was going to be a call whether the black kids should go home or stay at school and it was the first time that I thought there might be some issues. They told all the black kids to go to the boarding house – I don't know if they thought there would be a terrorist attack or something! – but after break we came back to school and everything was fine. I never had any issues with the white kids at the school; in fact, the only time I ever experienced aggression was when we played rugby against Monument. Coming from a liberal, all-boys school that had black kids on the team, the Monument guys kept calling us the K-word and all sorts of names. I think we were around 15 years old and we were in a maul when an Afrikaans kid called me the K-word and about five or six of my teammates just went at him!

'I stood back; I had resolved from an early age not to let that kind of thing affect me. It's not my problem that you see me the way you do – especially if you're going to see me in that light. We expected it from those boys – they were barefoot Afrikaans boys who were brought up like that. I wonder if things have changed. I think kids at Afrikaans schools might still be in a kind of silo, but maybe with black leadership and being exposed to more black people things have changed … although it all depends on the parents' attitudes, I guess.'

The schools that were chosen for Kabelo were done so for their excellent reputation, despite the financial burden they placed on his parents. 'They always did the best they could afford. I still need to sit down with my mom and ask her how they did it, because I didn't come from a wealthy family. I always had the right rugby kit, the right tennis kit. I always went on tour. It was a lot of money!'

Kabelo had no problem making friends at school, but one in particular would go on to play a significant role in the young man's life. 'I made friends with Tokollo Tshabalala right from the beginning as we were in the same dormitory. We were always exchanging music and talking about our dream to be big super stars. In fact in Standard 8 we put a demo together with money his mom gave us and one day we bunked school and took it to EMI out in Heidelberg – I can't even remember how we got there! We spoke to this guy who had a big watermelon on the table, which he ate as he was talking to us. He promised us all sorts of things that never materialised.'

The demo that the boys put together was a Kwaito one, with the two 'rapping in vernac and English on hip hop-like jazzy beats. Hip hop was the soundtrack to our lives although it was early days back then. We were ahead of our time in that particular market; we were just playing the music we loved. At school we were in the choir and school musicals – we didn't have any sense of the commercial side of business at all.'

Kabelo finished high school in 1995 and, despite being offered a place on a school rugby tour, he chose instead to travel to America on a short-term Rotary Exchange Programme to Florida. On his return he enrolled at Wits Tech for a Sports Management diploma, but left after six months. 'It just felt like it was Biology all over again! With Sports Management, they start with physiology and it wasn't what I was interested in. I wanted to know about the management of sport and putting tournaments together. My parents weren't happy; I moved out and slept on people's couches because when I was at home I'd have to listen to them nagging about what I was going to do with my life, so I stayed away as much as I could.

'Even as I grew successful my father refused to budge about the fact that he thought I should have finished my diploma. I remember after my first album went gold, the record company wanted to do a PR story about my family life, including a photo of me with my parents. My mom was happy for me but my dad said, "You know you've been successful in the business for six or seven years, but it still doesn't mean that I agree with you, or that I agree with you being in the business. I still stand by what I said, that you should have gone to school. I am not coming to take the picture." In a sense it taught me how principled he was. I know he didn't intend any malice – he just stuck to his guns when he felt strongly about something. In hindsight, if I had carried on I would have liked to have been part of the Local Organising Committee for the World Cup; the business of sport has become so lucrative in this country, but I've got no regrets. The music business is my calling and the foundation on which I've built everything.'

Kabelo's musical career began to look up when he and Tokollo recruited a fellow St Stithians scholar, Zwai Bala, who had joined the school from the Drakensberg Boys' Choir. As Zwai had already recorded a gospel album he had contacts in the industry, and together the three formed TKZee in 1996. 'The music industry was really growing at the time and record company execs were looking for new talent, so they asked Zwai to introduce them to musicians. There was a huge black market they weren't accessing, so they bought us a microphone, a little sampler and a keyboard, and told us to play.'

The trio would practise in Zwai's back room in Randburg and they released their first album, *Take it Eezy*, in June 1996 when Kabelo was just 19. 'It flopped dismally – we didn't know what we were doing! We sold 765 copies but we still believed in ourselves. We had a gang mentality and we thought that we were better than everybody; that they just didn't get the music.' The trio started to take note of what was happening commercially, visiting clubs at night and playing in the studio by day. 'We lived in the studio; we slept there, we ate there. We'd listen to music and sample and put things together. By the time we came to release our second album we had so much more material but we were still us; we wanted to make music that we loved and that we thought sounded cool. We were innovators on the South African music scene.'

Their second album, *Phalafala*, exploded onto the scene with sales of over 100 000 copies, followed the next year by massive success with *Shibobo*, which the band recorded in Amsterdam in collaboration with Bafana Bafana star, Benni McCarthy. In just a month the album sold over 100 000 copies, with the single becoming the highest selling in South Africa with over 280 000 copies sold. But cracks were beginning to show, with Kabelo becoming steadily hooked on a cornucopia of drugs. The more success the band enjoyed, the worse his addiction became. The release of their fourth and fifth albums, *Halloween* and *Guz 2001,* led to the trio winning an unprecedented five awards at the South African Music Awards (SAMAs), for Best Kwaito Album, Best Kwaito Single, Best Duo or Group, Best Single and Best Video. 'It was 1999 and we had been together since high school; we were always in each other's space – we'd even bought a house together. It came to a point where I only understood myself as a part of the collective. We had money and fame and I found myself in a place that I didn't sign up for: abusing drugs and living a promiscuous lifestyle.'

HALT

Tokollo left the band in 2000 and branched out on his own, with Zwai relaunching his own solo career shortly thereafter, which prompted Kabelo to follow suit. He released his first solo album, *Everybody is Watching*, in 2000, which was followed in 2002 by *Rebel with a Cause*, which would go on to win Best Male Vocalist at the Metro FM Awards and Best Kwaito Album at the SAMAs. But by this time Kabelo's personal life was in freefall, with his mother attempting three unsuccessful interventions. She eventually tracked down Hugh

Masekela who had also 'battled demons', but who had been clean for five years by then. 'My mom and Hugh spoke to me; he obviously had connections and he put me in touch me with some people and paid for my rehab. I still used for another month or so after that but he had really made an impact on me. Even though my mom is very overpowering, she was still my mom, but here was an industry person speaking to me and it really hit home. I was just sick and tired of being sick and tired, and I wanted to get my life back. You know, you can't help somebody who doesn't think they need help, but I knew I had had enough.'

Six weeks in rehab turned Kabelo's life around. 'They said to me when I arrived, "If you follow our suggestions and our guidelines you'll be okay." So I did everything they told me; I left no stone unturned. I didn't do it because I didn't want to go back there, but because I felt they were giving me a guarantee that I would get better, which is what I wanted. One of the most powerful things they taught us was the acronym, HALT. If you're feeling upset first check if you're hungry, angry, lonely or tired. If it's none of these, then you can work on figuring out what's bothering you.'

Kabelo left rehab two days before his 26th birthday a changed man. 'I think everything that happened to me was necessary; I couldn't have become who I am now without it, unfortunately. I heard a Christian lady, Joyce Meyer, speak once, and she said that "Life is all about how big your want to is." So if you want to lose weight, be a better husband or quit smoking, you can. If you can't lose weight, be a better husband or quit smoking it's because you don't want to. And I badly wanted to quit drugs.

'We all have an innate greatness in us and I've always known that my life was not cut out to end in mediocrity; that is what has gotten me through – to step up and show up. More than anything, I cleaned up because I felt a calling upon my life to say, "I'm doing it for myself and for all my other friends to show that it can be done." So I took all that pressure, all that responsibility, and put it on my own shoulders.'

To this day Kabelo speaks to young people about the realities of drug abuse, explaining that while it's easy to get started, it's not so easy to get out. 'I explain that there is only a 2 per cent recovery rate worldwide among drug addicts, so they might not be as lucky as me.'

THE ONLY TRUTH IS MUSIC

The year following his discharge from rehab Kabelo released his third solo album, *And the Beat Goes On*, which went to number one, which he followed up in 2004 with his fourth hit album, *Bouga Luv Album*. That year's Metro FM Awards and the SAMAs saw him take home statuettes for the Best Male Vocalist and Best Kwaito Album respectively, as well as the KORA Award for the Best Male Artist for the southern African region. A further highlight was being invited to open for international rap artists, 50 Cent and Ja Rule.

His winning streak continued in 2005 when he was again called onto the stage at both the Metro FM awards and the SAMAs, winning the Best Male Vocalist and Best Kwaito Album at the former and Best Kwaito Album at the latter. That year he also started his own record label, Faith Records, through which he recorded and released *BlackJack* with his new band of the same name. He also played for the world-renowned Black Eyed Peas as their opening act, while on a personal note he enrolled in Bible school. 'I had always had a sense of conviction that had never left me, but I had ignored it for years.' Kabelo earned another notch in his belt when he released *Exodus* in 2006, which went platinum.

His demanding schedule meant that sport had taken a backseat, however, and in 2004 he had decided to address this shortcoming. 'I signed a three-year endorsement deal with Reebok in 2004 to design a sneaker as the company were doing really quite innovative things at the time. They were one of the few sports brands at the time to have branched out to work with people other than sportsmen – for example, they did deals with 50 Cent and Jay-Z – so when my manager and I saw that happening we knocked on their door. The partnership made me rethink my attitude to my health and energy, so when I decided that I wanted to run the Comrades Marathon I spoke to the Reebok marketing team to find out about participating. They promptly assigned me a running coach in the form of Nick Bester, a previous Comrades winner.'

Kabelo completed the marathon for the first time in 2006, partnering with Harmony Gold to raise R250 000 for charity. 'I've run the Comrades eight times now; the competitive individual in me wants to better my time – wants to become better and faster. I get an awesome sense of reward at the end of it. It's also special because my gran and I used to watch the Comrades together religiously – that and Wimbledon. She was a big fan of Chris Evert-Lloyd because she was such a lady and she loved Ivan Lendl, but she didn't like Martina Navratilova! So we watched Bruce Fordyce win all those years and I think the seed was sown as far back as then.'

But Kabelo's decision to attempt the Comrades took some people by surprise, because when he made up his mind to run, not only had he not been running in years, but he also weighed in at 105 kilograms. 'I was huge! That was another reason I wanted to do something really, really hard, so that I could lose weight. Luckily my music brand was flying, so Reebok didn't mind that I was so big!'

One of Kabelo's professional highlights was to take place later that same year, when he was asked to be an opening act for Jay-Z's concerts in Durban, Cape Town and Johannesburg. 'I didn't meet Jay-Z, unfortunately, as he's my entertainment industry hero; I really admire the brand and the business he's built while still seeming to keep his humanity.' Rihanna was also on the bill, yet despite having played with these heavyweight artists and his phenomenal local success, Kabelo feels he has yet to experience the highlight of his musical career. A phonecall he'd like to receive would be from the renowned Nigerian musician Fela Kuti's son, Femi. 'That would give me amazing reach into the African continent. That's my next step – taking over Africa.'

In 2007 Kabelo returned to the SAMAs as both a host and a winner, taking home the award for Best Kwaito Album for the third time, before releasing his sixth solo album, *I'm a King*, the following year. In the meantime he continued to focus on his running, bettering his previous Comrades' times and becoming the first black man in the world to grace the cover of *Runner's World* magazine. To add to his sporting credentials, he was chosen by the South African Sports Confederation and Olympic Committee (SASCOC) to be an Olympic ambassador in 2008.

A reunification with his TKZee band members in 2009 saw the trio release a new album, *Coming Home*, as well as strike a multimillion-rand deal with MTN for the rights of their song *Viva la Pantsula*. Kabelo also became Patron of the Comrades Youth Run, and shortly thereafter was approached by Soul City to be an ambassador for their Phuza Wize Campaign. The aim of the campaign was to reduce violent behaviour among men aged 15–35 by 10 per cent by 2014, as well as to highlight the link between alcohol misuse and new HIV infections. To add to his already demanding schedule, Kabelo joined SABC 2 to become a presenter of a weekly multi-sport and lifestyle talk show, *Sport Nite*, while also finding time to perform with TKZee at the 2010 FIFA World Cup Opening Ceremony. Thanks to the success of *Sports Nite*, Kabelo added to his trophy cabinet by winning the Best Newcomer Overall and Best Newcomer TV Presenter at the 2010 SAB Sports Journalists of the Year Awards.

The opportunity to address an issue close to his heart presented itself that year when he was recording the Tears for Fears song, *Shout*, in the studio – only for his friend, singer Danny K, to overhear him. 'Danny suggested we start a movement around the song so we created the SHOUT Foundation as an anti-crime movement, using entertainment to convey a serious message. We use music and art to raise money to fund organisations in the crime-fighting space, but it's also important to look at the cause of crime. We have now fine-tuned our role to focus on education; our latest project saw us unveiling three libraries in primary schools in Cape Town, Soweto and Limpopo. Our financials are done for us *pro bono* and all the artists work for free, so the money goes straight to the schools that need it most.'

A new test presented itself in 2011, with Kabelo agreeing to be part of the Seven Summits Challenge. Having conquered Mount Kosciuszko in Australia and Aconcagua in South America, Kabelo agreed to take part in the Challenge in support of Mountain Heights, a charity for addicts that aims to actively demonstrate the conquering of physical challenges. That same year saw Kabelo be invited to act as an ambassador for the car manufacturer Kia, as well as the clothing brand, Tiger of Sweden.

Kabelo's media profile grew further in 2012 when he was selected to replace Randall Abrahams as a judge on *SA's Got Talent*, and was voted the ninth most influential TV media personality by *Star Tonight*. Another turn as a SAMA Awards presenter that year was good practice for the launch of his own TV show in 2013 – *Kabelo's Bootcamp*. A reality series, the show saw contestants compete against each other in physical and mental challenges to see who could lose the most weight while overcoming their personal trials. His involvement in the media industry expanded in 2013 to include a radio show with Gavin Koppel, the SHOUT SA Chairman, on 2000 FM entitled *Mind the Gap*, while he also launched an energy drink, Elements, with Danny K later that year. The highlight of his year was off stage, however, when he married the actress Gail Nkoane.

MULTIPLE PERSONALITIES

When it comes to making music, Kabelo is no different to other musos and occasionally suffers from a bout of 'writer's block', but has learned not to try to write in that state. 'I have learned to understand my rhythm, as it were. I know that when I am in a certain kind of space that is when I have to go for it. I also remind myself to have fun and focus on what makes me feel good. If I'm writing just for the sake of writing I can get too involved in the business side, and then the music bombs in the market.' Kabelo writes most of his own lyrics, but does enjoy collaborating with other artists, including the highly acclaimed lead singer of the Parlotones, Kahn.

For this singer, music is his muse. 'It might sound a bit spaced out but I think music itself inspired me from a young age because it was just so awesome. I would be sitting in the back of my mom's car and going to school with the radio on and there'd be a melody or chords that would catch me. My dad would play his jazz and my mom would play her Dionne Warwick records; they had a great collection and I also started collecting music as a child. Music just worked for me from day one. I love every genre; I'm almost OCD about music!'

Kabelo believes that everyone has different talents, but the trick is to find what makes you 'tick' and then make a career out of it. It is also important to him that he learns from his mistakes, although this is something that has taken years for him to appreciate. 'I've had to learn a lot along the way, including how to overcome my fear of failure and how to forgive myself and others. I've been known to hold a grudge, but you just have to let things go eventually. I've also learned to take constructive criticism. If someone says something with good intentions then it's easier to take on board. Rehab taught me to be aware of where I'm at. As I get older I've gained more perspective and have better self-esteem. I also still use HALT whenever I'm feeling upset.'

Kabelo considers himself an entrepreneur, thanks to his ability to exploit his brand on different platforms over the years. 'I get my brand to work for me and I love all the different projects I work on. I couldn't survive doing only one thing. By working across multiple platforms you guarantee your longevity, but music will always be my constant.'

Kabelo finds inspiration in the stories of entrepreneurs such as Herman Mashaba and Richard Maponya, particularly as they managed to grow extremely successful businesses despite living under the cloud of apartheid. As a leader in his field, he believes that authenticity in leadership is important for young people and that leadership is first and foremost service. 'You have to lead by example, but you can't do that unless you feed your body, spirit and mind; you need to look after yourself holistically. For me a person has character when what they say and what they do align.' A born-again Christian, Kabelo is proud of the man he has become. 'In difficult times, I try to let common sense, principles and character prevail.'

Kabelo never believed he would ever consider leaving South Africa to live abroad, but now finds thoughts creeping in that 'scare' him. 'I'm the most patriotic person, but the instability here is getting to me; what will be happening in 20 years' time? I visited LA recently and I loved it – it reminded me of Cape Town on steroids! If I were to live somewhere else I'd love to live in LA. The problem is my wife would love to live in New York!'

Despite his uncertainty regarding where he may be living in 10 years' time, one thing Kabelo does know is what he wants on his tombstone: 'Well done, thy good and faithful servant.'

This award-winning singer, TV presenter, athlete and entrepreneur has become so well-known across South Africa that one only needs to refer to him by his first name. Yet **KABELO MABALANE'S** life has not always been picture-perfect, with the Kwaito star being enticed into the dark side of the music business, becoming addicted to drugs and engaging in risky behaviour from a young age. His battle to overcome his demons has shown his legions of fans just what is possible given the right attitude and a measure of inspiration.

DEFENDER OF THE WEAK

THULI MADONSELA

WE SHALL OVERCOME

Thuli Madonsela does not have so much a family tree as a family forest. With her father, Bafana, having been married three times – the third marriage being to her mother Nomasonto – she was raised with an abundance of siblings. Neither of Madonsela's parents had much in the way of education, with her father, a Swazi, working as an informal trader and a taxi driver. Her mother went no further than Grade 6 and found what employment she could as a domestic worker and an informal midwife and social worker.

Madonsela was born in Johannesburg in 1962 and began her schooling in Soweto, but within a year she had moved to a Seventh Day Adventist school in Swaziland. 'My parents believed that we would get a better education in Swaziland and they had relatives there, so we stayed with them until we finished school. It was difficult being separated from our mom and dad, but we were fortunate that we were not in exile so we could still visit them in Soweto. In fact, as they got older my parents started spending more and more time in

Swaziland – although my mother loved Swaziland more than my father did. My father would drive the old long-distance taxis, which would transport people to Swaziland every Friday and then back to work on Sundays, so we used to come and go between the two countries on the weekends.' While her household was not a politically active one, her father supported the ANC and 'spoke about the liberation movement fondly'. It was when she would come home on weekends and for the holidays that her father would tell her what had been happening both in the township and on the greater political stage.

Madonsela again changed schools in her primary years, before moving for the last time to attend high school at a private Christian school, Enjabulweni High. In fact Madonsela was fortunate to finish high school because her father was sick for a year in Baragwanath Hospital, which meant that the family struggled to pay the bills. 'My father was of a generation that worked on farms so he believed that you just needed to study enough to be able to speak to your employers; he thought that completing Grade 10 was sufficient, so after that he didn't give us money to go to school.' Madonsela's mother, on the other hand, was very keen for her children to get as much education as possible. She had been handed over to missionaries as a child but ran away to work before finishing school, something she lived to regret. 'My brother went out to work, but fortunately he eventually pushed himself through school. I insisted on going back to school, but my father wouldn't pay for it so I ended up getting my schooling paid for by some foreign churches and then the United Nations paid for my tertiary education through a bursary scheme.'

When Madonsela completed high school she hoped to get a chance to study law at the University of Swaziland, but her pastor convinced her parents that she should not go into the profession, which was looked down upon for defending criminals, and said that she should rather study medicine. Madonsela was not accepted into the science stream, however, so she signed up for a Humanities degree instead. Despite passing well, she decided after the first year that it was not for her. 'I came back home and explored other options. I began teaching, but it was so unfair on learners; I was young and inexperienced and there I was teaching sciences to students who were the same age as me! I taught for a year but what I taught wasn't what I had learned at university; in those days, if you were seen to know something you were allowed to teach it. It was really part of the legacy of Bantu education. Fortunately Wits was running some courses on physical science … I was teaching Physics, Chemistry and Biology, so at least for the physical science part there was some training provided by the university at Bara Hospital.'

Madonsela's short-lived teaching career began at Naledi High School in Soweto and concluded in Swaziland, when she moved back to that country to wait for the university year to start. 'My mother was certainly very inspirational in terms of me getting an education. After I left school and was teaching, I really initially had no intention of going back to university. I was happy doing what I was doing, but she kept pushing me. Later my father came to realise the value of a full formal education and a profession and really supported me at university – both in terms of encouragement and financing.'

She restarted university in Swaziland in 1983 and forged ahead with her dream to study law. 'I really don't know why I gravitated towards law. When I look back, now that I am grown up, perhaps it is because of my experiences growing up with the impact of unjust laws. Firstly, for black people, with the enforcement of apartheid law, police would knock at night looking for people without passes; they used to be called the Black Jacks, if I'm not mistaken. And I also recall a lot of women losing their homes because of the enforcement of the Black Administration Act. In these cases, they were victims of their own relatives. If a woman's husband died, his family would really just emerge from out of the blue to kick them out of their own homes, because they would not allow a woman to own a house and if she didn't have a son of age who could take over and be the owner of the house, it reverted to relatives. My mother was also arrested when I was four for selling sweets at a school without a permit and my father would have to represent himself whenever he was arrested under the pass laws.'

After completing her BA in Law in Swaziland in 1987, Madonsela went on to study for an LLB at Wits University through a bursary from Beyers Naudé, which she completed in 1990. It was during this time that she became involved with the National Union of Printers and Allied Workers. 'It was accidental; once at home I got involved with the struggle informally, and we used to visit Mama Sisulu at her house in Orlando. During one of those visits I met Zwelakhe Sisulu, who was helping a union that had just started. He asked me if I could give my free time to the union, so I worked for them *pro bono* during all of my holidays.'

TO PROTECT AND SERVE

Upon earning her degree, Madonsela worked in various government departments and in civil society, including a role as the Presiding Officer at the Independent Electoral Commission, a law lecturer at Wits and Managing Director of the Office of the Status of Women in the Presidency.

Madonsela eventually joined the Department of Justice, during which time she created the Wellworth Law and Policy Research Agency. 'Because of my background and the issues of equality and human rights that bothered me, I used to advise people for free – so people struggling, for example, with IDs and permits, as well as issues of customary law and domestic violence.' The formal side of the agency advised and drafted policies and strategies for government departments, which exposed Madonsela to strategy development as well as legislation research and legal drafting relating to legislation. Upon her selection as Public Protector in 2009, Madonsela tried but failed to sell the agency, so she closed its doors because she was not allowed to earn a second income.

As far as her role as Public Protector is concerned, something she has struggled with for five years is getting people to accept that her findings are in fact binding in law. 'I think I am on the verge of giving up now. Even an ordinary ombudsman's findings are binding in law and the Public Protector is not just an ordinary ombudsman. When the Constitution was structured the provisions for the Public Protector were enshrined; recently there was a case that was decided in 2011 by the Supreme Court, which was confirmed by the FCA, that the Public Protector is *not* an ombudsman, they are an ombudsman *plus*. If you look at the Constitution, section 182, it says the Public Protector has the power, as regulated by law, to investigate any conduct in state affairs that is alleged or suspected to be improper and to report on that conduct. And section 182 1C says "to take appropriate remedial action". My understanding – and certainly a lot of legal eagles would agree with me, and have agreed with me – is that "take appropriate remedial action" is not the same as "recommend".

'So the Public Protector Act is very clear that the Public Protector makes findings and has to remedy the consequences of maladministration, but making a recommendation can't remedy the situation because making a recommendation is more like a commission of inquiry. A traditional ombudsman investigates and makes firm findings, and in addition to the findings they make recommendations.

'Ninety-five per cent of the time some action results, but in the other 5 per cent it's really frustrating if nothing happens immediately because some of the decisions made by the courts are not implemented straightaway. That is why, for example, some people have taken the government to court to get a sheriff to attach state property. So, for me, that sometimes there is a failure to comply is a source of concern, but it is not unusual. As in a court of law, though, if there is failure to comply it doesn't end there; the matter is not left to the complainant. I have the power to subpoena whoever is failing to implement my recommendations to come and explain themselves to me as to why they are not implementing them. After that I can request a debate in Parliament where they can explain themselves. Again, Parliament has no power – something that has been confirmed through legal opinion to Parliament – to review my findings. It can only apply its mind to the remedial action that I requested from the party. Only a court of law can review my findings, which are legally binding. It is the remedial action part that I would refer to as recommendation; that is not the same thing as a court order.'

THE NEXT STEP

The term for a Public Protector is seven years, with Madonsela's term finishing on 14 October 2016. While she would consider going back and reopening her agency, offers for her to go back to academia are more tempting. She also plans to join the Bar because although she has been admitted as an advocate, she would like to join one of the established Bars and practise formally. Her preference would be to practise constitutional litigation, as well as cases dealing with gender and race equality. 'I would also focus on administrative justice in the realm of human rights because the work I do as Public Protector has opened my eyes to the injustices in that area. There is a need to develop that area of the law. I will remain in the justice system as an advocate and I will be involved in teaching – partly human rights and partly constitutional litigation, but I also see myself teaching, writing and researching on the institution of the ombudsman and its variations. For example, in English-speaking countries we are called ombudsmen, but in French-speaking countries we are called mediators. Internally they can be called a Public Protector, an Inspector-General, an Investigator-General, a Commission for Administrative Justice or various other names.'

Madonsela was offered a scholarship to attend Harvard University in 1994 but turned it down because she was one of the 11 technical experts who was drafting the Constitution at the time. 'I don't regret turning that opportunity down at all. It was a question of being involved in a once-in-a-lifetime chance to be part of drafting the Constitution and we had just started. I really think I made the right decision. Of course, the idea was that I would go to Harvard some time later but I never did. I have just been reinvited to go to Harvard during my sabbatical, which I was entitled to starting from 2013. They said I should come for eight to 10 months, which is something I will seriously consider.'

Madonsela has two options: she could exit early from her position as Public Protector so that her long leave coincides with her leaving office, or she could take long leave in addition to leave she has accumulated and use that time to go to Harvard before returning to complete her term as Public Protector. 'I haven't really worked it out yet, because eight months is going to be a very, very long time!'

The unit at Harvard that has offered her this opportunity deals with governance in general, with a specific focus on corruption. 'I have been invited to do research and, from my side I have packed away an LLM that I had started, so it would be an opportunity to complete that during that period. Of course whilst I am there I would be able to give lectures as well, but that would be limited; the aim would really be to study and conduct research.'

Madonsela was recently nominated as one of *Time* magazine's 100 most influential people in the world, an award she picked up on a recent trip to Washington DC and New York. The award recognises 'the activism, innovation and achievement of the world's most influential individuals'. Madonsela welcomed the announcement on behalf of her team, but added: 'I really honestly am not deluded enough to think that I am one of the most 100 most influential men or women in the world, but it has been great in terms of highlighting the ombudsman institution as an important player in strengthening constitutional democracies in the world, particularly in emerging states.'

When it comes to making these important decisions, Madonsela is not one to lie awake after the fact, but does agonise beforehand. 'I am one of those people who sleeps well, but the most difficult time for me is when I'm about to make a decision – just before I put my signature on a report. My situation is not like that of an ordinary judge; it's probably more like being a Constitutional Court judge – where it's sort of a group process – but the difficulty with my role is that ultimately the decision falls on me. An investigator prepares the first draft under my guidance, and then it takes a long time to work with the teams to agree on something. Even if I ultimately make my own decision, I still like to convince the team first. I don't have to, but the system we have is such that I am more comfortable when I have made a decision that I have been able to justify to my staff before I have to justify it to the world!'

As time has passed Madonsela has become increasingly aware of the enormity of the power her office wields. 'I never used to think about it, but as people started dealing with me from a position of fear it became more apparent. I have also realised over the years that during the drafting of the Constitution not everyone understood the scope they were giving to this office. It is not very comfortable for everyone, and I think, because of people's reactions, I have come to realise that the decisions we make are very important.

'We never think that our cases are that big until we get the reactions. In one of our last cases we thought it would be run-of-the-mill; we expected the reaction to be for the people responsible to say, "Sorry, whilst we were not looking things went a little bit awry and we're really sorry and we're going to fix this." We thought it was going to end like that; that it wasn't going to be a big issue. Maybe I was naïve but that is what I thought.'

In fact, the reaction was so fierce that both of Madonsela's children, Mbusowabantu and Wensile – one of whom was living on campus at university and the other in a flat – moved back home as they were afraid of the repercussions of the anger shown towards their mother.

'I carry on with my job; I worry more about the impact on complainants than on my family. I also concern myself with the people I make these findings against. I usually hope that the outcome will be that there is no wrongdoing, and together my team and I work very hard to leave no stone unturned to find the truth, as well as to find any legitimate reason why they may have acted the way they did – in other words, was it a genuine mistake? When we finally arrive at a decision, it is always because it is the only solution.'

Something that does concern Madonsela personally is the impact on her children in terms of their inability to live freely. 'They can't say everything they may want to say or go everywhere they may want to go. In the run-up to the elections they had views on certain things but they had to censor themselves. They check with me before they say something as it might be attributed to me, so sometimes I have to ask them not to say something.'

Madonsela's children are from a relationship she had for 13 years, before her partner passed away. 'He asked me to marry him and he even asked my family, but at that stage I had a different view on marriage. I was sort of a feminist and had strange views about the institution of marriage and its impact on gender and its patriarchal origins. As a grown-up, I have different views on it.'

From a personal point of view, Madonsela is extremely proud of having raised children whom she considers to be great human beings. 'They have respect for their fellow human beings and a deep sense of justice. They are very compassionate and stand up for other people's rights, but might look the other way if their own rights have been violated. I'm not saying they're angels and that they've never been caught doing anything wrong, but their sense of humanity and justice and their respect for people make me very proud. They would treat you with respect whether you were a subordinate, a poor person or a rich person.'

From a professional perspective, Madonsela believes that her greatest achievement has been in creating teams and raising people to work at a level above what they thought was possible. 'I want people to operate more optimally, and more excellently, and to get excited about themselves. I may not have achieved that fully yet, but it doesn't make sense to talk about an institution that depends on one person; the idea should be to raise a team so that when I am not here my team can engage with people on any matter, and I don't need to worry that they're going to say something that I would not approve of, because we have learned and grown together. One of my proudest moments was when we did the last report and I was happy to go to a charity event in Joburg and be a speaker there while my team spoke to the media, because I knew that the ideas they were discussing were as much theirs as they were mine.' Madonsela sees her team members as having empowered each other. 'We are all professionals and although I make the ultimate decision, I have learned from the discussions and debates we have.'

Madonsela is a 'stickler for details', something she considers a flaw but which she realises is a good trait to have in a person in her position. 'I tend to want things to be done in accordance with the rules, happily, but sometimes that delays things and also makes me come across as being difficult. On the other hand, people tell me that my attention to detail is a strength. I also have great compassion for people and a deep sense of justice. I'm not easily rattled or excited; I tend to not immediately take sides just because I know one person and not the other. My friends call me Switzerland!'

Madonsela would like to see the corruption in South Africa be quelled before it reaches 'tragic' proportions. 'It's not as bad here as it is in West Africa, but it is endemic. There is a capacity deficit in internal audits in government departments as well as a lack of institutional memory. We need to consider the idea of creating a career civil service, so we won't have the situation where people are coming and going all the time.'

As if her plate were not full enough, Madonsela also finds time to participate in international forums and has assisted with the drafting of several countries' human rights reports. She is a member of the South African Law Reform Commission, Chairperson of the Centre for Reconciliation and Equality Studies, a member of the Business Women's Association of South Africa and the South African Women Lawyers Association, and Executive Secretary of the African Ombudsman and Mediators Association. She has also authored and co-authored books, chapters, journal articles and handbooks on gender, and writes reports on documents such as the Convention Against Torture and the UN Convention on the Elimination of all Forms of Racial Discrimination. In addition, she attends conferences such as the World Conference Against Racism, for which she had been involved in the preceding drafting process in Geneva. She also participated in the drafting of the Beijing Declaration, which was designed by the UN to advance the development of women around the world, and attended the follow-up conferences in New York over the next two years.

There are still some people Madonsela has not had the opportunity to meet on her travels, who she would enjoy hosting for dinner. This includes Barack Obama, who she would like to talk to about what drove him to think he could become President, and how he dealt with the inner voice that would tell him he couldn't do it. 'What kept him going when others said "no"? And why has he persisted with his ideas as well, bucking some trends on the way?'

Despite, or perhaps because of, her many travels, Madonsela is quite happy to spend the rest of her life in South Africa. 'I really think it is the best country in the world! I suppose because it is home, but I think we are a happy country; a resilient country. We have a spirit that defies what would appear to be negative circumstances at times. I have no plans to live elsewhere, but I wouldn't rule out working somewhere for a fixed amount of time, but I will always regard South Africa as home.'

When it comes time to being buried in her beloved country, Madonsela has thought about what she would like on her tombstone. 'I would want something like, "She left this world a better place, through ensuring justice and helping people realise their full potentials." Those things are important to me – justice and getting people to understand that they are more than they think they are. More than anything else, I'd like to help create an inclusive world. It really bothers me that after all these years we still see each other in terms of colour, even if we know it's irrational. I mean, for me to think that a white South African is the same as a Russian; I mean, rationally, we know that is not true! It's irrational to think that a black South African has more in common with a black Jamaican than a white South African. But those things still exist and that is something I would like to see myself contributing towards: a world where you don't really judge people by their colour, gender, disability or nationality. We should be judging people, as Martin Luther King said, by the content of their character.'

For Madonsela a person of character is someone who manages themselves. 'I believe, as a human, that the most difficult job we all have is to get ourselves to do the right thing, without waiting or worrying about "Will someone punish me? Is there someone who has authority over me who can make me do the right thing? Will the police arrest me?" It's the ability, even if you do make mistakes, to realise that you have made a mistake and fix it – not because there is somebody bigger or more powerful who can make you do the right thing, but because it is the right thing to do. Integrity is key, as it also encompasses genuine care for people.

'As a Public Protector, it has become important to me that when we look at someone we regard as a bad person or a person without integrity, it shouldn't only be somebody who steals money; it's also people who steal people's lives and their hopes. In other words, if I have a job that provides you with an ID or an RDP house or with health care, I should do that. If I don't because I am indifferent or because I am lazy, I'm as bad as somebody who steals.'

THULI MADONSELA has made a name for herself as a fearless public advocate and protector of human rights. Having had to learn how to overcome challenges from a young age, she put herself through university in order to realise her dream of becoming a lawyer, often assisting those less fortunate than herself with *pro bono* advice. One of *Time* magazine's Top 100 most influential people, Madonsela has perhaps become best known for her damning 'Nkandlagate' report.

BLACK LIKE HIM

HERMAN MASHABA

THE BOY WITH HOLES IN HIS SHOES

A cold wind snapped through the village of GaRamotse as Mapula Mashaba gave birth to her sixth and final child, Philip Samtseu Mashaba, in August 1959. The arrival of young Philip brought particular joy to his paternal grandfather, Koos Mashaba, who had claimed from the outset that the new baby would be 'no ordinary boy'. He was so adamant that his latest grandchild would be special and influential that he insisted on calling the child Highman – a name that dogged the boy throughout his youth. 'My name was the butt of jokes, and even though I managed to shrug off the teasing, I grew up resenting this grandiose label. Fortunately, I was saved from eternal embarrassment when, as a young adult, I came across the name Herman and realised it would be easy enough for me to make a change.'

GaRamotse was a 'typically rural village, so remote and insignificant that it did not even warrant a mention on any official maps'. Based in the greater Hammanskraal area, GaRamotse was just one of many villages and townships in the region, many of which Mashaba lived in as the family moved around during his youth. 'Such villages were generally drab, uninteresting places. Groups of modest mud homes huddled together amidst dense bushveld that, in summer, smelt sweet after an afternoon thundershower.'

Mashaba's parents were considered unconventional, because although Mapula had limited schooling, she was 'exceptionally independent', and the couple chose to live in a small house near to the family home instead of with her in-laws. 'My mother had excelled in her limited schooling, and as a young married woman she confided in her good friend and neighbour that she wanted to go out to work.' Unfortunately, for black women at that time, job opportunities were few and far between. 'The only job my mother ever managed to find away from home was that of a domestic worker – the bleak fate of many talented black women during the apartheid era.'

Although he did not fully understand it at the time, Mashaba's life took a dramatic turn when he was just two and his father, Matinte, died. 'My father's sudden death brought about drastic changes in the family – my mother had now become the family breadwinner. Like most villagers, my parents had enjoyed little more than a few years at school, so my mother was forced to look beyond the village for a job to support her family.' Mashaba and his three sisters were sent to live with his great-aunt, yet he considered the extended community in which he lived to be his family. 'It was accepted that a community looked after all the people who formed part of the community. That is how discipline was maintained and that is how attention and care were given to those who needed it. This spirit of caring, within and by a community, is the real meaning of Ubuntu.'

By this stage Mashaba's older brother, Pobane, had already left home, having only completed his Standard 6. The family were keen for all the children to get as much education as possible, but Pobane had run away to Pretoria to avoid the pressure of continuing at school. In his adulthood, Mashaba was sorry that his brother had not persevered at school. 'The opportunities, skills and knowledge that he would have gained, underwritten by maturity, might have allowed him to lead a much easier life.'

Mashaba's mother managed to find employment as a housekeeper for a white family, but this also meant that she was rarely home in the week to care for her own children. 'The small salary that my mother earned could not possibly cover all our needs. We fantasised about things like peanut butter, but usually we received nothing more than bare essentials such as soap powder and mealie meal. My mother's salary barely met the cost of transport between Johannesburg and Pretoria, and it was certainly not sufficient to pay school fees – even though they were only 25c a year.' Mashaba was close to his mother and missed her terribly, so her weekend visits were 'especially precious occasions. After my mother left and I was unable to sense her presence any more, a post-visit hollowness would descend upon the house for days.'

In the absence of a male figure in their home, Mashaba's next-door neighbour, Mr Parkies, and his paternal grandfather, Koos, filled that role. Koos was a 'big Shangaan guy' who lived in two worlds. As a security guard at the Ga-Rankuwa municipal offices, he was only able to come home once a month, where he exercised his authority on the family with an iron fist. Herman later reflected that his grandfather, despite his size and the influence he wielded at home, was in fact defeated by his circumstances and robbed of his dignity by the effects of the apartheid era, hence the power he was determined to exert at home. It was the stories that Mashaba heard from people like Koos that led him to believe that all white people were 'evil creatures'. Until his early twenties, everything he heard and experienced about whites was that they were 'violent and lacked compassion'.

Life took a small turn for the better when a new family moved to the village. The Baloyis brought with them a wind-up gramophone that 'set our hips rolling, our knees pumping and our minds dreaming. The songs that came out of that brown, beat-up gramophone hinted to us that there was a world beyond the place where our sun rose and set every day. With my spirits buoyed by my love of music, I was a cheerful person and a fairly popular kid at school. Teachers always singled me out to deliver a speech or to be the leader of a group when we had group activities; this is probably because I have always been comfortable and confident in the limelight. I was fortunate to have teachers who liked me and made time for me.'

INVESTING IN EDUCATION

School was not an easy place, however. The teachers had no tolerance for students who broke the rules, which was often challenging for Mashaba, who had to finish his household chores before he could leave the house in the mornings. The teachers on duty were remorseless, particularly for those students who struggled to pay their school fees. Beatings and humiliation were common, which left a lasting impression on Mashaba. 'As a result of my own experience, I believe that free education is absolutely essential to developing countries. Without access to education the potential of a learner is significantly curtailed; many of my peers had to drop out of primary school. It is short-sighted for governments to ignore the necessity for free education. If citizens are educated the chances of their being self-sufficient are high, but if they are uneducated they represent a loss of talent and labour and are a permanent drain on the economy.'

Mashaba was also fortunate to be raised by sisters who created a peaceful and harmonious home environment. 'My sisters did their best to give me guidance and stability, and I have always tried to emulate their example; on the occasions that I strayed, I can only blame myself. What I appreciate most about my sisters is that even though our family was fragmented, we were not dysfunctional.'

As the eldest, Esther in particular played a key role in the young boy's life, and, along with his mother, encouraged him to complete his education above all else. Support from his family, as well as an awareness of how little control over the direction his life could take, led Mashaba to focus on the one thing he could control – his schooling. He was well-aware of how limited the opportunities for black people were at the time, and knew that if he were to move beyond his circumstances and earn his independence, learning was critical. Upon reaching Standard 6, one of Mashaba's teachers left an indelible impression on him. He went out of his way to encourage the students to study, offering Saturday school for them. 'We soon realised it was imperative that we attend those extra classes if we wanted a better future for ourselves. Mr Khase sacrificed his family leisure time to teach us, and our efforts and his devotion paid off.'

AN ENTREPRENEUR IN THE MAKING

Yet the realities of life in GaRamotse were never far away. As Mashaba moved into high school, his mother's salary was no longer able to support the whole family, and hunger was an ever-present reality. Theft was common in the township – not as a malicious act, but one of survival. Growing up in this way it is not hard to see why Mashaba and his friend, Louis, turned to crime. Their first foray into delinquency saw the boys selling dagga, the profits from which they could feed themselves. This business soon grew and Mashaba added knoxman to his résumé – someone who controls the dice during a gambling session. 'The knoxman was feared and respected, and I tolerated no bad behaviour. I had some lucky escapes – not only from gamblers, but also from the police who constantly patrolled the township.'

When his mother fell ill it was up to Mashaba to provide for the household, but because he did not earn enough from dealing dagga he and Louis decided to focus on gambling. While his friends travelled every weekend to work as gardeners in the suburbs of Pretoria, Mashaba had 'no intention of allowing anyone to strip me of my dignity. While my friends worked as weekend labourers, I stayed home and studied and socialised, but by 5pm I was at the train station to welcome them home with my dice. Everything they'd earned over eight hours, I won from my friends in eight minutes.'

But Mashaba was always on the lookout for the 'next big thing'. An opportunity came when a friend told him of a stolen welding machine, the location of which he was willing to share with Mashaba and Louis for a share in any profit. Despite not having any idea of what he planned to do with it – not to mention the problems he would face if caught by the police in possession of it – Mashaba was determined to lay his hands on the machine and worry about the rest later. By this point the family had moved to Leboneng where most people did not have electricity. This did not bode well for the sale of the welding machine, but Mashaba was not one to shy away from a challenge. He finally settled on trying to sell the machine to Moersekont, a drug dealer with whom he had previously had some dealings.

During the negotiations with the gangster, Mashaba played it cool, a lesson he had learned avoiding arrest in the township. 'I realised early on the power of showing no emotion, especially when it came to negotiating. It was a lesson born out of fear and intimidation, and it proved invaluable in developing the negotiation skills that I later used in all my business dealings.' By selling the welding machine Mashaba suddenly had more money than he had ever dreamed of – the princely sum of R100. He was tired of being hungry and having to walk to school in broken shoes, and his early foray into entrepreneurship was his way around that. While Mashaba considers himself lucky to never have become addicted to alcohol or drugs, he does admit to having sniffed benzene to stave off hunger pangs, and he now credits God with 'steering me away from addiction and a wasted life' – something Pobane unfortunately could not claim.

Another defining aspect of Mashaba's young life was apartheid, and he grew up – as did many young black people – with a strong sense of black consciousness. When the homelands were created, Hammanskraal found itself part of Bophuthatswana, but although many of his friends were excited at the prospect of being free from the apartheid government, Mashaba believed that one restrictive government had simply been swapped for another. The situation for black workers remained dire and exploitative, but when reporters came to Hammanskraal to look into a story about the treatment of factory workers, they were too afraid of losing what little money they did earn to risk being interviewed. Mashaba felt that he had to intervene, and by taking a train into Johannesburg and giving the workers' payslips to a journalist, he felt 'liberated' at the chance to stand up for his people.

By the time Mashaba entered matric he was doing relatively well, and his mother turned a blind eye to his money-making schemes. He was not to know it then, but that year he met his future wife when he attended a beauty pageant to 'fish for girls'. The winner of the pageant was a young Connie Maloka, but despite Mashaba's attempt at flirting, he was gently rebuffed.

A ROAD LESS TRAVELLED

He continued to work hard, forming study groups and helping others to learn from past matric papers. His final exams saw him pass well in everything except for Afrikaans, a language he detested and refused to learn. He was the first in his family to pass matric, with his sisters only making it as far as Forms 2 and 3. It had long been Mashaba's dream to go to university and, despite the family's poverty, they worked together to make that dream come true. One way in which his mother assisted was by insisting that he convert to Catholicism when she landed a job at a nearby seminary. While he resisted at first, he soon came to be grateful when the Church paid for half of his annual university fees. The remainder of the loan came from Barclays Bank, with Esther and her husband standing surety.

Mashaba enrolled at the University of the North in 1979 where he hoped to study law, but his hatred of Afrikaans and all that it stood for destroyed those ambitions, as his matric mark was not high enough. He turned to a BAdmin degree with majors in Political Science and Public Administration, but because he had no intention of ever working for the apartheid government he instead set his sights on becoming an academic. 'Entering university was a defining stage in my life; I was embracing adulthood and leaving the waywardness of youth behind me. I accepted that I could no longer sell drugs or set up a gambling school on campus, and that I'd have to find other ways of surviving. My sister, Conny, always helped me out with a few rands when I needed it, but I refused to give up my education to go to work, as I knew that the only way to live my life on my own terms was to make the best of the opportunities given to me at university.'

It was when he was home on holiday from university that he was to get a second chance to woo Connie, which he did with rather more success this time round. When it came time to introduce her to his mother and family, he wrote a letter home asking if he could bring Connie round to the house to meet them. This told them all they needed to know about Mashaba's feelings for his new girlfriend, and she and his mother instantly developed a rapport that would last until his mother's death in 1996. His sisters also fell in love with the soft-spoken girl.

On Mashaba's return to university he and Connie communicated through letters, but he still considered himself single – until he had a ring on his finger he was not about to deny himself the joys of university life. Looking back, this is something he regrets. 'If you grow up womanising, you kill your value system and cause damage in your community. I see this happening now in South Africa.'

But the realities of life in apartheid South Africa intervened in 1980, when rioting on campus about what should have been a relatively minor argument led to the police being called in. This resulted in multiple arrests and a student body was formed to negotiate with the police for the release of the detainees. Never one to be a spectator, Mashaba was the youngest student elected to the committee, which he believes was due to his ability to keep a calm demeanour, which in turn conveys credibility.

As the committee went back and forth between the university council and the students, they came to realise that the council did not intend to address any of the students' grievances; classes were cancelled and one morning Mashaba awoke to discover that the police had surrounded the campus. The students were encouraged to return to their homes to avoid bloodshed, and an extremely disappointed and frustrated Mashaba took the train back to Hammanskraal. A few weeks later he received a letter from the university, stating that only those students who 'adopted an attitude of commitment to their studies and undertook to adhere to the university's rules' could return to campus. Mashaba knew in that moment that he would not complete his university degree, because he believed he would be sacrificing his dignity if he went back.

He did not make that decision lightly, however, because he had financial obligations to his sister, the bank and the Seminary. 'This period of my life was difficult and confusing: I felt disappointed, demoralised, angry and depressed.

For a brief period I feared that my usual optimism might degenerate into complete hopelessness. If I gave up my studies I would have to find a job to pay back my loans, but I didn't want to fall into the hand-to-mouth existence of so many of my friends and Pobane.'

His greatest desire was to leave the country to join Umkhonto we Sizwe. 'I wanted to leave the country, get the Russians to give me AK-47s and come back to kill all the scaly creatures,' but after weeks of trying to arrange to go into exile, he realised that his contacts had let him down and he would have to do the 'unthinkable' – he would have to find a job working for a white man.

TAKING THE HIGH GROUND

For weeks during that winter of 1980, Mashaba felt like his soul was being crushed. The country was in a state of upheaval and he was unable to find work. He did not want his family to know how depressed he was about both his own and the country's circumstances, so he pretended that all was well when in fact he was becoming concerned for his mental health. When his brother-in-law told him of an opening at a Spar distribution warehouse, Mashaba was in two minds. 'The South African Council of Churches was promoting study opportunities for black students to study abroad. I wasn't sure if I wanted to leave the country to pursue a military training programme, or to get a bursary from the SACC to study. And I still had serious reservations about working for whites. After careful consideration, I decided to apply for the job at Spar and tried to suppress my racial prejudices.' Looking back, Mashaba considers himself extremely lucky to have made the choice he did. 'People who were in those environments now don't go out to work for the public, they have their own personal agendas. I'm really disappointed with the current situation in the country.'

Mashaba landed the job and was proud to at last be able to contribute his monthly salary of R180 to the family, but the reality was that the job was menial and demeaning. Although he was forced to deal with petty racism on a daily basis, he was keen to avoid confrontation – a trait that has stayed with him throughout his life. Seven months later, he managed to get a job as a clerk at a small furniture-manufacturing company outside Pretoria, where he was not subject to the same racism he had suffered at Spar. It was also here that he learned a valuable lesson – by sitting and listening to what others had to say he found he could learn a great deal.

At the same time Connie had taken a job as a bookkeeper at Southern Sun, which meant that the couple were relatively well off, yet Mashaba continued to lie awake at night wondering when he would come up with a 'big idea' that would enable him to work for himself and be in charge of his own destiny. He was still all too aware that he need to pay off his student loans, and he also wanted to marry Connie so he needed to save money for lobola. 'I never rushed into things without careful planning, so once I had paid off the student loan, I decided to ask Connie's parents if I could marry her.' An amount of R800 was agreed upon for lobola, which Mashaba paid in June 1982.

It was at the same time that Mashaba came up with his first initiative. The show, *Ipi Ntombi*, was playing in Johannesburg and Mashaba wanted to bring it to Shoshanguve. The cousin of a colleague hired out halls so Mashaba went to the Alhambra Theatre to speak to the manager about doing a run in the township. To Mashaba's great surprise, not only did the manager agree to speak to him, but he also agreed that, for a deposit of R3000 – Mashaba's life-savings, he would put on the show for three nights. 'I felt as if I was floating as I left the theatre; I was filled with confidence, amazed that I had simply asked and my request had instantly been granted.'

The venture, however, turned out to be disastrous. Mashaba had delegated duties without conducting any oversight and had done very little marketing. Not only did he lose his deposit, but he was also humiliated. 'I decided that the next time I undertook a project I would take full control of everything, without relying on others to ensure its success.'

With Connie earning a steady income, Mashaba decided that it was time for him to find a job in sales where he could earn commission. Connie had accepted that he would never settle for mediocrity and that she would be the stabilising influence in their lives, so after listening to his plan to leave his job to go out on his own, she eventually agreed. 'While Connie had grave doubts about my decision to resign, she nevertheless stood behind me. Her own dreams for our future were as big as mine, yet she seemed instinctively to know that there was room for only one maverick in our relationship; and that one of us had to feel the ground under their feet.' Their first stop was to buy a car – despite the fact that Mashaba did not know how to drive. His enthusiasm was not dimmed by the fact that he reversed the car into a tree on the first day, and two months later he passed his driving test and bought insurance – just in time for him to have another accident.

Mashaba resigned from his job and was gratified that his boss and colleagues wished him well. 'Leaving the company in such a dignified way allowed me to maintain an enduring relationship with the owners, one that remains strong to this day. Many such long-lasting business and personal relationships have stood me in good stead down the years.'

After their wedding in February 1983, the couple set off to Durban on honeymoon – an extremely rare occurrence for black people in those days. 'That visit to Durban opened our eyes to the extent of the country. We realised that perhaps GaRamotse was not big enough to warrant a dot on a map.' Upon their return they bought a four-square-metre Zozo hut, which they put in Mashaba's mother's garden as a bedroom. Their new life had begun.

Mashaba began work as a sales agent for an insurance company, but it did not take long for him to realise that he would never be successful because he simply did not believe in the product – he could not in good conscience convince the poor people with whom he interacted to spend what little money they had on insurance they did not need. His integrity was something he valued highly and which he still credits in large part for his success today. He moved on to selling crockery and cutlery, but although this went well, he still desperately wanted something that would challenge him. He added linen and fire-detection systems to his inventory and started to learn a lot about the art of salesmanship, but he was concerned that with what he was selling he would never get repeat customers. Constantly having to travel to new areas, find new customers and generate new business was made extremely difficult by the pass laws that restricted his movements.

With this in mind Mashaba continued to scan the employment ads; he clearly remembers the day he saw an advert for SuperKurl, a company that manufactured black hair-care products. Having his hair done for his wedding had been a wonderful experience for Mashaba, and he knew that this was a product he could sell. A meeting at the factory with the owner, Leon Thompson, was all Mashaba needed to see that the product would offer him sustainable sales, and despite them initially looking for a white salesman, Thompson agreed to give him the job. Mashaba worked on a 30 per cent commission on the wholesale price, which he agreed to, given that it allowed him the freedom he so longed for. The next day he was given lessons in the hair-care industry and met both black and white entrepreneurs – it was a thrilling start to his new endeavour and he could not wait to get started.

Mashaba soon gave up his other sales jobs to concentrate on SuperKurl, quickly becoming the company's top salesman. 'I'd got into the business at the right time: black hair care was burgeoning and informal salons were springing up on every street corner.' Thompson and Mashaba got on well and it was not long before Thompson took him on a road trip to neighbouring African countries to market SuperKurl. Yet Mashaba was all too aware that he was unlikely to become a partner in the business and he still wanted more from his life. 'I didn't just want the gold watch when I retired from SuperKurl in 25 years' time – I wanted to own the gold mine.'

THE BIG GAMBLE

So it was that Mashaba and Joseph, a colleague he had brought into the business, decided to approach Johan Kriel, the company's pharmacist, because they knew that Johan was thinking of going out on his own in competition with Thompson. Although it was unheard of for a black man to approach a white one to start a business, Johan agreed to the venture – with some persuasion from his wife – when he was not given the partnership he had been promised by Thompson.

Now that Mashaba had the people, all he needed was the funding. He approached Walter Dube, a friend of Joseph, who owned a distribution company that had imported black hair-care products from the US before losing the licence. Dube soon taught Mashaba and Joseph some lessons about doing business when he asked them at their first meeting for their business plan. Sheepishly, Mashaba and Joseph returned with a business plan, at which time Dube peppered them with questions that led them to revise their plan until Dube was finally satisfied. Dube's conditions for a R30 000 loan were that he would be a 25 per cent partner in the business, that Mashaba, Joseph and Johan would each put up R3 000 as security, and that they would repay the loan at prime plus 10 per cent. Despite Johan not having the R3 000, Dube accepted the R6 000 and granted them the loan. 'The relief I felt at securing that start-up loan was immense; step by step, I was creating the reality that I had envisaged for myself. That small boy in Hammanskraal with holes in his shoes would finally get to stand on his own two feet and walk the path he had always dreamed of walking.'

That year was not all plain sailing, however, because Connie fell pregnant and then went into early labour at six months. Having already lost a baby to an ectopic pregnancy, the loss of their little girl was doubly difficult. 'I cannot even articulate how Connie's pain affected me; I have loved her since the day I first saw her and seeing her suffer was one of the most shattering experiences for me.' Fifteen sessions of in vitro fertilisation followed with no success, when Louis' wife, Sally, offered to be a surrogate mother for them. She fell pregnant immediately but also suffered an ectopic pregnancy, at which point the Mashabas decided that they had done all they could.

One of the first decisions the team had to make was what to name their new company. At a meeting Dube told them about a book called *Black Like Me* by John Howard Griffin. The book was about a white American man in the 1950s, who darkened his skin to get a real sense of the repression black Americans were dealing with at the time. The four agreed unanimously that that would be the name of their business. 'What appealed most to me about the name was that it suggested black pride, a consciousness of what our new company aimed to promote, and what it would offer to consumers.' The next step was to find premises, but blacks were not allowed to own or operate businesses in white areas, so Johan went out to a business park in Ga-Rankuwa where he secured a 200 square-metre factory. 'When I visited that mini-factory for the first time, my mind exploded with the vision of a busy company pumping out products for me and Joseph to sell.'

Mashaba's job was to develop the brand for the company, so he approached two women he had become friends with at the top hairdressing training academy in Johannesburg. Their knowledge of American marketing concepts and strategies helped Mashaba to conceptualise and develop the business's brand strategy. Because he was aware that he needed 'proper training' he attempted to study at night through Damelin, but he missed so many lectures due to work that he eventually gave up and decided to teach himself through reading.

While it was evident that each of the partners had doubts about the others' loyalty, apartheid having effectively entrenched distrust between blacks and whites, the group had no choice by this stage but to move ahead, and Black Like Me became a reality on Valentine's Day 1985.

A decision was made to create an entirely new product range from scratch, with Johan substituting chemicals to reduce the cost of the products in order to maximise profits. From the outset the salons loved the products – on their first day, both Joseph and Mashaba returned to the factory at 3pm to restock their cars because they had already sold their entire inventory for cash. The team were confident that they would be successful in what was a very competitive market, and brought Connie on as a full-time office administrator, as well as a young man to help with mixing and bottling. Within seven months, Dube's loan had been repaid and the partners began to earn well. 'Inevitable obstacles and challenges cemented the foundations of the partnership in the new business; during those difficulties we all came to realise that we were doing our best for the company and that we could trust each other.'

This trust came to be crucial when Thompson set about trying to undermine Black Like Me, beginning by offering a 'buy one, get one free' promotion.

Mashaba and his partners decided to do the same, forcing them to reduce their turnaround time in order to keep up with demand. 'Having Johan's expertise and resourcefulness was a major boost in keeping staff spirit buoyant – and indeed in keeping the business afloat. Those early days proved that we were all fighters, and we faced the challenges that arose with calm optimism and a dedication to building Black Like Me into a major contender in the market.'

Joseph and Mashaba ensured that they spent plenty of time visiting their customers, with Mashaba becoming a firm believer that face-to-face contact was essential to the maintenance of client relationships. Johan then managed to have phone lines installed, which meant that clients could phone their orders in. This set Joseph and Mashaba free to expand their customer base, but it was a hostile environment with barricades and patrols enforcing the state of emergency that existed.

Mashaba also began to spend more time on marketing as he was keen to make Black Like Me a market leader. 'There were times when my partners shook their heads at some of my unconventional ideas, but I persisted nonetheless and the company's visibility grew.' One of his ideas was to get onto TV, and following negotiations with the SABC, Black Like Me sponsored a 13-part hair-and-beauty grooming series in 1986. The response from the industry and the public was overwhelming, and the programme was such a success that before the first one had finished airing the producer phoned Mashaba to tell him that the SABC had commissioned an additional 26-part series. 'This programme was the foundation of a long and rewarding relationship with the SABC. Ironically, this success came during the time when the national broadcaster was controlled by the old regime, but despite this, the top management of the SABC gave the company an important break and we developed a working relationship.'

This was also a personal turning point for Mashaba, who dealt with Bessie Louw, manager of all the SABC's TV stations. Bessie believed in a non-racial future for South Africa, and this proved to be music to Mashaba's ears. 'The support and understanding we received from the SABC had the effect of opening my eyes to my prejudices. My unyielding opinion that all whites were racists who didn't consider the welfare of blacks had been challenged by Bessie's attitude, and I had to acknowledge that maybe it was time for me to get rid of my preconceived ideas.'

Mashaba went on to invite one of Johannesburg's most popular hairstylists, Anver Saferdien, to consult to them, which led to a glamorous launch and hair show at one of Johannesburg's top clubs. A year later, Anver joined the team and ensured that Black Like Me promoted itself as a far bigger company than it actually was. Boxing sponsorships and road-safety campaigns followed, blazing a trail for black-owned companies in South Africa. This campaign was in part due to the tragic loss of Pobane in a car accident – an event that affected Mashaba terribly.

The same year Mashaba and Connie decided that the time was right for them to buy a house, which they did for what seemed to be an exorbitant price of R30 000. It was also important to Mashaba that he buy his mother a house, which they managed to do the following year. 'I had begun to realise that having money is like travelling – you cannot enjoy it on your own. I wanted to share my good fortune; it is in the shared experience that things become special.'

By this time, the team had taken on so many people and had so many orders to fill, that despite having taken over five units in the business park, they could no longer fit into them. Again Johan went out and this time secured them a 1 500 square-metre factory nearby. This meant that they could buy bigger equipment and bring on extra workers, as well as employ more administrators and a financial director. The new factory did not last long, however – rapid growth in the salon industry meant that the team outgrew it almost immediately. Mashaba thought the best option would be to build premises that would be designed specifically for their needs, but because they could not get financing they were compelled to use the partners' money to buy a building.

It was now 1990 and Mashaba and Connie took advantage of the scrapping of the Group Areas Act and bought a house in Pretoria North. Before they had the chance to move in, the local newspaper ran a story indicating that their would-be neighbours were not happy about having a black family living in the area, which made them reconsider their decision. However, on the day they moved in they received visits from neighbours, as well as an invitation from one in particular, Pik Botha, to a 'Welcome to the Neighbourhood' cocktail party. The rest of the community protected the Mashabas from the right-wingers and they developed friendships that still endure today.

On the business side, Joseph was becoming increasingly unhappy with the way the business was growing and was reluctant to take on more responsibility. Despite the other partners urging him to keep his shareholding, Joseph wanted to sell, but he was not happy with the offer on the table. Bringing a lawyer in to manage his departure did not end well for Joseph, who ultimately left with less than had initially been offered. Johan was the next to leave, deciding in 1992 to sell his shares to Mashaba in order to become a farmer. That year was notable for Mashaba for other reasons, too, when he was invited to be the first black member of the Johannesburg Chapter of the Young Presidents Organisation (YPO).

GOING UP IN FLAMES

In 1993 a multinational competitor offered to buy Black Like Me for R65 million, but Mashaba turned it down. Instead he entered into a marketing deal with African Bank and began to train hairdressers, salon owners and distributors on the business of the industry. Mashaba decided to increase production and with the blessing of the management team, the company went into 24-hour production. That night the factory burned to the ground. Mashaba had suspicions about an ex-employee and approached the police with evidence, but the situation in the townships was so volatile at the time that the police did not have time to devote to the case. In desperation Mashaba offered a reward, but to no avail, and the case remains unsolved to this day. Shortly before the factory fire Mashaba had also lost a butchery he owned to fire, but did not get a payout from insurance because the company declared bankruptcy. He had a similar shock when the insurance company for Black Like Me would only pay for the building and not the contents, and he was forced to replace the factory contents out of his own pocket. This was a real setback for both him and the company, and the enterprise was forced to reduce its product line and once again do the bottling manually. Fortunately the staff pulled together to ensure that the company would survive, but production still plunged. Another setback came in the form of crime, which spiked post the 1994 elections. Employees were hijacked and salons were robbed, which meant that those salons that had bought on credit could no longer afford to pay their bills. This forced the company to change its policy on credit, which in turn left many clients unable to buy from them. It took 18 months to rebuild the company, with the staff complement reverting to 160 by the end of 1994.

When Black Economic Empowerment (BEE) was introduced, Mashaba was approached to sell Black Like Me while retaining a seat on the board, but that was not for him. 'To be honest, I felt insulted at times when I watched as some of my peers allowed themselves to be wooed by corporates, only to end up occupying the corner office with nothing to keep them busy other than the view from their office window. I have always had a strong work ethic and I had no inclination to be a *ja-broer* [a "yes man"] on a corporate board.'

EVOLUTION

The year 1994 was not all gloom, however, because the Mashabas' greatest miracle materialised when Connie fell pregnant and gave birth to a little girl – Nkhensani. Mashaba's mother moved in to help, eager to make up for not being able to spend much time with her own children when they were young. The Mashabas also made time to travel, which Mashaba credits with having exposed him to the world and its diversity of cultures. 'Travel taught me much by exposing me to the world's expectations of me; all I needed to do was open my eyes to the opportunities that existed and seize them. My exposure to open-minded people who had grown up without the shackles of hatred made me adamant in my refusal to tolerate any expression of racism in my presence.' This spilled over into his dealings with his staff, believing as he did that good relationships with employees, as well as suppliers and clients, makes good business sense.

Mashaba decided that the best way forward for the company was to go global, so he began to look into other markets in Africa. 'Initially we established distribution contracts in Zambia, Malawi, the DRC, Lesotho, Namibia and Swaziland, and then Louis and I visited Kenya and Zimbabwe to forge links with suppliers there.'

Despite the rapid increase in markets thanks to the new democratic dispensation in South Africa, foreign expansion was not a picnic. Unpaid debts, poor communication and problems with customs and excise left Mashaba wondering if going global was more challenging than it was worth. Although his limited education meant that he relied in large part on his gut to run the company, he still felt that Black Like Me needed to expand internationally, but that it needed mature business experience to really make it work. 'When Colgate-Palmolive approached me, I looked at the offer coolly and decided to give it due consideration. That company's penetration into international markets was well-established and it had a body of corporate expertise that would fill the gaps in my style of management. Colgate-Palmolive had the capital and credibility I needed to reach the level of success I'd envisaged.'

The offer from Colgate-Palmolive was not the only one, but it did allow Mashaba to stay on at the company and keep a 25 per cent share. When the agreement was finally drawn up and signed in July 1997, it was 'the size of the Bible'. The year 1997 was a milestone for the Mashabas in other ways as well, as not only did they celebrate the birth of their son, Rhulani, but they were also invited by then-President Nelson Mandela to visit Robben Island along with other local and international dignitaries, including Hillary Clinton and Bill Cosby. It was on this trip that he really appreciated the learning that the prisoners had gained from reading, a similar theme to his own upbringing. 'Books have been a constant companion in my life. It is through the solitary pursuit of reading that I have managed to educate myself and broaden the foundation of the inferior education I received as a boy. Through books I am constantly exposed to ideas that have resonated with me and helped me to consider and solve specific issues in my personal and business life.'

Three years into the partnership with Colgate-Palmolive, Mashaba could no longer ignore the fact that the company had a problem. 'In spite of the buy-out, our market share continued to slide. Yet I went against my better judgement, ignoring my gut feeling that things were not going according to plan. I persevered, patiently allowing alien systems and controls to be implemented.' Eventually he spoke to Connie, explaining that he could no longer 'stand by and watch as Black Like Me slides into obscurity'. It was one of the 'lowest ebbs' of his life when he decided that he needed to extract himself from the business. But what he had expected to be Colgate-Palmolive buying him out turned out to be quite the opposite, with the company offering Mashaba their 75 per cent. After long discussions with Connie, he realised that not only did he still care deeply about the staff at Black Like Me, as well as all the community outreach programmes they sponsored, but he also wanted to be in charge of his own business as well. Lengthy negotiations saw him buy back Colgate-Palmolive's 75 per cent share in August 1999 for less than he had sold it to them for.

Mashaba then set about reforming Black Like Me and building his own profile. By 2001 the company achieved 'phenomenal' sales, and by expanding its product range, modernising its packaging, including French products for Francophone Africa and hiring an export manager to deal with business on the continent, 2002 saw 40 per cent growth. Yet in spite of its growth the company had only captured 10 per cent of the South African market, which was worth approximately R600 million at the time. Mashaba knew that he had to refocus his efforts on foreign expansion. It took two years for him to study the UK market and develop an entry strategy, which with just three million people making up the market was valued at a remarkable R740 million. In April 2002, Black Like Me entered the UK, having formed a joint venture with Renbow to distribute their products.

Mashaba had learned the hard way that large corporate structures were not the only way to conduct business and that 'emerging small-to-medium businesses are the lifeblood of sustained growth in a developing country'. He decided that the time was right to look into BEE, and was disappointed to see that in many instances it was not truly empowering those who needed the most help. 'The truth is that South Africa needs entrepreneurship, which benefits the economy by providing sustainable economic growth. It is vital that educational institutions and businesses teach entrepreneurial skills – self-motivational skills, time-management skills, financial skills, administrative skills, and sales and marketing skills – all of which can and need to be taught, not only to students, but also to employees.'

MOVING ON

In 2001 Mashaba announced that he was going to establish a BEE investment company. He canvassed several prominent politicians and business people, eventually creating Leswikeng Mineral & Energy (Pty) Ltd with partners such as Max Sisulu, Ronnie Mamoepa and Jane Phiri. But it was not long before the company was put to the test, when in 2002 Mashaba decided to bring another partner, Dr Noel Machingawuta, on board and give him equal shareholding. When he approached his partners they were adamant that they would not give up any of their shares, which infuriated him. It was only when he declared that he would dissolve the company that they finally agreed to include Machingawuta. Shortly thereafter the first deal was concluded, with Leswikeng buying the Mogale Alloys smelter in Krugersdorp.

But back at Black Like Me problems had begun to resurface. Connie had left the company in 1997 to pursue further education and to spend time with the family, only returning to the business in 2002, and Mashaba realised that the company was in desperate need of a strong leader who could devote the necessary time to the business and its people. He thus approached Connie with the idea of collaborating with Amka Products, a competitor he knew ran an extremely good business. Connie was reluctant, recalling the problems of the Colgate-Palmolive acquisition, but Mashaba was adamant that things would be different this time. Although Connie was even more against the idea when she realised that staff would have to be retrenched, Mashaba knew that this was an opportunity that he could not pass up and that if things stayed the way they were, Black Like Me would not survive. 'At the end of the 49 per cent sell-out to Amka, only 10 of the 90 personnel kept their jobs.' Connie stayed on as Managing Director at Black Like Me, which continues to thrive in the partnership with Amka.

Mashaba began to use the network he had developed from his days selling crockery from his car boot, and the exercise soon paid dividends. A meeting with Tom Henry, CEO of Stocks Building Africa, was arranged through an old friend who had built the Black Like Me factory in Mabopane. Despite Mashaba's reservations, agreeing to the meeting turned out to be one of the best decisions he had ever made. 'I always say that I haven't really had a mentor in my life, but insofar as a mentor guides and teaches, I would have to say that Tom Henry came the closest to playing this role. It didn't take long for Tom to persuade me to become a shareholder in Stocks Building Africa.'

As Mashaba wanted to buy 30 per cent of the company he had to approach RMB Ventures, which held 72 per cent of the shares. Unfortunately their offer was so low that the initial meeting lasted less than 10 minutes, forcing him and Tom back to the drawing board. A few months later, though, a deal was struck. Mashaba's new position as Chairman was intimidating for the boy from Hammanskraal, as he worried that he would be managing a group of highly educated board members. As always, Connie was on hand to reassure him, telling him, 'You're streetwise and wise, Herman. That's got you where you are today. People like you don't need certificates to prove their competence.'

As Leskwikeng has grown, Mashaba has faced criticism of his choice of investments, yet he believes that all have been 'deliberate and strategic'. If wealth creation is not at the core of a business plan, he has no hesitation in turning it down – his strong belief is that job creation should be the result of a good business plan, not the cause of it. Chemistry is also a strong predictor of success for Mashaba, as is liquidity. Where possible he and his partners only invest in companies that require the least amount of debt to be incurred, which ensures that the debt can quickly be serviced and liquidated.

To satisfy his need to interact with a diverse range of stakeholders, Mashaba went on to create the Phatsima Group and Lephatsi Investments. All three companies have the same vision: 'To become a leading non-racial entrepreneurial and socially responsible company, and to be at the forefront of the economic empowerment of previously disadvantaged groups in South Africa.'

LEADING FROM THE FRONT

Entrepreneurship remains close to Mashaba's heart, and he believes that there are many factors that can play a crucial role in the success of an entrepreneur. Education, self-belief, reading, mentors, salesmanship, creative flair, vision, access to finance and luck are some of the attributes he sees as important, and he has been inspired by entrepreneurs such as Robbie Brozin, Mark Shuttleworth, Felicia Mabuza-Suttle, Donald Gordon, Sol Kerzner and Richard Branson. This passion for entrepreneurship, as well as community upliftment, has led him to support programmes such as the St Mary's Alexandra School Project and the Field Bank Foundation. He also gives talks to young people about entrepreneurship and the importance of education, and funds students who have a genuine need and desire for education. Black Like Us, an art initiative that helps artists to improve their business skills so that they can make a living from their profession, is another brainchild. 'Daily I am fortunate to encounter ordinary South Africans who are active in being responsible citizens. I learn from them and our interactions refine my views and opinions about things. I could read a thousand books and study at almost any university, but neither are substitutes for the wisdom I have encountered in my meetings with people from all echelons of society. I have found that to be a learner, you must first be a listener.'

Yet Mashaba is all too aware of what allows him to help communities in South Africa – his success in business. 'Business cannot live in a vacuum. Business is part of a working civil society and without a functioning democracy and functioning systems, business will suffer.'

When it comes to measuring his success, he looks to his relationships with his family and friends. Having lost his father and brother, he does not take anyone for granted, and respect for human life is so important to him that he has decided to dedicate the remainder of his life to fighting discrimination. Another cause close to his heart is the promotion of capitalism, which he does through the Free Market Foundation. Through these causes, he hopes his children will never turn to him and ask why he did nothing when he saw the problems the country faces. 'I am a privileged South African and I never want someone to say that I did nothing; that I didn't really care. So instead of going to the Russians and asking for an AK-47, now I look to the Constitution and civil society to change things for the better.'

Mashaba is adamant that a life as a politician is one he would never consider, preferring to be an independent civil society activist. 'I look at what our government is actually doing for our people, particularly black people; it is such an insult that our government strongly believes that black people are not capable of doing anything for themselves. We need to conscientise our people not to accept that nonsense! If you want to destroy this country it is for civil society to do what we did in 1994, because in 1994 we all went to sleep and what we are seeing now is very scary. We need to wake up today because we are really facing a serious crisis.'

Unsurprisingly, Mashaba is not concerned about his tombstone. 'If people want to remember me, there are plenty of photos they can look at.'

A born maverick, **HERMAN MASHABA** knew from an early age that he was not cut out to work a 9-to-5 job. Despite his impoverished background, he used his intellect and street smarts to seize opportunities where others saw none. Having built a multimillion-rand business from the boot of his car, Mashaba is living proof that your background and material circumstances do not need to define your future.

WE SHALL OVERCOME

BRIAN MOLEFE

SCATTERLING

In June 1958 the apartheid government passed Proclamation 150 and 151, which listed the areas that would be subject to forced removals. Eight years later, Lady Selbourne, a township on the outskirts of Pretoria, was added to the list, with one of those affected being a young Brian Molefe, who had been born earlier that year in a local Roman Catholic maternity hospital. Following the forced removals baby Molefe went to live with his maternal grandparents in Atteridgeville, until his parents married and he went to live with them in Ga-Rankuwa at the age of six.

'My parents were very young so my grandparents decided it would be best if I went to live with them while my father went to university and my mother finished teacher training college. My father came from a very poor family, but he was extremely bright. He wanted to study medicine and had earned distinctions in Maths and Science, but when he got the forms for university he had to put down the occupation of his parents. As his father was dead and his mother would be arrested if he put down that she sold illegal home-brewed beer as her occupation, that seemed like a dead end, but fortunately his maths teacher arranged a bursary for him to study social work at the University of the North, so he went there and got a degree and became a social worker. Eventually he did a postgraduate degree in Social Work, a Masters degree in Social Work and then a doctorate in Social Work. I remember on his graduation day he said to me, "I always wanted to be a doctor!"'

Molefe's mother went on to become a high-school teacher, having three more children – one daughter and two more sons – many years later. When Molefe moved back to his parents' home he missed his grandparents, as he had grown very close to them and his grandfather in particular was an inspiration to the young boy. 'He worked as a labourer in a construction company but when people were removed to new locations they were given houses with no windows, doors or floors. It was a great opportunity for him – he started putting in windows and doors, laying floors and stoeps. He made so much money that he bought himself a big car, even though he couldn't drive! He was a bit of an entrepreneur. In those days black people were not allowed to drink spirits unless they could prove they were educated above a certain level or that they were a professional, like a teacher, social worker or doctor. My grandfather used to work hard in the day and he'd be very dirty, but after work he would wash and put on a black suit, especially on a Friday, and my grandmother would iron his shirt and starch it, and he'd walk to the bottle store and the guys standing outside would pay him a fee to buy them something and they didn't even ask for ID inside! I remember how excited I was when my grandfather bought me my first bicycle.'

When Molefe was 14 the whole family moved to Mafikeng, where he was sent to boarding school. Although both his parents strongly encouraged him to get the best education possible, 'unfortunately, I was a very disappointing student!' It was during high school that Molefe discovered politics, which took precedence over academics. Although he was accepted into the University of Natal to study a BCom in 1985, he dropped out after one year, went back to

Ga-Rankuwa and joined the ANC. 'Then I registered with Unisa and, to my surprise, I did very well, so I finished that year and then went to Rhodes in 1987. I think I did well at Unisa because I could manage my own time and do what I wanted to do. It didn't matter if I woke up at 2am in the morning to study or only went to bed at 4am; there were no lectures and no structure and I did very well in those circumstances. Because I did so well, though, my parents wanted me to go to a "proper" university, which is why I went to Rhodes, but I only stayed there one year.'

MATTERS OF STATE

In 1988, Molefe returned to live with his parents in Limpopo, where he became very involved in politics. 'My parents were very disappointed that I was more interested in politics than academics. Their political views were aligned with mine but they were not activists at all; they never lifted a stone in anger and didn't want politics to be something that consumed my life, which unfortunately it did. They used to raid my room looking for literature they considered dangerous because they were worried that the police would raid our house and find it.

'I'm not exactly sure where I got my passion from, although there was an incident in Atteridgeville that I remember well. I must have been 10 or 11 years old and the municipality had built a swimming pool right next to the stadium, but it hadn't been opened yet. There were riots going on, which we didn't comprehend, and when a group of children climbed over the wall of the pool to swim, the police came and fired live rounds and a child died. His name was Patrick – he lived diagonally across the street from us. He was just an ordinary fellow who was not political; he must have been about 13. His funeral was something. For the first time I heard about how Kruger and Vorster wanted to kill all the black people and that started it for me. At that moment I became interested and I never looked back.'

Although he had not been born at the time, the Rivonia Trial was something that would inspire Molefe throughout the course of his life. 'The principles of Nelson Mandela and the Rivonia trialists, as well as the friendship between Mandela and Oliver Tambo, really made an impact on me. To see how they built an organisation and saw it through despite all they had to overcome. I first started hearing about Mandela in the late 1970s, but by the time I reached matric I really understood what was happening. I've always thought that business-school academics should write a case study about an organisation that was not allowed to operate in its primary market, which was not allowed to recruit staff, and which had half of its leaders living in exile in another country and the other half living on an island. But every time they sent sales people to come and sell the product, which was an idea; the sales people, who worked without remuneration, did so at the risk of being imprisoned or killed. And the leaders somehow inspired the sales force to go in, over a 30-year period, to sell the product until they took over market share completely. Imagine if I was selling goods here in Johannesburg, but half my sales force was in Harare and the two couldn't talk to each other. They have no salary and they might be killed, but we get them to want to do it. So it comes down to a vote between people who have had no meetings for 30 years against the incumbents who have all the resources in the world, and the former win because their product is better. How do you do that? And if that can be done under those circumstances, why is it so difficult to build an organisation in an environment of freedom?'

During his time living with his parents in Limpopo Molefe got a job working as an administrator for the ANC, immediately after the organisation was unbanned. 'I remember I was interviewed for the job by Lesetja Kganyago who is now Deputy Governor of the Reserve Bank, as well as Collins Chabane and an old man called John Phala who had just come back from Robben Island. He had been imprisoned on the island in 1977 and was an amazing old man. He only asked one question during the interview, which was, "What is the ANC's policy on witchcraft?" Luckily I knew that the ANC doesn't have a policy on witchcraft, but the context was that there were quite a lot of activities against people who were perceived to be witches and who were burned in their houses, which was something the ANC wanted to contain. So what he really wanted to know was, "What do you think about witchcraft?", "Do you believe in witchcraft?", and "If you work for the ANC, are you also going to instigate people to burn witches?"

'The answer I gave was, "Look, there's no witchcraft, but it doesn't help the ANC to tell people something that they so fondly believe in does not exist, so we have to find a balance between allaying people's fears about witchcraft's existence and alienating them because we don't think witchcraft exists." He said, "You're hired!"'

Molefe was then elected into the provincial executive of the ANC in Limpopo and was the head of economic planning, despite still having some courses outstanding from his BCom. During a meeting in Johannesburg in 1992 a decision was made to create development forums through the country, so Molefe resigned from his ANC job and became the first convener of what was then the Northern Transvaal Regional Development Forum. 'The forums were civil society forums but they were led by ANC people. They were very successful; I established a regional development forum that was comprised of religious people, among others, which was great because we wanted to incorporate as many people as possible in development issues.

'Some of the funding came from the Nedbank Chairman's Fund, while the rest came from local and international NGOs. I remember, when Chris Hani was killed in 1993, that there was going to be a memorial service in Polokwane, and the Chief Minister of the Lebowa government, Mr Nelson Ramodike, was also angry about the killing and gave a donation for the memorial. When everything was set up at the taxi rank outside the Pick n Pay in Polokwane, Ramodike arrived in his Mercedes-Benz and the people chased him away because they saw him as part of the system. That made Mandela very angry. He came to the Limpopo ANC office a week later on a Saturday morning – I remember it very clearly – and he said: "Why did you chase Ramodike away? If you chase him away from an ANC meeting you are driving him towards de Klerk. We are negotiating to go into an election and we need to bring people towards us, not drive them away." He was told that "It wasn't us, it was the people that didn't want him there", to which he responded, "You are the leaders. You must lead! You cannot fail the organisation."'

Molefe had not been at the event but apologised to Mandela, along with the rest of the executive, and then the ANC called Ramodike to arrange a time to meet with him. 'He said he would come to us but Mandela said that we had to go to him, so we went to his house and apologised. After that there was food and wine and we started drinking, but Mandela didn't drink and he suddenly said, "Some of you are very young. We can't all go to Parliament so some of you have to go back to school."'

It was not long before Molefe got a call telling him to prepare to go to school in London to do a postgraduate diploma in Economics through the School of Oriental and African Studies (SOAS) at the University of London. 'I wanted to go to Parliament and I was on the list but I was told I was too young; I was only 26. I still didn't have my BCom so that's why I did a diploma, but I also registered to finish my BCom at the same time. I stayed in a flat with Lesetja and two other girls, and it was a struggle to complete my BCom at the same time as my diploma; I remember I wrote the exams at the South African Embassy. I was also elected President of the Association of South African Students in Great Britain; it sounded like a great title!'

Before he had left for London, Molefe had been attending a meeting in Johannesburg in March 1993, when he was told that he should attend an ANC course in Rustenburg. As he had thought he would only be away from home for the day he had no clothes or toiletries with him, so he bought what he could from the ANC shop on the ground floor of Shell House and made his way out to Rustenburg. 'There I was, all dressed in ANC gear, and little did I know that I was about to meet my future wife!' Portia Derby was an academic who was studying for her Masters in Economics at the time, and was attending the course on Central Banking, which was being run by the Bank of England. Between March and that September when Molefe left for London, he saw Portia 'two or three times' as she was living in Pietermaritzburg and he was living in Polokwane. He came back home from London in December of that year to marry her. 'That's romance!'

Molefe returned home after the elections in 1994, having earned his degree and diploma, and moved to Johannesburg. The ANC wanted to send him to the Reserve Bank but the bank refused, so they called Viv Bartlett, treasurer at First National Bank, who agreed to take him on and train him as a forex dealer. Once his three-month training was complete, Molefe joined the Development Bank as an Institutional Specialist in 1995, but the then Premier of Limpopo called him to ask him to return to the province to continue his work in the Development Forum, which by this time had evolved into the Reconstruction and Development Programme (RDP). This position lasted for two years until he received a phone call from the then Minister of Finance, Trevor Manuel, who invited him to work at the Treasury, where he took on the role of Director of Intergovernmental Relations, before becoming the Chief Director of Asset Management. It was during his time at Treasury that his first child, Itumeleng, was born.

Most of Molefe's learning came from on-the-job training. 'Look, education is important, but in my case there was actually very little knowledge from what I had learned at school or university that I applied. I mean in Economics II you cover forex, but you don't get a chance to trade currencies, for example. Education does help you to go through the thought processes though.'

Two years after joining the Treasury, in July 2003, Molefe became the Deputy Director-General of Asset and Liability Management, which involved managing the country's debt portfolio. During the same year, Molefe earned his MBL from Unisa and was appointed CEO of the Public Investment Corporation (PIC). His position as CEO of the PIC lasted for eight years before he moved on to become CEO of Transnet in February 2011.

GETTING DOWN TO BUSINESS

When it comes to his own leadership style, Molefe looks to carry on in the vein of Mandela and Tambo by making sure that Transnet inspires people as a brand. 'People should be inspired to want to work hard in Transnet; to turn it around and make sure it functions. I worry about how much there is to do so I spend a lot of time on organisational work, spending Fridays talking to workers and going out to the various areas.'

With 64 000 employees, Molefe has his work cut out for him. 'The big challenge is we want to get the trains to work and we want to get the ports to work, but they won't unless we can show every person – from the lowest workers or the basic units of the organisation, which we call gangs who go into a shift together – how important their roles are and the bigger picture or scheme of things. For me that is a challenge; getting people to understand what we are trying to achieve as an organisation and as a country.

'The best way I've found to do this is by talking to people. You would be surprised that, although money incentivises people, it does not do so entirely. People need to understand why they are doing something and buy into it, then there is no stopping them. What makes people sit for three months in Kiev's Independence Square? It's not money, it's because they believe in something.'

Molefe believes that one of his flaws is that he is too emotional and soft on people. 'Professionally and personally, I get too emotionally involved, but also if I decide I want something I can be hard-headed, obstinate and push at all costs. That can be a weakness because sometimes you have to know when to stand back, but it's also a strength because you must stick to what you're doing sometimes and be able to distinguish what's important and what isn't. When you're running an organisation that becomes very important because you can be consumed by all sorts of detail and nitty-gritty stuff. I consider myself quite good at that; I can see when unnecessary details come creeping in and always maintain a view of the big picture.'

There are certain things that Molefe acknowledges he hasn't figured out yet, but they are complex constructs such as how the mind of a teenager works. Bringing up his children leaves him with little time to worry and overanalyse the decisions he makes. 'I think things through, but if I can't decide straightaway I put it away and come back to it at the right time. When I do make a decision then I'm happy that I've made the right decision and I don't revisit it. I'm very decisive in that way. I find that if I'm having difficulty making a decision, I think about it quietly by myself then I see things from a different angle and the answer comes to me.'

Looking further down the line, Molefe doubts he would go into politics but thinks that teaching would be something that would appeal to him. 'I'd like to learn a new language and meet new people. Eventually I see myself teaching at a small seaside university; I don't mind where, as long as there is sea close by. If I do live overseas for a while I'll always come back to South Africa though. If I were to get an overseas posting I think South America would be interesting. I had a crush on Gabriela Sabatini when I was in high school!'

As far as South Africa is concerned, Molefe believes that significant progress has been made in the past 20 years. 'From a human rights, freedom of speech and intellectual engagement point of view, there is much more tolerance now than there has been in this country for centuries. These are all important values for me. Sometimes people abuse their right to express themselves as they please, but as long as no one gets hurt in the process, it's good that they can because that's what people fought and died for.'

When it comes to talking to young people, Molefe believes he has a way with words and with stories, although that holds no water with his 17-year-old son, who is not sure what he wants to do when he leaves school. 'He doesn't like science, commerce or figures. I think he wants to write. But he said to me, "Dad, we need to acknowledge that I am lazy. I may just become an overt cynic!" I'm not sure if it's because he wants me to push him or he wants to see if I will push him to become something else. Or maybe he's just trying to provoke me because a lot of teenagers seem to do that; they just want to get a reaction. He did say to me, though, that he doesn't want to be rich and he doesn't want to be branded as my son. He told me that he wants to be a "forward-thinking leader".

'I then spoke to a friend of mine who has a daughter who is studying Actuarial Science and I asked him what I should do because my son wants to be a cynically overt leader, and he said, "I'm not surprised. I can hear you speaking in him! Just think … your father wanted you to go to university and everybody thought you were just going to waste, and look at you today! Your son must see something in you that he's unconsciously emulating."'

The state of leadership in South Africa is something that concerns Molefe, who believes that 'leadership now comes with a lot of trappings that never used to be there. Leaders generally start off facing true north but then somewhere along the way they get distracted and go off course completely. I think they lose touch with the ordinary people and forget what is happening down on the streets. There are some leaders that I would like to meet, like Bob Marley. I find his lyrics very inspirational; he had foresight. I'd also like to meet President Barack Obama – not because I always agree with him, but because he's gone from being a skinny kid with a funny name to the President of the United States; I like that.'

Molefe has himself received various awards recognising his leadership over the years, including Financial Services Achiever of the Year in 2003, Investment Specialist of the Year in 2004, BEE Leader of the Year in 2005, Newsmaker of the Year in 2006, the Empowerment Leadership Award in 2007 and Institutional Investor of the Year in 2008. He has also held various board positions, including at SASRIA and Airports Company South Africa (ACSA). He has also found time to be a member of the South African National Defence Force's Reserve Force, all the while training to be a pilot, learning to play the saxophone and attending various specialised management and leadership programmes at institutions such as Wharton Business School, Harvard Business School and the Kennedy School of Government.

When it comes to taking other people's opinions into consideration, Molefe believes they must be taken from whence they come. 'You have to learn to field them. You can always tell when you get feedback that is meaningful. I spoke once at a function where there were students present and 12 years later somebody came up to me and said that what I had said about the importance of being diligent had stuck with him throughout that time.'

Molefe has learned to overcome his fears – with the exception of his fear of snakes – as he taught himself that 'you only have fear for something that has not happened. You don't have a fear for something that has already happened or that is happening, and there's no point in fearing something that may not happen.' Molefe also does not fear dying and has decided what he would like on his tombstone. 'Here lies Brian Molefe.'

A tragic shooting at the hands of the police when **BRIAN MOLEFE** was just 11 years old led to his passion for social activism, which despite his rigorous schedule continues to this day. This schedule includes his role as CEO of Transnet as well as various directorships, being a father, continually advancing his education and learning to play the saxophone, among others.

A FORCE OF NATURE

YOGAVELLI NAMBIAR

THE MEANING OF LIFE

Common sense characterised both Yogavelli Nambiar's parents, Bala and Ambie Nambiar, and that more than made up for what they lacked in formal education. The youngest of four children, Nambiar was born in Chatsworth, the largest Indian township in Durban, in 1973. Her parents stressed the importance of education, as well as values and ethics to all their children, with religion also sharing centre stage. Some of the values that resonated most with Nambiar were being open-minded, liberal and generous – traits she observed in her parents, who believed in living the values they cherished.

As a construction worker, Nambiar's father often had to accept contracts that took him away from home for long periods. Where possible, however, the family travelled with him for the lengthier contracts, including two years spent in Cape Town, before the family finally moved to Johannesburg.

As she was growing up, Nambiar's parents did not emphasis entrepreneurship, but rather 'like most Indian families, they wanted us to get into a good job.

Certain sectors were viewed as "higher" than others – the law and medicine, for example. But my parents never forced us to study something we weren't interested in; they never pushed us along a path, but just said there must be *some* path. We were encouraged to make a choice, which we could change later if necessary, but we had to get a good education first. I only discovered entrepreneurship later on in life really. Or entrepreneurship discovered me!'

Although Nambiar was raised in middle-class communities, growing up she was all too aware of the inequities of life in South Africa. 'I think I was almost born knowing that there were inequities. I am not trying to martyr myself by any means, but I would just pick up on something that seemed unequal or unjust and when I would raise it with someone else, like my friends at school, they hadn't noticed any differences. I was quite an activist at school, so I fought the way that the caretaker was treated, for instance; I would fight the cause of the underdog. If the principal or a teacher scolded a child for something I believed was wrong, or I had seen what really happened, I would speak up, even though it had nothing to do with me. And normally I'd end up getting into more trouble than the other child!

'I felt the need to speak up for people who didn't, in my little mind at the time, have a voice or who couldn't speak up for themselves. I think, because of that, I grew in confidence in my ability to fight a good fight; to fight for a good cause where something I saw was wrong. There was an instance when a helper's daughter and I were friends. She is black and we wanted to go together to the community library but they wouldn't let her in. I started fighting her case and shouting and creating a big ruckus and told them that it wasn't right. I think I was, maybe, 10 years old at the time. Both of us got kicked out so the story doesn't really have a great ending, but it made me realise that there is always something that I can do or say, even if the result isn't always what I wanted to achieve.'

Despite Nambiar's boldness in speaking out, she claims she does respect authority, but not always the figure in authority. 'I have a brain and am able to add value in an argument. I'm not going to argue with someone who is an authority on nuclear science because I don't have that kind of expertise, but

I believe in my ability to listen and create sensible opinions, and I'm open to being wrong. I have a healthy, but not a blind, respect for authority.'

Nambiar continued with her activism throughout her school years, and yet had a 'pretty normal childhood'. She was, however, a victim of bullying during Standard 9 when the family moved to Johannesburg, where she was the only Hindu at a Muslim school. 'It got really terrible – I had shoes thrown at me and it was very bad, so my parents removed me from the school after just six months.'

Nambiar finished matric in 1991, at which time she began studying Public Relations at the Durban Institute of Technology (then ML Sultan Technikon), and her results were such that she was allowed to complete her final year while working in Johannesburg, where she had acquired a job with Sun International in their corporate communications and eventing team. This was an eye-opener for Nambiar, who until that point had never even stayed in a hotel. 'It was great work; I was going out and seeing the wealthier side of the world. The very first hotel I stayed in was the Palace of the Lost City, so it could only go down from there! I was enjoying the good life; this young executive, growing in the company. My bosses liked me and I was doing well and travelling internationally.'

After three years Nambiar was headhunted by Vodacom, but life took an unexpected turn in 1999 when she and her brother were doing a search on the Internet for their surname. As fourth-generation South Africans they were not aware of any other families that shared their last name who they were not related to, so they began e-mailing every Nambiar they came across to learn more about their heritage, with the result that she decided to go to India to meet some of them in December that year. 'I went to India for three weeks and what I saw there was a massive *klap* on the side of the head!'

Nambiar travelled to Mumbai, Bangalore and Chennai, where she saw massive disparities between the rich and poor. 'It was different to South Africa, because here there are a lot of poor people but it almost feels segregated; you could almost live your whole life without seeing them. In India you could not escape it. That trip was the biggest education of my life; it's where I really connected with my purpose.'

When Nambiar returned from her trip, she resigned from Vodacom, sold her car and told everyone she was moving to India to 'sort out all its problems!' Although Nambiar realised that South Africa had problems of its own, she did not view them as being as urgent and overwhelming as India's. Her parents were not political and she had never been politically active, so her understanding of the realities of daily life for the majority of South Africans was limited – despite the stories she heard from her father, who would sometimes describe the treatment of the Indian and black construction workers at the hands of their white compatriots. 'A bus used to take the workers from the hostels to the construction sites, but the white workers would stop the bus and force the others to walk. His telling of these stories wasn't political, though – we knew it was wrong, but we were never involved in discussions about it or protests. We were sheltered to a large extent, so when I got to India it was an eye-opener. I was also older by that time and more comfortable with having worked and seen the world. I was naïve thinking I could solve all of India's problems though!

Nambiar's family was shocked at her momentous decision, but they were used to her doing things differently to her siblings ('I was always the one doing the crazy things!'), and understood her motivation. Her friends and colleagues, however, were horrified – particularly at her decision to leave Vodacom where she was earning a much higher salary than her friends and advancing rapidly up the chain of command. At a year-end function Alan Knott-Craig had spoken to her parents, saying, 'Yogi is going to change the world, she's going to the top!' Little did he know that she would end up trying to change the world from the other side of it.

A PASSAGE TO INDIA

Nambiar initially went to Bangalore because she had friends there and had also liked it most of the three cities she had visited in December. She set up her immediate accommodation and one of her friends – who was later to become her husband – introduced her to the Asian Women's Human Rights Council where she was offered a position. 'I was hoping to do research on the social aspects of poverty in India – what the challenges were and where the need was greatest.' When she arrived at the Council they were in the throes of arranging a World Conference on Women against War, for Peace, with their definition of war encompassing all human rights violations against women. 'I think that Indians believe in fate quite a bit. The conference was to be held in Cape Town and there I was, so it all seemed quite fortuitous!'

Not speaking a local language was challenging for Nambiar, because while she may have looked like other Indians, she did not dress, speak or act like a local. Fortunately, everyone in the organisation and all of her friends spoke English, yet she had a strong sense of going in blind – both in terms of language and ability. 'I had not experienced any of the issues we were talking about and I didn't really understand the environment; the only things I had going for me were goodwill, a desire to make a difference and the willingness to learn. Those three things helped me to get through it all.'

The conference saw 45 women from developing countries around the world gather in Cape Town in 2000 to talk about the human rights violations they had experienced, which for Nambiar was a real education. 'There were discussions on issues I had never known about growing up – witch killings, dowry deaths, comfort women, female genital mutilation, ethnic cleansing and genocide. I met three Filipino women who had been stolen to be comfort women for the Japanese in the Second World War; I think I cried more in the three days of the conference than I had in my entire life.'

That year also saw her attending conferences in Thailand to help NGOs draft UN legislation on migrant workers, refugees and trafficked women, which led her to decide that she wanted to stay on in India – partly for work and partly because she decided that she wanted to get married, which she did in 2001. The following year she left the Council to join the Foundation for Action Motivation and Empowerment (FAME), an organisation started by a wealthy Indian philanthropist.

One of the reasons Nambiar left the Council was her concern that little progress was being made in the fight for women's rights. 'At the end of one of the conferences we were going to a party the organisers had arranged, and there was a woman who had attended the conference whose daughter had died in a dowry killing. She was an older woman, thin and very sad looking. We felt bad leaving her behind so I asked her to come with us. I will never forget her response. She said, "I came here because I believed you educated people. I believed that you were going to find me answers, you going to get me justice for my daughter. I did not come here for a party. You have had this conference, you have talked about all this, you have heard all these stories, but you are going to have a party now, to say that you are done. This is not done for me. This is my love; I have lost my child and I came to you for answers."'

This shook Nambiar to her core, and she realised that while the conferences were important, they achieved few practical gains. She went back to the Council after the conference but it felt like more of the same – talking, poetry and stories with nothing being achieved. Although the team was also working with women who were prostitutes and was helping women who had been trafficked, Nambiar felt that she needed to work more directly with affected people. When the offer to run FAME came in 2002, Nambiar jumped at the chance.

FAME's purpose was to work with people with disabilities, specifically children with mental retardation, Down's syndrome, muscular dystrophy and cerebral palsy. 'Before joining FAME, I didn't even know someone in a wheelchair, let alone anything about running such an organisation, but the man who started FAME was the father of one of my husband's friends who had heard about my work at the Council, so he asked me to run the place. He had just five kids enrolled and two people employed, in one room in a house, but we built it up to be a substantial player in the disability sector. I was there for five years and by the end we had about 100 kids in new premises.'

During her time at FAME Nambiar helped to grow the organisation, overseeing everything for the building of a new school – even down to the handrails for each bathroom. 'It was an amazing experience, because through it all I was learning so much and I think that for me is a common thread throughout my life – I believe it's crucial to always be open to learning. Words like "specialist" and "expert" start making people feel that they almost can't learn any more. But you can learn from anywhere, from anyone, no matter how they look, what they are dressed like, where they are from, what work they do, how old they are – anything.' The role she played led to Nambiar spending a good deal of time in the slums, which also gave her an insight into how the cycle of poverty grinds people down. 'If you are the poorest of the poor and live in a slum, then you have a terrible life, but if you then have a child with a disability, life gets that much worse. And if that child is female, things really get desperate.'

From a staffing point of view Nambiar had to work hard to build the respect of staff who were not sure what to make of this young South African woman. 'I made an effort to dress a bit more suitably for the environment, but I didn't come from a poor background and I didn't have a child, let alone a child with a disability, so I had to show both my colleagues and the parents that I was open to learning from them. I really led from behind, I think, but I also pushed or challenged them to try things they didn't really think they could do. I supported them and when they achieved something they felt more confident and empowered by the fact that I believed in them and saw their potential. I won the teachers over much sooner than the parents; it took time to build trust. Even the male/female dynamic was difficult with the parents; a father would speak to a junior male rather than look directly at me; they couldn't process having to deal with a woman in my position. I persevered, though, and I think there was a lot of love generated. So much in India is about relationships; if you can respect people and create good relationships, people learn to overlook other issues. When I left I had three farewell parties thrown for me and even people who lived in the slums who had one meal a day would bring food to me and feed it to me as a sign of respect. It was extremely moving.'

During her tenure at FAME, Nambiar also studied for a degree in Community and Health Psychology through Unisa, which she completed in 2006.

HOMECOMING

By 2007 Nambiar was experiencing problems in her marriage and felt she wanted to come home to her family and support system. She had managed to come home every other year, with her parents visiting her in the alternate years, but she felt it was time for a new start so she and her husband moved to South Africa. The marriage only lasted another year, however, before her husband moved back to India.

Before leaving India, Nambiar had been contacted by a company looking for South Africans who had a communications background, social development experience, and who knew India. 'I say I don't believe in fate, but actually a lot of things happened fortuitously, which seem almost predestined in hindsight.' Nambiar started with Kaelo Worldwide Media immediately upon her return home, heading up the company's corporate social investment consulting department and their CSI communications platform – the biggest in Africa at the time. And then, two years later, Nambiar decided that it was time to strike out on her own, having started a travel company, Stratos Lifestyles, with a partner from India in the interim, as well as a social development consulting business. 'The company was doing well – we were doing experiential luxury travel – but I felt I wanted to step away and concentrate more on the social development business.' Her contracts at Unnathi Social Development Advisory included being one of a team of four who wrote the government's Youth Development Strategy and undertaking 25 case studies on social enterprises across South Africa for the UN's ILO. At the same time she completed her Honours in Development Studies through Unisa.

It was while writing Tiger Brands' CSI strategy that she came across the Gordon Institute of Business Science (GIBS). Goldman Sachs was looking for a business school to partner with on their *10 000 Women* Initiative, a women entrepreneurship programme, which Nambiar brought to the school and ran from 2011. Then, with the programme due to end at the end of 2013, Nambiar was asked by the Dean of the business school to create and run an Enterprise Development Academy (EDA) at GIBS, with the aim of using a scholarship-based model to take entrepreneurship and business education to entrepreneurs of a lower socio-economic level. 'We want to teach people how to run their business as a business, even if they are social entrepreneurs. In one of our programmes we are teaching spaza shop owners how to run their stores more efficiently and profitably. We've started off really well and are confident that we'll really make an impact in the creation and growing of new enterprises, which will lead to more jobs.'

Although the Academy is for both men and women, women's issues remain a focus for her. In fact, she is so motivated by her work that she admits to living an unbalanced life, but explains that it is a conscious decision to be out of balance for a while so that she can help the most people possible. Helping women to be self-supporting is a key focus, and she cites studies that show that an investment in women and supporting female entrepreneurs goes further than for their male counterparts when it comes to savings, education and uplifting their communities. One way in which Nambiar tries to encourage sustainable entrepreneurship is as a member of the group that created the Enterprise Development Council of South Africa, which looks at how to bring all the players in the entrepreneurship and business space to create a supportive environment for entrepreneurs, and what both the government and the private sector can do to move this forward. 'On one hand we have such stiff targets – 90 per cent of all new jobs need to come from the small and medium enterprise sector by 2030 – but on the other, the Global Entrepreneurship Monitor shows that South Africa is one of the worst-performing countries in terms of entrepreneurship. If we support entrepreneurs to learn skills and not be dependent on using what little money they have available to access education, then there will definitely be a major change.'

A NOBLE CAUSE

Nambiar sees women as being more collaborative. 'We see it in the classroom and in their businesses; women engage with each other and aren't as confrontational. They build on ideas, form associations and create partnerships. Men like Nelson Mandela and Mahatma Gandhi had values and behaviours such as doggedness and fairness, which I find inspirational, but there are also so many women I really look up to, including Thuli Madonsela, Michelle Obama, Ellen Johnson

Sirleaf and Mother Teresa. Like Mandela and Gandhi, these women are not afraid to show weakness. We often get to a point where we idolise leadership qualities but we forget there's a human being behind them. The higher you place someone on a pedestal the harder they fall when they make a mistake. That's why I take praise on an equal footing with criticism. I learn from both; I'm not broken by criticism but neither am I elevated by praise to the point where I can't see that I'm fallible.'

Other people who inspire Nambiar are some of the social entrepreneurs she has worked with, as well as her parents, who she credits with being grounded and sensible. 'They espouse the values of education and Ubuntu. I'm also inspired by the Dean of GIBS, who had a vision and the leadership to build consensus among many very intelligent, diverse, ambitious, efficient and impactful people to develop a business school like this.'

Someone who inspires Nambiar on a personal level is her friend, Rehema, who has 'an incredible ability to rise above the pettiness of a situation and to see a broader picture. I think that's an important quality in a leader; someone who is able to see what is going on on the ground. Rehema has a magical way with language; she can create a situation with words that really makes you stop, sit back and let it all sink in.' Nambiar also takes motivation from her brother for his level-headedness and balance, as well as her sisters. 'One of my sisters, despite going through a difficult divorce, still has an amazing sense of hope and a vision for the future. I think those are important leadership qualities – that in the midst of whatever is happening now, you can see beyond where other people can see and you are able to show them that something better is to come.'

Nambiar's second sister juggles a high-powered job with being a mother of two, something that Nambiar admires greatly. 'I'm always overwhelmed by mothers in general, but working mothers in particular, who are able to juggle so many things. That's another thing with leaders – you're managing what someone can take on and working with them to challenge them, to see what more they can handle. When you're with one person you need to make sure that they feel they are the only person in the world at that time. When someone walks into my office I never continue typing on my laptop. It's a pet hate of mine that people engage with machinery when someone with a live, beating heart is standing in front of you and needs your attention. You need to stop what you're doing and give people time. If the work is urgent you can ask to reschedule, but ultimately I think time is what people want; they want to feel recognised. I have the most amazing team here at GIBS. Not once in the last three years have I ever had to ask someone to come in early, stay late or work over weekends. Everyone is so innately empowered and motivated and passionate about what they do innately.' Nambiar does get frustrated, however, with people who are driven by ego. 'I like dealing with and being inspired by people who are driven by purpose.'

If Nambiar could host a dinner party and invite anyone she pleased, entrepreneurs would fill most of the table. 'I'd like CK Prahalad and Muhammad Yunus and Richard Branson, and it may sound clichéd, but I'd also like Michael Jackson to have come over – I'd want to talk to him not as a performer but as a person; why he handled certain things the way he did, what motivated him, how he dealt with his incredible fame. In that way, I'd also like to chat to Princess Diana. And maybe Winnie Mandela – that would be an interesting one! I'm really interested in the psychology behind these kinds of people.'

Nambiar hopes that if she were to meet the mother who changed her life all those years ago, that she would be proud of the woman that she has become. 'I was a good person before I met her, but now I've evolved into a person who is good but with a purpose and a focus on getting results. My actions have an impact and I am conscious of the actions I take.'

The feedback Nambiar gets from the people she has worked with over the years bears testimony to the impact she has had on their lives. 'When somebody has experienced a positive change because of something I have done, I feel I have been successful. I think that women often have "imposter syndrome", where we feel that we're never quite good enough, so when I really make a difference it's good to know that I'm not faking my way through life! One of the most touching moments was when I was leaving India and there was a little boy from the slums who wanted to say goodbye. He had mental retardation and also had autistic features, but when he saw the other kids and their families giving me gifts, he felt really bad. He asked his mother for something, but she said they had nothing to give, so he thought and thought before he reached into his pocket and found a mint that had been there for so long it was on the verge of being black. I still have that mint. He gave it to me with so much love and he so desperately wanted to say thank you. I went back to the school three years ago for a visit and there was mayhem when I walked in; even though the children there suffered from mental and physical disabilities, they came running or crawling out of their classes to greet me. It was incredibly moving.

'I also worked on a project in India with prostitutes and I heard after the fact that of the 15 women, 12 had managed to get out of prostitution because they had set up successful micro enterprises. That's a significant change, but not all change has to be like that; sometimes it's just someone you help to gain confidence.'

Nambiar is not sure where she will find herself in five years' time, but she intends to adopt a daughter with whom she hopes to travel and teach to be a conscious citizen of the world. 'I see us with our backpacks, exploring cultures and understanding how we are one part of such an amazing universe. And that we have a responsibility that comes with that; if we have been blessed in some way, we have a responsibility to others who have not been.' Professionally, Nambiar would like to have grown the Academy to have touched thousands of people who would otherwise not have had the opportunity. I worry that I'll die before I have helped enough people. When I was in college I counselled raped and abused women and I want to keep making a difference. I hate the cliché of teaching a man to fish. I agree with Bill Drayton – I want to revolutionise the whole fishing industry! I want us to be disruptive in the way we look at social change, and there's so much to do on that that if I could I'd live to be 200!'

Nambiar has two ideas for her tombstone, but has yet to decide which she'll go with. 'One is "Never before has there been a person who has eaten so many bunny chows!" My second is "One person breathed easier because she lived". What I experienced in India really left an indelible impression on me. One woman I worked with had been gang-raped and tortured, and the fear I felt when I went bungee jumping didn't come close to the fear I experienced doing some of the profound and dangerous human rights work we did. It's hard to experience those things and come back and act like everything is lovely and all is good with the world. But I am still in love with life and optimistic about the future. If someone is worried about territory or petty issues then I step back, because all that's really important is making an impact. I'm invested in my work so I try to see things at the macro level.'

A social entrepreneur at heart, **YOGAVELLI NAMBIAR** has given her life to better the lives of others. Having spent a sometimes harrowing seven years in India, she returned home to South Africa in 2007 to continue her mission – assisting those from disadvantaged communities to improve their lives and the lives of those around them. The current vehicle for her mission is the Enterprise Development Academy at GIBS. The Academy teaches entrepreneurs how to run and grow a successful business, thereby ensuring a positive impact on job creation and economic growth.

FASHION FORWARD

NKHENSANI NKOSI

CUT FROM THE SAME CLOTH

Thanks to the strong values and work ethic of her parents, Nkhensani Nkosi (née Manganyi) did not have to look far for role models as a child. 'My father, Chabani, grew up in an impoverished rural area with an illiterate mother, but despite his circumstances – which at one time even saw him working as a gardener – he went on to become a clinical psychologist, a writer, the Director-General of Education in Nelson Mandela's government, the Vice-Chancellor and Principal of the University of the North at the time Mandela was rector, and Vice-Principal of the University of Pretoria. He also spent time as a Senior Research Fellow and Visiting Professor at Wits' African Studies Institute and was awarded an honorary doctorate in Literature from Wits in 2008. My mother also came from humble beginnings, yet she earned a postgraduate degree and went on to become the Head of Information Management in the Gauteng Legislature. They are both honourable people who had to work extremely hard for everything they made manifest in their lives. My aim is to live their legacy and hand that on to my children.'

Born in Baragwanath Hospital in June 1973, Nkosi is the youngest of two daughters from her parents' marriage, and also has three stepsisters. The first eight years of Nkosi's life were spent in the Transkei, but as her parents' careers began to take off the family moved back to Johannesburg, where they lived in Diepkloof, Soweto. 'I attended Sacred Heart College in Observatory and during the State of Emergency I would have to get from school back to the township; I struggled to create my own identity in the midst of everything that was going on at the time.'

Things began to fall into place when in her Standard 9 year Nkosi was selected to take part in a programme called Edutrain. 'They took a group of school leaders and put us on a train through KwaZulu-Natal. There were all types – liberals, far left-wingers, right-wingers. There was a lot of heated discussion, but by the end of our trip we were all firm friends. The experience changed my life and it's really something I'd love to organise for other groups of young kids these days.' Nkosi also studied drama at school before she went on to study a BA at Wits, with majors in Industrial Psychology and Sociology, and graduated in 1994.

'My parents believed that education was the key to economic freedom, which is why it was unthinkable in our household not to want to go to school. Coming from an academic family meant that there was no way we would ever be allowed not to pursue at least one university degree!'

INSPIRATION STRIKES

During her years at Wits, Nkosi took part in student marches and looked up to activists such as Helen Joseph, David Webster and Ahmed Kathrada. She thought that she would choose a career in politics upon completing her degree, but fate intervened when a friend suggested she attend an audition at Wits Drama School. This paved the way for her professional career in the performing arts, during which time she travelled extensively and won a number of awards along the way. 'My first role was in *Sophiatown* when I played a schoolgirl called Lulu. I loved it! My parents were there almost every night in the front row and I couldn't get enough of the applause!' Nkosi went on to act in plays such as *The Coloured Museum* and *Marabi*, which toured internationally, as well as in films including *Legend of the Hidden City*, *Tarzan: The Epic Adventure* and *Kickboxer 5*. 'Travelling overseas was a real eye-opener for me. I had lived in America for four years while my father completed his doctorate at Yale, but when I was older I understood more about what I was seeing and experiencing.

'I had always been creative and I really wanted to be an actress, but my parents were baffled as to why I would want to pursue such a "frivolous" career! Luckily they always supported me; they believed that I had the power to make my dreams come true and have supported all my ventures in life.' Another valuable lesson her parents taught her was the importance of having a social conscience and being aware of what was going on around her. 'They taught me about integrity, humility, compassion, persistence and perseverance.'

Life took another turn in 1995 when Nkosi was acting in *The Colored Museum* at the Market Theatre. 'Some friends brought Zam to the play. He and I went for drinks afterwards and then sat in the car talking until 6am! That was the start of everything – although it took us nine years to get married!'

Nkosi started work as a trainee script evaluator for Penguin Films in 1995 and went on to become a scriptwriter for the show *Going Up* with Joe Mafela and Roberta Durrant. She was also the first black stand-up comedian on M-Net's *It's a Funny Country* and created her own production company, Vicious Funk Productions, in 1996. It was through Vicious Funk that she produced inserts for *Options*, an SABC 3 magazine programme that she also presented in 1997 and 1998, as well as corporate videos. She later went on to sell the company to AME, a listed media company, in 1998.

Another big break came in 1999 when Nkosi was selected to be a host, spokesperson and scout for the M-Net model competition, *Face of Africa*. 'It was an incredible experience as I got to travel all around Africa and was really exposed for the first time to the African aesthetic. I saw an Africa that no one was talking about; her soul, her people, the dynamism and creativity, as well as the innate rhythm that underscores everything that happens on the continent.

It was then that I realised what I wanted to do, which was to create a unique lifestyle brand through products that would redefine the way people see Africa in the 21st century. I was also reading Richard Branson's book, *Losing My Virginity*, at the time, and I was very inspired by him. He's a creative activist and that's exactly how I see myself, so I thought, "If he can do it, so can I!"'

Nkosi's parents again showed their faith in their daughter – who had sewn clothes for her dolls as a little girl – by cashing in policies to assist her financially, while Zam provided the moral and emotional support that gave her the courage she needed to take her leap of faith. So it was that Stoned Cherrie, the extremely popular urban African fashion label, was registered as a business in 1999, with their store opening in Rosebank, Johannesburg, in 2000.

WHAT'S IN A NAME?

'The name Stoned Cherrie first came to me when my sister was writing a script called *Black Stoned Cherry.* It really resonated with me because "cherrie" is township slang for "girlfriend" and "stoned" implies strength, so I thought it was a really unique and iconic name for the brand I envisaged building to celebrate strong, hip, urban, dynamic African women. Not long after that I was in a supermarket and saw a tin of black stoned cherries. It was meant to be!'

While building the company, Nkosi kept her acting and TV career going by finding time to do voiceovers, host two series of the reality singing show, *Coca-Cola Popstars*, in 2002 and 2003, and co-produce and co-present the popular TV magazine programme, *Mojo*, on SABC 1 with Zam from 2003 to 2005, which went on to win a South African Film and Television Award.

By 2004 Stoned Cherrie had become a household name and had changed many people's perceptions of African fashion. Some of the designs the fashion house became best known for were T-shirts sporting the images of anti-apartheid heroes, such as Steve Biko. This came about when the company entered into an agreement with Bailey's Historical Archives in Johannesburg to have the exclusive use of the front covers of *Drum* magazine from the 1950s. The mixture of modern fashion with the faces of iconic South Africans led to recognition from a variety of news channels such as CNN and the BBC. 'I wanted to take the images of a terrible time in our country's history and turn them on their head; to make our history part of popular culture.'

A chance meeting when Nkosi was speaking at the Design Indaba led to her next big thing. 'At one of the dinners I happened to be sitting next to the MD of Woolworths. I was teasing him about them copying our designs, which obviously planted a seed in his head as it wasn't long after that that his team phoned me to talk about a collaboration. I really had two options open to me in terms of growing the brand at the time – opening more stores myself or getting a retailer to stock our products – so when Woolworths contacted me it was perfect timing. I realised that it was going to be a challenge to position ourselves as a boutique brand at a national retailer because our clients didn't want to be one of thousands wearing our designs, so we conducted extensive research into how brands like Ralph Lauren manage to retain their exclusivity while accessing lower price points and markets. Essentially we had to create a diffusion line, which was an amazing learning experience.

'A retail environment is very different to operating a boutique store; I was lucky as few designers ever get such great exposure to a retail environment. I would strongly recommend that young people who want to pursue a career in fashion spend several years in retail before branching out on their own. There is so much potential in the South African fashion and design industry, but it does require some development. Working with Woolworths really brought a rigour and discipline to what we do, which has stood us in good stead over the years. I could have expanded by creating new stores but I didn't want to be a retailer. One minute you're designing clothes and the next you have to worry about manufacturing, leases, and all sorts of other issues, which wasn't what I was interested in. I also didn't want to be involved in manufacturing as I realised that I didn't know what the real cost was of producing the clothes, because we would change the designs as we went. It was impossible to keep track of the time, resources and money we were using, so in 2005 we decided to outsource. This meant that we could pay a set price and let someone else – actually a former employee – worry about making a profit from manufacturing. We also launched our eyewear range that year – it was a busy time!'

BUILDING THE BRAND

Nkosi used a variety of means to learn as she went along, including reading and relying on mentors. 'I consider myself fortunate to be surrounded by positive, supportive people, and I'm not afraid to ask for help when I need it! I've found that people are happy to lend a hand or provide advice when you ask for it.' Something Nkosi is not a huge fan of is self-help books, because she believes that 'we all have the answers inside ourselves'. She is a keen observer of people and situations, and has found experience to be a compelling teacher. Her course has not all been smooth sailing, however, with one of her biggest learning curves being to understand how to build a profitable and sustainable business. 'The issues related to the fashion industry were easy to learn and overcome, such as manufacturing and buying cycles; it was the business principles and doctrines that took time to master. I was fortunate to have a mentor in the form of Eric Parker, a franchise guru and businessman who has supported and guided me throughout my career.'

Recognition for her entrepreneurial flair came in 2005 when Nkosi was selected from 200 candidates across various fields to be one of six winners of a place on the US-based Endeavor programme for entrepreneurs. This culminated in 2006 when she shared a stage with the founder and Chairman of Yahoo!, Jerry Yang, at the Endeavor Annual Gala in New York, when they spoke about their experiences as entrepreneurs.

Never one to sit still for long, she also released a compilation music CD entitled *Stars at Play,* on which Nkosi also co-wrote a song, 'Stoned Cherrie', the same year – and followed up in 2006 by accepting the role of Goodwill Ambassador for the UN World Food Programme's 'Catwalk the World' initiative in Ghana.

With the rapid growth of Stoned Cherrie, which by this time was selling eyewear in over 450 stores in South Africa, Kenya, Uganda, Ghana, Mauritius and Canada, and the company's tenth anniversary approaching, Nkosi felt that it was important to take a step back and refocus. As part of the process, she took part in a leadership conference in Boston in 2009, which helped her to concentrate on what she wanted Stoned Cherrie's core business to be. 'We all had to state our companies' missions in one sentence. It took me a while but I eventually realised that our mission is to inspire.'

One of Nkosi's proudest moments came when the brand was invited to take part in the New York Fashion Week that year. 'There was real enthusiasm for the brand, which was very exciting for us, and being given the opportunity to design some of the outfits for the FIFA 2010 World Cup also enabled us to show the world what South Africa is capable of.'

A further opportunity arose in 2010 for Stoned Cherrie to open stores-within-a-store at 48 Foschini outlets throughout the country, but this meant that Nkosi had to make the difficult decision to conclude the relationship with Woolworths. 'It was the most challenging business decision I've ever had to make, but the opportunity with Foschini allowed us to stock all of our merchandise offerings, from clothing to eyewear and accessories at the branches, so it enabled us to really establish ourselves as a diverse and top-to-toe brand.'

Some of the diversification driven by Nkosi included creating woven upholstery fabrics, a bespoke couture service, homeware and uniforms. In addition, she developed an upholstery range that was used by architects and interior designers on designs for offices and restaurants, and secured a licensing deal for tailor-made books.

'Diversification is important to me because although we were a first-mover in the market, now there are plenty of imitators. I don't believe in following trends for the sake of it; I like to think that we are deeper than that and really bring out the core of what it is to be an African in our products. I also want to create something that has soul – too much now is copied and churned out by the thousands.'

An exciting new project came about in 2011 when Nkosi was invited by Volvo to design accessory elements for their customers, as well as the interior of their XC60 model. In addition she renovated the studio to turn it into a showroom and also did an online flash sale on City Mob.

Some of the awards Nkosi has gathered on her path include the Top Success Story of the Year, Top Women in Business and Government, Young Business Achiever of the Year, Young Business Achiever: *Black Business Quarterly*, Best Ladies Wear: SA Fashion Awards, PAWE Young Artist Award, Best Actress for *Sophiatown*: Vita Award, Entertainer of the Year International: Crystal Awards – Women in Film, Best-Dressed Designer: Style Awards, Woman of the Year: Tribute Achiever, two-time Best Designer: *Style* Magazine, and The Next Hot 100: *Mail & Guardian*.

BODY, MIND AND SOUL

During her student days Nkosi always made time to give back, which included reading for blind students. The company also now works with the African Feeding Scheme and other groups of crafters, which provides disadvantaged women with training and work opportunities. 'It's important for me to create a balance in life. If I take care of my spiritual, emotional and physical needs, I find that I can take care of the needs of my family and my business. Having a positive outlook helps – I really believe that it's your attitude that determines if you will overcome a challenge. I think that anything's possible. I also believe that success is not about how much money you have in the bank or how many houses you own; I measure my success by how happy and fulfilled I am in the various aspects of my life – my family, career, physically, spiritually, mentally and emotionally.'

Nkosi gets her energy from being around her children, three of which are her biological children and the eldest of which is her niece, whom she regards as her own. 'My kids make me appreciate life and I love going on holiday with my family. Between us we've tried lots of different things including skydiving and scuba diving, which I absolutely loved! I love living in Joburg and thrive on its energy, but it can also be really difficult to switch off, so my secret relaxation technique is to watch reality TV!'

Nkosi's latest work is inspired in part by tribal designs and in part by her belief that at the core of every person's DNA is love. 'Over the last few years I've been developing a range of hand-painted graphic prints and ceramics – from baths to cake platters and chandeliers to forks. It's all part of my vision to position Stoned Cherrie as a lifestyle brand, and at the core of each of the new designs is a heart.

'I love being a designer as I get to realise my vision in my creations. I dream big, which flies in the face of my upbringing because my parents are strong believers in logic and caution! I do believe, though, that if you want to achieve anything big, then you have to start with a big vision. Obviously it needs to be realistic, but the bigger the better! I tend to start with the end goal in mind and then work backwards. My motto in life is "Leap and the net will appear". Fear is the absence of faith.

'I'd like to foster entrepreneurship in South Africa with the government and business schools like GIBS. Inspiring young people is very important to me – my dream is to instil in young people a sense of infinite possibility. I really enjoy giving talks both at home and abroad and motivating people by sharing my experiences. My concern is that without quality leadership to motivate young people, they become inspired by material acquisition and the discreet charm of the bourgeoisie. Education is the cornerstone of our children's future; it is critical if we hope to build a powerful nation.

'South Africa is at a crossroads and where we land up depends on the decisions we make today. If we do not critically assess the areas that see us failing to address the crude disparities that continue to create dangerous levels of segregation, we will have dug ourselves deeper into our murky socio-economic crisis. On the other hand, we have a spirit of resilience, which saw us overturn a political system that had been entrenched and rolled out over years. It really depends on the quality of leaders that we are able to birth and cultivate in the next couple of years.

'People like Herman Mashaba and Richard Maponya really inspire me – the township boys who made it big during turbulent times. They had a vision and were never derailed by circumstance. Other South Africans I admire include Chris Hani, Nelson Mandela, Archbishop Emeritus Desmond Tutu and Steve Biko, who all blazed a trail with a firecracker spirit. They set the agenda for change and made an impact wherever they went, with passion, purpose and focus. I also find the Dalai Lama to be hugely inspirational because, like Nelson Mandela, he believes that love is the only real solution to world problems. All of these leaders had certain key characteristics in common – integrity, courage, tenacity, compassion, tolerance and passion. I don't believe you can achieve much without the latter. Leaders should have the ability to lead by example and act every day on their passion, seeing opportunities where others see difficulties.

'I'm also inspired by beauty, but I do believe that if you are open to it, inspiration can come from anywhere and anything. I find beauty in so many places – the complexity or simplicity or life; the intricacy, delicacy and robustness of nature; the resilience and tenacity of struggle heroes' resolute stances; culture, history, art, expression – everywhere.'

For someone as passionate and inspiring as Nkosi, her epitaph will not be a stretch.

'In her own special way, she helped transform the lives of many.'

NKHENSANI NKOSI is best known as the founder, CEO and Creative Director of the fashion label Stoned Cherrie, but the designer is also an entrepreneur, actress, television personality, speaker and mother of four. Nkosi's passion for Africa led to her decision to create the unique Stoned Cherrie brand, which now has a presence in countries as diverse as Canada, Uganda and Mauritius.

THE AGE OF ENLIGHTENMENT

TERENCE NOMBEMBE

A CULTURE OF LEARNING

Terence Nombembe was born in the small Transkei village of Qumbu in September 1961, to parents who were both educators. Neither parent taught in the Transkei, however, because job opportunities were scarce in South Africa at the time, which led to them to spend most of their working years in Swaziland. Both taught at a missionary school in Mahamba and later moved to Gege, with Nombembe Senior acting in a dual role as principal. But when Nombembe and his siblings – a brother and two sisters – were in primary school, they moved from Swaziland back to the Transkei where they lived with guardians, who were important role models in those formative years.

Nombembe only saw his parents once a year at Christmas. 'Our guardians took us as their children and we took them as our parents. They were instrumental in the choice of careers we pursued.' In particular, Nombembe's paternal guardian, Mr Lubando, was very encouraging of the young man. 'He was amazing. He was energetic and very, very supportive. He made sure we got the best education we could. While I was at school I used to visit him in his office – he was an administrator for the Transkei government at the time. He was a very positive, supportive and inspirational man.'

Upon reaching high school, Nombembe was sent to the Umtata Commercial and Technical College where he completed his matric, studying only commercial subjects. 'The choice of this school was one that my parents and guardians made for me, my brother and one of my sisters. My other sister was sent to study science. They must have seen some ability in me that I couldn't see then, and I am thankful to them for having such foresight and assisting in the career choices I have made, as I have never had a reason to want to change this career, and have never regarded myself as having pursued the wrong career.'

In 1976, Nombembe was in Standard 7 when Professor Wiseman Nkuhlu, a Transkei local, qualified as a chartered accountant. 'I didn't know about it at the time but I heard from Mr Lubando that the first black person had qualified as an accountant. He told me that Prof Nkuhlu was opening up a firm of accountants and said that I should also become an accountant. Mr Lubando was resourceful, motivational and inspirational in terms of giving me a sense of focus and purpose in life.'

It was in 1979, when Nombembe was in his final year of school, that his father decided to return to the Transkei, taking up a position at Mdeni Senior Secondary School in Qumbu. This reunion ended tragically just three months later, however, when Nombembe's father was killed in an accident. This meant that upon attaining his matric, Nombembe's mother, who had moved from Gege to St Pauls in Manzini, had to take out a loan so that he could begin studying for his BCom at the University of Transkei (Unitra) in Umtata (Mthatha), yet there was never any question but that Nombembe and his siblings would attain the best education possible. 'My parents and guardians were very firm and very clear about our education. Education is what we needed to liberate us in the end. My mother, in particular, single-handedly helped with our growth and development and did everything she could to assist us in our pursuit for education.'

Nombembe was one of the first students to study at the newly launched Unitra campus in 1980 and was the first ever occupant of room 272 of the men's hostel at Unitra, where he remembers juggling 'a combination of fun and hard work' for the three years he spent there. The hard work took precedence, however, as he was determined to earn high marks in order to qualify for a bursary. His exertions paid off when he secured a bursary for both his second and third years, while also working at Coopers & Lybrand during his holidays learning practical auditing and accounting work.

He credits his years at university as laying the foundation for his 'open-mindedness about the issues of the profession', as well as his clarity of thought when it came to his purpose in life. 'Having Prof Nkuhlu as the head of the accounting department at university and one of my lecturers was a real eye-opener. To know that here was someone who was the first black chartered accountant, who was running his own firm and who had produced two other accountants – that was inspirational. The other two accountants who worked under Prof Nkuhlu's supervision, Sabelo Magwentshu and Wakeford Dondashe, qualified in 1981 when I was still at university and it dawned on me and my colleagues that this thing was not an impossibility.' Another significant benefit of attending Unitra was that it was here that Nombembe met his would-be wife, Nokwanda, who was studying education at the time. She coincidentally also lived in room 272 in the women's hostel when she came to Unitra in 1981.

Through his part-time job, Nombembe also got to know people who were making a name for themselves in the profession. 'Suresh Kana was one of the first black partners at Coopers & Lybrand so it was a very prominent story in the firm at the time. When I met him for the first time I said to him, "You know, I knew about you back in the early '80s!" Vassi Naidoo was another prominent trailblazer I knew of. We were tracking people who were qualifying and they were very inspirational because they were demonstrating that this was possible.' Despite only six or so members of Nombembe's era at Unitra successfully qualifying as Chartered Accountants, this was a significant achievement for the BCom graduates of the early 1980s at Unitra.

Speaking at the University of the Western Cape recently, Nombembe encouraged the students to follow his lead by tracking people ahead of them in their professions, and to 'feed off their strength and enthusiasm'. This motivation, he believes, should inspire people to realise their ambitions, as it did for him.

RISING TO THE CHALLENGE

Although there was no shortage of opportunities at Accounting firms in Umtata at that time, after graduating in 1982 Nombembe decided not to pursue articles; his intention was to find a better-paying job so that he could support himself as well as his mother and siblings. 'I went to this government entity. It was called TRACOR – the Transkei Agricultural Corporation – and the finance director there, Clive Berlin, told me that he had a suitable job opening, but that he was not going to give it to me. He told me, "Go out of that door and go and do articles." That is when I went to Alex Aitken and Carter (now KPMG) and fortunately Sean Mulligan, who was partner at the time, had an opening and I spent three years there under his supervision, doing my articles. I am still thankful to Clive to this day.'

Nombembe stayed on at KPMG as a supervisor for a year following his articles, before deciding in 1987 to move to a bigger city in South Africa from the Transkei in order to earn more experience. 'Initially I wanted to come to Johannesburg, but I got a position with KPMG in Durban. It was my first experience of what it was like to work in a segregated environment. I had been a supervisor in the Transkei so you would expect that at least I would get to supervise people, but I never supervised a single person in Durban.'

But after nine months, he realised that he was not going to get the broad exposure he was looking for if he stayed at KPMG, so decided to look for a job elsewhere. 'At the time Unilever was experimenting with the appointment of professionals, and CAs in particular. I was lucky because normally Unilever would take on university graduates and groom them from there into the various areas of development. Linda Yanta – another role model of mine who qualified as a chartered accountant at a very young age in 1985 – and I were the first few accounting post graduates in that programme in 1988; I was fortunate to get into Unilever and I never looked back.'

Nombembe was a member of the internal audit portfolio that conducted audits of the various factories and operations at Unilever, which proved fortuitous because he was preparing for the Board exam but was struggling with Management Accounting. 'I wanted experience in a factory environment because Management Accounting was giving me nightmares. Getting an opportunity as a factory accountant at Unilever Lipton Tea factory in Pietermaritzburg gave me a really clear insight into what Cost and Management Accounting was, because I was seeing it with my own eyes every day and living it every day.' Unilever, and particular one of Nombembe's supervisors, was instrumental in assisting Nombembe to overcome his 'shortcomings'. 'Phil Cox was my mentor at internal audit and he was a very, very supportive Australian guy. He actually facilitated my migration to the Lipton factory because he knew that that was what I wanted.'

Despite failing three times, Nombembe persevered and passed the Board exam on his fourth attempt in 1990. 'I never, never thought that accountancy wasn't for me. I knew what my limitations were, which is why I continued to pursue opportunities that would expose me to all aspects of accountancy.' That year was a special one for Nombembe for another reason, because it was then that he married his sweetheart, Nokwanda.

In 1991 Nombembe left Unilever and moved to Cape Town to join BP. 'Colin McClelland was the finance director at the time and he was responsible for a campaign to get some young professionals into their fold.' Through BP, Nombembe was offered an opportunity to work at BP Botswana as a finance manager, a position he held for two years. 'It was a lovely experience. It was my first job with a different culture and a different language, and I really enjoyed it.' However, despite spending two years in the country, Nombembe did not learn to speak Tswana, a fact he attributes to his fear of failing. 'The guy I appointed to teach me to speak Tswana said, "Just speak, don't be afraid of making mistakes", but I simply couldn't. I just couldn't associate myself with that and I ended up giving up. I am very careful about the way I convey myself as I am scared of making a fool of myself and am very scared of failure!'

Nombembe returned to Cape Town in 1996 where he took on the position of Market Research Manager at BP, before joining Gobodo Incorporated in 1997 as a partner. He remained at Gobodo until 2000, at which time he became Deputy Auditor-General of South Africa. Six years later Nombembe became Auditor-General (AG), succeeding Shauket Fakie on 1 December 2006.

For Nombembe, the fact that he was the first black African AG was 'not an issue. It never registered; it was not something that preoccupied my mind at all.' What did preoccupy his mind was taking over from Fakie and continuing what he had started. 'When Shauket became AG his focus was to professionalise the office and establish a good sense of independence, so that people would respect it for its stature. I was lucky to have inherited an office that had a good workforce, so my role was basically to make its good stature be known and for people to experience what an independent and professionally run office could do for the country. I think that I achieved that and I have no regrets from my seven years there.'

Nombembe explains that his focus as AG was to create awareness and appreciation of what the roles and duties of running a proper government institution are, in the various formations that exist, such as municipalities, public entities, national government, provincial governments, Parliament, provincial legislatures and municipal councils. 'To a large extent, I would say I achieved that, because I spoke to almost every leader in all those formations and most of them understood and concurred with what we were promulgating and advocating. No one ever demonstrated a push back on the importance of running government ethically and in a responsible manner. The only thing that remains to be done, which I guess the team that is left there will have the task of continuing with, is to get people to act on what they now understand to be necessary.'

Despite this, Nombembe does not consider the AG's role a political one, and in fact has never had any desire to go into politics. For him it is all about being someone that makes a difference in the lives of the citizens of the country, which is why he enjoyed his job as AG and decided at the end of his seven year tenure to take on the position as CEO of the South African Institute of Chartered Accountants (SAICA). 'For me is it important to do a job where I'm making a positive impact on the country. I chose this job at SAICA because I wanted continuity from what I was doing in my previous job, and this was where I could comfortably express that desire.' He believes that there is much untapped potential at SAICA and hopes to engage SAICA members directly as he did at the AG's office, where he visited every municipality in the country during his seven years. 'I want to motivate SAICA members to go out there and be better leaders with a passion for nation building.'

As far as the outcomes of his tenure as AG are concerned, he asserts that there was an understanding of the responsibility that lay with the various governmental organisations, but that a lack of education in governance principles hampered delivery. When it comes to fostering the ability to attain clean audits, he thinks that an academy of governance is part of the answer, as is 'constant awareness and monitoring of leadership among themselves. The notion of leaders not being accountable is what in my view retarded and delayed the programme of implementation, because accountability may have been there for lower levels, but I don't believe accountability is firm enough for the people who are at the helm of running these institutions.'

For Nombembe, this includes more than just a peer-review mechanism. 'I think that there should be firm accountability; people should not be a law unto themselves. If people fail, they wait for elections to be judged. I think a speedy manner and a firm manner with which political parties can hold their leadership responsible is something that should somehow be institutionalised. I think the lead time is almost unreasonable for government and political parties to realise that we are going down the wrong way in that particular municipality or government department. That is why I think we need to blend schooling, accountability and monitoring at the appropriate level.'

GETTING THE HOUSE IN ORDER

When Nombembe concludes his time at SAICA, he would like to explore the possibility of an academy of governance in more depth. 'What I envisage is a platform – and there can be many of these platforms – where there is continuous dialogue among leaders to air their views, their frustrations, their limitations, their vulnerability. For someone to give them feedback on the tactics of working around those issues and confronting their limitations, because here we're talking about people who have limited time to go and sit in class and be taught. Theory, for most of them, is something that they are aware of and familiar with, but practice is something that they have got limited ability to execute. They need someone to help them facilitate finding their own solutions.' Nombembe also feels strongly that government leaders can learn from business leaders in South Africa, but is concerned at the lack of opportunities for this to take place.

Despite having enjoyed his time in Botswana, it is not an experience Nombembe would repeat because he relishes living in South Africa and feels fortunate to have worked with colleagues from many countries around Africa and the world. 'I have made so many friends and networks and connections, which I really would still like to use on the basis of, "How do we develop a better Africa; a better South Africa?" There is an immense amount of wisdom and experience sitting with the Auditors-General of this world yet most of them retire and basically disappear into a quiet space. I've encouraged them to make a point of taking their experience and knowledge and sharing it for the benefit of others.'

Nombembe regards himself as a teacher, explaining that he likes to 'simplify things – to break complex concepts down to easily understandable terms and scenarios. I like to find solutions that will make things work for others. I'm not the kind of person to try to replicate what others have done; I've got my own way of doing things and I prefer to do things that I believe work, on my own terms.' This is linked to his drive and focus, which he maintains is crucial to success. 'A lack of focus means that you tend not to know what you want; you will be unprepared and ill-equipped to achieve what you need to.' This drive he attributes to some internal strength learned from his parents and guardians, which he describes as being able to do 'effortlessly'.

This trait of following his own path could be described as stubborn – something that Nombembe acknowledges – but he also describes himself as a patient man. He also admits to not being a good reader, preferring to think and listen. 'I take my patience as an amazing strength in the kind of environment we live in, because if you're not patient you are going to lose people and become disconnected from reality. I managed to do my job at the Auditor-General's office for 13 years not because I read it in a book, but because I sat down, studied the environment, listened to what was required for the organisation, and said, "What is the best way to do it?" I just moved at the pace that I thought was right at the time.'

Nombembe strives to give people the opportunity to really excel in their careers. 'I like engaging them, helping them, educating them and empowering them. I also believe strongly in talking *to* people before you talk *about* them. That philosophy worked well for me in my previous job as I never said anything about the government without them knowing that I was going to speak about those issues.'

As parents, Nombembe and Nokwanda have been instrumental in encouraging their three children to get the best education possible, but they have also agreed that they will not force them into a particular field of study. 'They need to find out what it is that they are most interested in and passionate about, and we just support them in developing that passion of theirs. One thing we keep emphasising to them, though, is they have to take whatever they like academically to the highest level. If needs be they must go up to the PhD level, because if they take their studies very seriously they will become prominent, autonomous and successful in life.'

Nombembe believes that South Africa ought to set the pace of what it means to be a well-run country over the next decade, despite the 'perceptions that government has not necessarily got its act together'. His view is that the knowledge is there; it's just the implementation of that knowledge that is problematic. His discussions with politicians have led him to the conclusion that most want to 'do the right thing', but limitations are placed on their abilities. The accounting profession is one he thinks can 'infuse excellence into commerce, industry, government and small business', particularly with what he sees as a wealth of talent that can be transmitted into the economy. 'When this happens, there is no reason why South Africa ought not to be a trendsetter and replicate that throughout the continent.'

This lack of technical skills is not limited to the public sector, however. Nombembe states that 'the reality is that the private sector is very, very vulnerable; they are struggling in terms of technical skills at the lower levels and leadership skills at the higher levels. The entire economy is really bleeding because of that.' Nombembe fears that the biggest challenge facing leaders today is that they are not giving themselves sufficient time to take control of their environments. 'In many instances, when we get to these leadership positions we are misdirected by the noise around us and we don't focus. I don't care if you're a Minister or a President, at the end of the day you have to supervise the people within your reach because that is where your downfall and your glory are going to come from. It's a simple principle – you have to get your own house in order and lead by example.'

Nombembe is the type of person to lie in bed at night and deliberate over things rather than 'let them go'. One issue that keeps him awake is what it is that makes Africa a continent whose governance practices are deemed to be shambolic. This is something he hopes to disprove in his pursuit of governance excellence. 'This is a myth; insufficient time and attention are paid to issues of good governance. It is taken as an afterthought – as something that is a nuisance to how governments should be run. I want to figure out what makes people think along those lines. It is a myth within ourselves that we are creating.' In fact, given the opportunity, Nombembe would relish the opportunity to sit around a dinner table with heads of state to discuss with them the importance of mixing good governance with political ambitions.

Looking to the future, Nombembe is not sure what it holds for him, but he hopes to always be an advocate for good governance. His staunch belief in good governance is a trait he inherited from his mother, who was 'very, very firm' about doing things ethically. He acknowledges that some people consider him 'too strict', but for him, life is about doing things right, and he finds it hard to forgive himself when he errs. As a Sunday-School teacher, he takes pride in seeing young people who exhibit behaviour that is progressive and responsible. 'When I see what drives people – the material things, the unethical and irresponsible behaviour – we need to protect children from falling foul of what they believe is a normal life.'

And when it comes down to it, what would Nombembe like to be inscribed on his tombstone? 'I want something punchy and very inspirational. I haven't formulated how it should read, but it should be something about the fact that I lived on this earth for good governance, and that I did everything in my power to make good governance a way of life on this earth and in Africa in particular.'

TERENCE NOMBEMBE'S strengths and attributes were clear to his family from a young age. A firm believer in education, he overcame the many hurdles he faced to become an accountant, before rising through the ranks to take on the role as the first black African Auditor-General of South Africa. His seven-year tenure saw him lauded as a 'model civil servant' who was both efficient and effective. Having concluded his role as AG, Nombembe is now the CEO of the South African Institute of Chartered Accountants (SAICA).

IRONS IN THE FIRE

SIZWE NXASANA

A MOTHER'S TOUCH

Even to the apartheid government, Sizwe Nxasana's potential was evident from a young age. His selection in Standard 4 to attend a school for high-performing children meant that the young Nxasana looked likely to fulfil his mother's fierce ambitions for him.

Born in August 1957 to a schoolteacher father and a nurse mother in Newcastle, Nxasana was the fourth in line of what would eventually be seven children. When he was just two his father and a friend decided to move their families to Lesotho, where his father took a position as a maths and science teacher at a high school and his mother stopped work to look after the family. They moved around at various intervals, with Nxasana, his brother and Robert Sobukwe's two sons even spending some time in a girls' boarding school. 'It was quite an experience. There wasn't an appropriate primary school close to the high school where my father taught, so that's why we ended up in a boarding school. I remember having a little partition around our bunk beds!'

Those early days were challenging for Nxasana. 'Growing up in a boarding school in a foreign country, you have to learn a new language and it was terribly cold in winter. It built a lot of resilience in me. If I look back, I had to start taking responsibility for my actions, which built character.' Nxasana would see his parents when they could get away, but with so many children to get to their visits were infrequent. Holidays were special, however. 'My dad was from Durban so we went there every holiday by train and spent time with the extended family.'

When Nxasana was eight his father moved the family again – this time to his own hometown. 'He decided he had had enough of teaching in Lesotho so he got a job at a school in Umlazi township and my mother started training to be a midwife at King Edward Hospital.' It was when he was 11 that Nxasana's potential was spotted and he was moved to one of two 'special' schools in Umlazi. It was an unusual situation for black children to find themselves in at the time; and upon reflection, Nxasana wonders whether it was a visionary school inspector who selected the best of all the local schools to attend. These schools had much higher standards and better teachers, and the competition was fierce. Having been at one of the special schools, Nxasana moved into Standard 6 but then skipped Standard 7 and moved up into Standard 8. Given that he missed some of the basics in Standard 7 he had to work extremely hard to keep up, but for the most part he enjoyed school.

Nxasana's mother was adamant that all her children would receive the best education possible, and took it upon herself to ensure that their teachers knew this. 'My mother always took a huge amount of interest in selecting the schools we went to and stayed close to what we were doing at school. She was a typical Zulu maiden, I guess – she took no nonsense from anyone, including the teachers. I even knew her to physically confront teachers she thought were not up to standard and we moved schools if she thought they weren't doing their jobs properly. I had moved schools every year before I went to the special school and we all also had to go to boarding school in our senior high-school years as she thought that that would build character.' Maths and science were a particular focus in the family, and those children who struggled were 'taught and drilled, as how can your dad be a maths and science teacher and you are dumb in those subjects!'

As Nxasana progressed through his schooling alcohol became increasingly problematic for his father, and his addiction meant that he was not always able to work. This meant that much of the financial and emotional burden was placed on his mother, who had to work full-time as a nurse while raising all seven children. 'My mother really inspired me as I grew up. In fact, until the day she died she was an amazing woman. When she went to school you could do a Junior Certificate, which was the equivalent of Standard 9, and then go on to train as a teacher or a nurse. When my dad died in 1977 my mother went back to school and did her matric – at age 50. She then decided that she didn't want to be a nurse any more, so did a degree in Nursing in order to complete a postgraduate degree in Psychology.'

Despite his father's failings, Nxasana recalls him as an extremely smart man. 'He was very clever. Much cleverer than I could ever hope to be. He was the only boy in a family of three and he was spoiled. His grandfather was what was called an "exempted native" – in other words, an esquire – so my dad was the third generation to be educated and he didn't have to struggle for anything; he was very easy-going. In a sense, my dad was a role model for me in that he influenced negative reinforcement. He didn't want to do anything that was too hard, and yet he was probably the smartest person around. There are a lot of things in my life and maybe even in my character that are my dad, but there are things that didn't work in his life, including alcoholism, that scare me to death.

'I want to avoid his failings and take the positive side of what he had; to be a better version of him. That is a huge influence in my life. I deliberately made good choices because, as a youngster you try alcohol and smoking and all those things, but when I was about 18 I realised that I had so many things in common with my father, which were small things but important things in how my life might play out. I dumped all the friends I grew up with and made new ones who I wanted to know me in a different way; as a person who is different to how I was shaping up to that point.'

Nxasana's family were Anglican and his oldest siblings went to an Anglican boarding school, but by the time Nxasana reached Standard 9 his mother decided that the standards of the Anglican schools were not high enough, and had her children – from the third child down – rebaptised so that they could attend a Roman Catholic boarding school in Mariannhill outside Durban. Nxasana believes that his mother was right about boarding school building character, because it taught him and his siblings how to be independent, as well as to make decisions and be accountable for them.

The lessons he learned from his mother have stood him in good stead throughout his life. To this day, if he has a challenge he is struggling with he continues to ask himself what his mother would have done, and then makes a decision based on that. 'My philosophy around women's development and empowerment comes from my mother's example. For many women, they get their degree and start work, but then in their thirties they may get married and have children and often have more responsibilities than their partners. But when the children are grown up, women should be encouraged to go back to work and focus on themselves and their careers. My youngest brother was in high school when my mother decided to go back to school and she worked until she died at age 70.

'As companies, we need to think differently about women empowerment and development. From my mother I learned that you should never stop learning, and that you can do anything you want to as a person. Very often we hold ourselves back. My mother was doing matric with children younger than me at the time and she didn't care; she knew what she wanted. I remember coming home and Mom was sitting with these kids and doing assignments with them! Other people might think that they're too old or too old to learn from kids, but not her. I grew up believing that I could do anything I set my mind to.'

A PROCESS OF ELIMINATION

Becoming a chartered accountant was not something Nxasana ever considered during his adolescence; at school it was his dream to be a pilot. His grandmother lived near the old Louis Botha Airport in Durban, so he and his brothers used to go to the air-force base next to the airport and watch the planes come in. 'Even today, if I had to create a bucket list, flying is one of the things I would still want to do.'

In fact, he 'stumbled' into the Accounting profession. 'When I passed matric I had good results, but my mother was done with you when you had finished school; you had to make way for the younger kids. I had no money and no clue, so I started working as an issuing clerk in a clothing factory.'

It didn't take long for Nxasana to realise that this was a 'crap job', so after three months he began to seriously start thinking about what he wanted to do with his life. He applied for and received a bursary from the then KwaZulu government to become a land surveyor, which saw him move to Pietermaritzburg for a month before being sent out to a construction camp in Tugela Ferry. 'The construction team worked for the government and was building roads and irrigation systems along the Tugela River. It was quite an experience for a township boy!'

Fortunately, this 'township boy' loved the outdoors – as well as driving cars, trucks and tractors. 'I was a youngster and it was a fascinating experience. I got to do surveys and then climb on a grader or tractor and show the operator what to do and where to cut. It was a lot of fun.' And yet, while he enjoyed it, he also knew that this was not something he wanted to do for the rest of his life, preferring the idea of working in an air-conditioned office. His elder brother had completed a BSc, so when he encouraged him to pursue commerce, Nxasana thought it had to be a good option.

Nxasana applied for a BCom Marketing at Fort Hare University and began his studies in 1976, with his first year paid for through a combination of his savings, a partial bursary and a loan from Standard Bank. At the end of his first semester there was a great deal of excitement when one of the lecturers – Professor Wiseman Nkuhlu – became the first black African CA. In fact, until that moment Nxasana had not even known what a CA was. Along with some of his classmates, he decided that he wanted to switch to Accounting, but Fort Hare did not offer Auditing or Tax and Accounting only went up to third year.

But Nxasana was nothing if not determined. He had found Nkuhlu's stories of studying for Accounting after he was incarcerated on Robben Island extremely inspiring, particularly as Nkuhlu's origins were in a rural village in the Transkei.

For his second year of study, Nxasana secured a more substantial bursary, but his education was interrupted by the death of Steve Biko. 'My mother and older siblings were very political – very driven, very aware and very active. When I was in second year we decided as students that we were going to stop going to lectures until apartheid was killed. Some of us ended up in prison for causing chaos and demonstrating against the apartheid regime. It took a lot longer to get my degree than I had imagined because we kept getting kicked out of university and then having to reapply.' While Nxasana was at university he had a relationship that resulted in a baby daughter, but it was not until she was a young adult that he really developed a relationship with her.

Upon receiving his degree in 1979, student loans and family responsibilities meant that Nxasana had to get straight to work. He had initially hoped to do his articles but very few firms hired black people in those days, so he found a job in the Accounts department at Unilever and registered through Unisa to do the courses from second and third year that were not offered at Fort Hare.

Nxasana was eventually accepted to do articles at a small firm of accountants, Gouws, Strauss and Partners, which did work for the KwaZulu government. 'When you look at all the black CAs who were qualifying at that time, most worked for audit firms that worked in the so-called independent homelands – so development corporations, the buses and the breweries, etc.' He then completed his Honours during his second year of articles in 1983, which allowed him to write the Board exam and become the sixth black CA in the country. That year also saw him marry Judy Dlamini, a fifth-year medical student at the University of Natal.

It was not long before Nxasana became a manager and then an audit manager at Gouws, Strauss and Partners, but in 1984 he decided to move to Pricewaterhouse. 'Things were beginning to change a little and firms were starting to take on black articled clerks and managers. I was probably one of the first black managers at Pricewaterhouse in Durban, but after a year I decided that I wanted to go and do something else and left to join the Small Business Development Corporation.'

At the time, the Small Business Development Corporation (SBDC), now Business Partners, was running a campaign aimed at helping black business people. 'It was a cool thing to do, I thought. I would be helping our people establish businesses. I only worked there for six months, though; I didn't like the culture so I quit.'

Following his time at the SBDC Nxasana's next job was at SA Sugar Distributors, a joint venture between CG Smith Sugar and Tongaat Hulett, which dealt with the marketing and distribution of sugar and sugar products. His role as CFO lasted three years before he finally decided it was time to start his own firm, which then took a further 18 months to set up. With a young family, it was a daunting prospect, but Judy had by this time qualified as a medical doctor and had started a practice as a GP, which meant that the family had a reliable source of income. Nxasana started his firm in 1989 and, given his wife's profession, initially looked to medical practitioners to fill his client roster. 'I called the firm Sizwe and Co., but it was just me and my secretary-cum-bookkeeper so she was the "Co."!'

Because there was a huge demand for Accounting services among black professionals, the firm grew quickly. At that time, the only other black-owned Accounting firm was Nkuhlu's in Umtata (Mthatha), although some Indian firms also existed in Durban. In the second year Nxasana took on another partner and hired his twentieth employee. 'In those first two years we had mainly doctors and lawyers as clients, but also traders, supermarkets and bottle stores. In our third year we started doing NGO work, particularly international NGOs.' He enjoyed the consulting side of the business the most so focused on that, leaving others to manage the auditing. In the evenings he also taught Accounting, Auditing and Tax to part-time students at the University of Zululand.

As the firm grew and other black firms started to flourish, Sizwe, Sango Ntsaluba and Sindiswa (neé Nkonki) decided to merge their audit firms to create Nkonki Sizwe Ntsaluba. We sat around the table and said, "Let's create one big firm." We were getting in each other's way but we knew each other, so joining together made sense.' By 1994, under Nxasana's guidance as CEO, Nkonki Sizwe Ntsaluba Inc. had grown to seven offices around the country with over 200 staff.

Under the new dispensation the team began to take on work for the government, but even the consulting could no longer hold Nxasana's attention. After three years he knew that this was not what he wanted to do for the rest of his life. He had told his wife and family that he would stay with the firm for 10 years but no longer; however, in 1996 at the age of 39, he had had enough. 'I didn't know what I was going to do, but I just decided to go and do something else. I remember telling all the partners at a strategy meeting – there must have been about 20 of us by then – and they thought I knew something terrible they didn't. Everyone thought it was bizarre as the firm was doing really well and we were growing, but they came to understand that I was serious about this decision.'

DEFINING A CORPORATE IDENTITY

Nxasana decided that it was time to venture into the corporate world and started applying for jobs, but it was just before he left the firm in March 1998 that Telkom advertised for a new CEO in the *Sunday Times*. 'Initially I didn't take any notice but I was commuting up to Joburg every day and I was meeting a client at the Sandton Sun and we got to talking about Telkom. We were doing an audit of Transnet and Transtel at the time so I sort of knew the space from that point of view, and I was also doing some consulting work at Transtel. As I was flying back to Durban that night, it just clicked – I decided to apply for the job and after a whole series of interviews I got it.'

Judy had been running a successful practice in Umlazi, seeing more than 100 patients a day, but she and Nxasana had also ventured into other businesses, including owning Chicken Licken franchise outlets, a Dial-a-Movie and a 24-hour bakery next to her medical practice. Upon locking up one night she was held up at gunpoint for the takings from the practice and the bakery, and so the family decided to leave the township. 'Within a month we had sold everything – the businesses, the practice, the house – and we left.'

The family moved to Umhlanga and Judy started a practice in town, but it was just not the same. 'She had gone from being a community doctor to having people who were just looking for sick certificates, so she lost her passion for the job and decided she didn't want to do it any more.' At the same time Nxasana was offered the job at Telkom, so the family decided to move up to Johannesburg. Nxasana took over the reins at Telkom in April 1998 and Judy elected to study for her MBA. 'I really see similarities between my mom and my wife. Judy works very hard and is just an amazing woman. She started off as a medical doctor, then changed course and became a businesswoman. She has done a great job of it.'

The move to Johannesburg was also a good one for Nxasana. 'Telkom was really fun because we were doing so many things, restructuring the company and preparing the company for an IPO both on the Johannesburg Stock Exchange and the New York Stock Exchange. I didn't quite know what I was letting myself in for. I went from running a firm that had maybe 350 people to one with 62 000 people.' Risk is not something that he shies away from, however. He believes his training as an accountant has shaped him and created his philosophy around rules and compliance, which he mixes with a dash of calculated risk.

As an accountant, he was used to moving from industry to industry and understood what the company's key drivers were. He was also confident in his own abilities, which he attributes to his mother.

While running his own firm, Nxasana had sat on the board of the Natal Building Society (NBS) with Paul Harris and GT Ferreira, but when he left to join Telkom he resigned from the board – partly because of the potential conflict of interest, but also because he wanted to focus on Telkom. In 1998, after just three years at the helm of Telkom, Harris and Ferreira approached Nxasana to join the FirstRand Board. Initially he turned them down due to his demanding schedule, but they were persistent and, after Telkom listed on the

JSE and NYSE in 2003 and most of the restructuring had taken place, Nxasana decided to look for listed company experience outside of Telkom, and finally agreed to join the FirstRand Board.

By 2005 Nxasana had 'had enough' of Telkom and planned to start his own business in the mobile virtual operating space, including offering mobile payments. The concept of his business plan was similar to that of Virgin Mobile: 'Ride on the networks, create a different brand, start to look at mobile payments as part of the offering. There was a big opportunity there, but the guys told me I could do the same thing at FirstRand. At that stage, Laurie Dippenaar was retiring and Paul Harris was going to be CEO of the Group so they were looking for a CEO for the banking group, so after seven years I left Telkom in August 2005, and in January 2006 I took up my position at FirstRand Bank Limited.' By the time Nxasana left Telkom, the share price had more than trebled since its listing.

For a man like Nxasana the inevitable question is, 'What next?' 'I don't think of myself as an entrepreneur. Telecoms was great and I had a passion for it at the time, and starting the business was a no-brainer as there was a captive market. Now I travel a lot on the continent and see how resources are extracted without nearly enough manufacturing taking place, and that's what I want to focus on when I'm done here.'

Nowadays, he takes lessons and inspiration from people around him. The characteristics he admires in people are hard work, caring for others and living a good life. While there are no particular leaders, local or international, that really inspire him, he would like to have a conversation with Barack Obama. 'I was listening to him the other day and, having listened to him many times, I look at what he says and how he articulates his views and ideas, and he is very good at what he does. I wish I could orate like he does.'

IN ADDITION

Nxasana is also passionate about education and 'playing a little role in creating opportunities for people who come after me. There are so many bright young kids in the townships and rural areas. I studied Accounting and came from a middle-income family so I was lucky; there are these young kids that you come across and all they need is a break and someone to talk to them about opportunities and how they can live their lives in a better way. I was talking to someone recently who is a senior executive in a company who told me that I had once spoken at his school and if it weren't for me he wouldn't have become an accountant. That really makes it worthwhile for me.' As CEO he also takes the opportunity to employ young graduates as his personal assistants, which gives them a unique insight into the office of a CEO.

Along with some friends, Nxasana created the Association for the Advancement of Black Accountants in Southern Africa (ABASA) in the early 1980s. 'I was never a prefect, I was never on the SRC, and even though I may have been locked up I was in a group, so I was never a leader in any other situation until I decided I was going to do something about the benefit that I ended up with and the inequity in the country.' Nxasana became President of ABASA in the late 1980s and, in his role, gave talks at schools, spoke about the Accounting profession and tried to overturn the barriers to the profession. 'We were activists and I think I am still an activist in that way. I'm now the Chairperson of the National Education Collaboration Trust, so I've always been involved in education one way or the other.'

Nxasana has been awarded honorary doctorates from the University of Johannesburg, the Durban University of Technology and the University of Fort Hare, although he claims he's not sure why he got those; he would rather measure his success by the success of his nuclear family. 'Children are their own people and there's no greater reward than seeing them successful and enjoying what they do.' His eldest daughter, Nandi, is a medical doctor, while his youngest daughter, Nkanyezi, is a CA and an analyst at JP Morgan. Despite receiving a kidney from his father, an aortic aneurysm claimed Sifiso Nxasana in 2012 when he was just 27 years old.

Success in business is also important to Nxasana. 'I have some insecurities and one of those is waking up one day to find myself like my dad. I work as hard as I do and live my life the way I do to compensate for that fear. I am petrified of addiction, so occasionally in winter I will drink tea, but I am petrified of it. If you see me drinking Coke you must know I'm in trouble because I'm petrified of being addicted to Coke. I have a sweet tooth and a sugar addiction is a real addiction. Knowing my character, how my make-up may be and how my father was, I say, "Okay, maybe I'm addicted to sugar, but maybe its fine" – otherwise my life might be boring. I try to channel my addiction by going to gym every single day. I know I have an obsessive-compulsive character but I try to channel it into something positive.'

Nxasana keeps any obsessions he might have under control with a full diary. His previous and current duties have included acting as Vice-Chairman of the SARS Audit Committee, Deputy President of Business Leadership South Africa, Non-Executive Director of Business Against Crime, a member of the Income Tax Special Court and a Non-Executive Director of the Development Bank of South Africa. In addition he makes time to give talks at gatherings such as SAICA's Leaders in Finance Summit and chairs the Thuthuka Bursary Fund, which assists young black would-be accountants with bursaries and academic and life skills support.

His plan is always to be involved in education in one way or another, and 'tapping into young people to solve the problems we have. There are all sorts of opportunities I would like to explore, so it may be housing, water or communication – I have no idea what it would be at this stage.' Politics is not an area that Nxasana would like to be involved in, however. 'I'm quite happy playing on the periphery. I work with government quite a lot in the context of the NDP. We hosted an education dialogue here at FirstRand at the end of 2012, which resulted in the creation of the National Education Collaboration Trust. We want to address the problems of the quality of education in the country.'

Nxasana also enjoys cooking and gardening and is extremely interested in history; on his many travels he tries to engage with locals to understand the history of their countries and people. His own history and heritage are also important to him – so much so that he and Judy wrote their family history and created a family website, which was 'a journey of discovery for us'.

On the whole, he considers himself to be 'pretty easy-going', although he has been known to be stressed by traffic and selfish people. 'If you want to drive me up the wall, just be selfish!' He does admit to caring about what people think of him, adding that 'we all have egos and vanity. I do care about how I look, how I dress. I love fashion and I love cars. Whether the cars are for me or about how I look, I have no idea, I just love them.'

Nxasana isn't sure what he would like on his tombstone, although he does know that he wants to leave behind a legacy of having made a contribution to educating young people. 'If I could be remembered as someone who played some role in improving the lives of others through education, I would be happy. I am also here to prove something to myself and to whoever cares to listen, that as an African person you can be as good as anybody else in the world, not just here. I set myself a standard to be a role model for black youth. If I can change even slightly the attitude in our psyche as black people, then I'll be happy.'

And will he ever retire? It's unlikely. 'That word isn't in my vocabulary at all!'

One of the first black chartered accountants in South Africa, **SIZWE NXASANA** has risen to prominence and now occupies the position of CEO of FirstRand Bank Ltd. As an entrepreneur, businessman and philanthropist, he has made his mark on the financial services industry, the professional services industry and education in South Africa.

FORTUNE FAVOURS THE BRAVE

FRANCOIS PIENAAR

THE FOUNDATION YEARS

South Africa owes a considerable debt of gratitude to a lady who changed the course of the country's history by rescuing Jacobus Francois Pienaar from possible death in 1974. At just seven years old, Pienaar was playing in the veld with his friends when a rival gang from the neighbourhood 'captured' him, put a noose around his neck and left him hanging from a tree. Had it not been for Miss Laubscher, a teacher at Pienaar's primary school who happened to be passing by, the history books may have told a very different story.

It was the dawn of a new year when Jacobus Francois was born to Jan-Harm and Valerie Pienaar in what was then the rural mining town of Vereeniging. The first of four sons, young Francois and his brothers were not born into a wealthy family, but what their parents lacked in money and education, they made up for with unconditional love and support for all four boys. With circumstances having led both Jan-Harm and Valerie to leave school before attaining matric, they were determined to provide their children with a better life, and instilled a strong set of values in their children.

Pienaar's working-class background was typical of many Afrikaner communities in the 1960s and 1970s, which a young Pienaar was ashamed of in his youth, leading to his determination to change his circumstances through education. Now in his forties, Pienaar is embarrassed at the memory of asking his father to drop him off a distance from school so that his friends would not see their dilapidated old car.

Looking back, Pienaar is aware that there were many others worse off than him, and is grateful for the free and adventurous way in which he grew up. Playing outside in the sun with his brothers and friends, Pienaar was encouraged to be active, explore and experiment, all of which led to an independent spirit and a love for sport and the outdoors. The boys were brought up with Christian values at the core of their parents' philosophy on child-rearing. These values centred around honesty, a profound love for family, a strong work ethic, a determination to succeed and pride in being an Afrikaner, all of which Pienaar is still proud to lay claim to and which he believes laid a solid foundation for his later successes, as well as his ability to deal with failure.

Working in the steel industry, Pienaar's father was a quiet and resolute man who led the household with authority. The young Pienaar was close to his mother as a child, and was not initially as tough and uncompromising when it came to a physical test as he became renowned for on the rugby field. He was expected to be a role model for his brothers; this was a responsibility he took seriously and extended beyond his family life onto the rugby field and into the boardroom.

Known for being the serious one in the family, Pienaar realised early on that, given his limited circumstances, sport was his best chance at attaining the level of education to which he aspired. What would turn out to be an illustrious rugby career began with the future No. 6 playing in bare feet on the baked dirt outside AJ Jacobs Primary School in Vanderbijlpark. Starting off as a centre, Pienaar did not take long to move to No. 8, but his first attempt at selection ended badly when he was not chosen for the Transvaal Primary Schools side.

His father was furious and believed that it was because Pienaar attended a poor and 'unfashionable' school, and in hindsight Pienaar realised that it was his first brush with the 'self-interest and ego' he later discovered to be rampant in the world of rugby.

While Pienaar was still at primary school, his father took up a job with Sasol and the family moved to Sasolburg. Pienaar joined Voorslag Primary School and quickly became involved in every sport he could, but soon showed an aptitude for the high jump and cricket. This led to his selection for Transvaal for the South African athletics junior championships when he was just nine, as well as for the Triomf Cricket Week. Pienaar learned early in his career that injury is an occupational hazard for a professional sportsman, yet despite cutting his foot during the high jump at the athletics championships, he still earned a respectable third place.

It was at this time that Pienaar was first introduced to business by his Uncle Kobus, an entrepreneur with a tyre business in Johannesburg. Kobus drove a Mercedes, which seemed to the young Pienaar the ultimate symbol of success, and he was thrilled when his uncle took him on to help with wheel alignments during the school holidays. Pienaar's first wages were spent on an electric carving knife and an electric fan for his mother. He continued to play rugby throughout this time, and remembers watching matches on the television with his father whenever he had the opportunity. At the time Pienaar realised that segregation existed in the country, but was taken aback by the outcry at the third Test between South Africa and New Zealand in Auckland – politics did not belong in rugby, he believed.

Yet despite Pienaar's love of rugby and his success on the athletics track, cricket dominated his high-school years, with the teenager batting and bowling for the Transvalia High School team. Upon representing the Vaal Triangle, Pienaar went on to be selected for the Country Districts provincial high-school team to play at Nuffield Week. However, a serious cut on his hand, gained during the celebrations after his selection, meant he had to play with stitches in his bowling hand. This was the beginning of the end of Pienaar's cricket career, as Border took advantage of his lack of control to smash him out of the park. When he was not selected for Nuffield Week the following year, he turned his attention to rugby.

All the while, Pienaar was well-aware that he needed to get good marks to win a scholarship if he were to escape Sasolburg. Pienaar's leadership abilities were already apparent, and he was chosen to be a prefect in his matric year. He went on to pass his final exams, but he decided to retake his matric because he wanted to do better in order to win a scholarship to university. In truth he was also not keen to start work or do military service, and fortunately his parents – who by this time had moved to Witbank with his younger brothers for his father's work – agreed with his choice.

This was the type of sacrifice that Pienaar's parents were willing to make. It would also have made their lives considerably easier if he had gone out to work and supported himself. It was during his second matric year in 1985, at Patriot High School in Witbank, that another Mercedes had caught his eye – this time it belonged to a friend's father who was a lawyer, and predictably it planted a seed in Pienaar's head. Given his modest background, it was not surprising that Pienaar measured success in rands and cents, and he set his sights on studying law.

But the Mercedes was not the only game-changer at Patriot High. A broken ankle the previous year meant that Pienaar was unable to play in Craven Week, a rugby tournament known as a launch pad for many provincial careers. Yet this had not stopped him from continuing with his physical and demanding style of play, which stood out at Patriot, not known for its rugby prowess. While playing in trials, Pienaar, who was now at flank, 'tackled two guys into hospital', and together with his brother, Kobus, at flyhalf, the two were instrumental in securing Patriot's win at a local rugby week. Pienaar was also not afraid to assert himself off the rugby field, which led to accusations of arrogance, but still his rugby and leadership skills saw him being chosen to represent South Eastern Transvaal at the 1985 Craven Week. It was at this competition that Pienaar was offered his first opportunity to be captain; it was, however, strongly suggested by a teacher that being captain would interfere with his ability to play, so unusually for him, he decided to withdraw from contention.

One thing led to another and Pienaar found himself being selected for the South African schools rugby team, which apart from being a source of great pride for his parents, was key to his application for a university scholarship. Offers came in from the universities of Potchefstroom and Pretoria, but it was the proposal of an annual bursary of R3 000 from the Rand Afrikaans University (RAU, now the University of Johannesburg – UJ) that saw Pienaar heading to Johannesburg to study law.

REACHING FOR A DREAM

It was during initiation, in the first few weeks of university, that Pienaar really began to appreciate what it meant to be part of a unit. The hazing of the new boys in the university residence was harsh at times, but Pienaar soon felt a strong sense of camaraderie with his fellow students. Studying while playing rugby was also a challenge, as he was not allowed to miss any practice sessions or matches. This led to long nights of studying other people's notes from classes he had been forced to miss. Having the security of a professional qualification was a non-negotiable, however, so he soldiered on.

As far as rugby was concerned, Pienaar's first challenge was to be selected for his residence team, which he duly achieved. Once this had been accomplished, he made it onto the university's under-20 side, and then tried out for the Transvaal under-20 team. Despite having been virtually guaranteed a position, Pienaar was shocked to find himself left out of the team. As had happened with Craven Week, politics and dishonesty had conspired against him. Having been told by one of the conveners that he did not need to attend the final training session, he soon discovered from his coach that the convener had told the selection committee that Pienaar had made himself unavailable.

Fortunately, Pienaar won a place on the provincial team before the season closed, and went on in 1987 to play for both the RAU and the Transvaal under-20 teams. His hard work and determination paid off when he earned a place on the South African under-20 team, which played against the British Bulldogs later that year. Yet, despite all the effort and sacrifices made, the amateur status of the game in South Africa meant that the Transvaal players were only paid R30 a game.

Money was important to Pienaar – not only as a means to put food on the table, but also as a symbol of success. When his father secured him a holiday job at Highveld Steel in Witbank, it was fortunate that Pienaar was not afraid of long hours or hard work because the position involved cleaning the heavy equipment and drills. Pienaar's shifts were 12 hours long and he also volunteered to work 16-hour shifts on public holidays to maximise the opportunity for double pay. Part of the impetus was to show his father that he did not consider himself special simply because he was studying at university, and that he was as capable as his father of performing hard, dirty work.

A persistent feature throughout his school years was Pienaar's reputation for getting into fights, and this did not change at university; his reputation was extremely important to him and he did not want to be seen as weak or not up to a challenge. In Pienaar's words, 'I desperately wanted to be strong, wanted to be a winner, wanted to be someone who people respected and admired.' It was clear that Pienaar's reputation as a leader – and as a force to be reckoned with – was growing when he was asked to be head of security for RAU's Rag Week.

When Pienaar was only 21 he was appointed captain of RAU's first team, tasting victory in his first match as skipper. For Pienaar it was a defining moment and his obsession with rugby, and being a leader grew exponentially. Being selected for the Transvaal B team was another move in the right direction, and Pienaar's strategy for achieving success one step at a time was bearing fruit. He was a strong believer in setting annual, achievable goals, because he believed that 'in sport, consistent progress more often leads to longevity at the top of the game'.

But because it was not just rugby that Pienaar was passionate about, he continued to come up with ways to make money. Opening and running the first hostel bar at RAU before selling it for R3 000 – an amount equivalent to a year's living and tuition expenses at the time – was just one of his bold ventures in what was already a packed schedule. Having earned his BProc, Pienaar elected to stay on at RAU for a further two years to complete his LLB – a feat that not many rugby players can claim to have achieved.

The training continued, with Pienaar working hard to build himself up so that he would be in contention for a place on the Transvaal team. It was in 1988 that his exertions really began to pay off, and towards the end of the season he was drafted into the Transvaal team. But, as with all sporting endeavours, his place in the team was not guaranteed, and rivalry with other loose forwards meant that he had to rise to countless challenges. His selection for the provincial team was accompanied by an initiation that was so brutal and degrading that it cemented in Pienaar's mind what leadership was not; his desire to be part of a cohesive unit and to create a family atmosphere in any team he led was defined at that point.

As captain of the RAU team again that year, Pienaar led the side to the finals of the national club championships, where he distinguished himself by allowing his team members flexibility outside of the training and match schedule – a foreign concept at the time. His idea was to 'treat the players like adults, to leave most of the discipline to the players themselves and to focus on the rugby'.

Winning the championships was another crucial moment in Pienaar's life, because it took him to a new level of self-confidence, which remained with him despite suffering yet another injury that saw him lose his place in the Transvaal team for part of the year. The year 1990 was also a landmark one in South Africa that saw the release of Nelson Mandela from prison. The changes in the country that followed were far-reaching, and included the unification of the South African Rugby Board and the non-racial South African Rugby Union. Following years of international isolation, this opened the door to a new level of rugby for Pienaar and his peers.

The following year brought with it a new influence in the form of Harry Viljoen. A former provincial rugby player, Viljoen had become a successful businessman who was 'driven by an infectious enthusiasm and an exciting willingness to dare and be different to the rest. He respected the past, but he was not imprisoned by traditions.' This appealed greatly to Pienaar's own views on leadership, and Viljoen's new professional outlook, training regimen and focus on having fun led to a resurgent Transvaal, which was aided by Viljoen's promise of a R500 bonus for the biggest tackle of the match. Considering that the team members were by then only earning R600 per match, this was a significant incentive.

As Pienaar's reputation grew, he began to receive offers of money to take part in invitation and provincial matches. This, of course, was against the rules of amateur rugby, but as the regulations were never enforced, Pienaar knew that he would not be penalised for it. The idea that he could really make money from rugby took hold when the University of Pretoria offered him a place on the university's rugby team and at Northern Transvaal. Upon hearing of this, Louis Luyt – then CEO of Transvaal – matched their offer and Pienaar decided to stay on at Transvaal. His revised remuneration was R2 000 a month plus match fees, leaving him with over R4 000 a month – a sum he was very happy about until he discovered that two players he had been recruited with already earned that amount. He realised at that moment that he would have to fight to be remunerated fairly, as no one would pay a cent more than they thought they could get away with. When a similar situation arose in 1995 with the Springboks, Pienaar was to remember the lesson he learned that day.

Another lesson Pienaar learned early on was that, as a public figure, gossip is an ever-present reality. He soon learned to be pragmatic about it, however, saying that 'Anyone in the limelight simply has to accept the fact that people will gossip about them, and most of that gossip is going to be unflattering. It goes with the territory and I was able to accept that from an early stage in my career.'

PUTTING YOUR BEST FOOT FORWARD

Pienaar's progression to the top was enhanced when Transvaal reached the finals of the Currie Cup in 1991 – which they lost to Northern Transvaal – and the following year he was one of 60 players invited to participate in the first Springbok trials since readmission into the international arena. From first trying out with the C side, he was moved up into the B side before being asked to captain the A side in the final trial, yet when the squad for the upcoming home tests was named, Pienaar was not in it. 'I was hopeful of being included in the squad at the very least, but something went wrong. I am not sure what concerned the coach, but I was not only left out of the Bok squad to play the All Blacks and Australia, but I could not even find a place in the Junior Springbok team. With no explanation, no word of encouragement from anyone, I was left out in the cold.' Seeing the way that the Australian team were hailed as heroes, however, was further incentive to Pienaar to work even harder to attain his dream of earning a Springbok cap.

In the meantime, problems were afoot in the Transvaal changing rooms, where the administrators – and, in particular, Louis Luyt – insisted on changes following the team's defeat in the Currie Cup final. Pienaar's name was being bandied around for the captaincy, but 'such speculation damaged the morale of the side and affected my approach, not least because I knew in my heart that I was not quite ready to take on the mantle of captaincy'. Despite Pienaar's protests to Luyt, the administrator put him in as captain and the atmosphere became increasingly difficult. Viljoen 'appeared not to agree with the move and would typically spend more time discussing tactics with Jannie than with me – and I could hardly blame him. Jannie should have remained captain.' When, after just four matches, Pienaar told Luyt that he was relinquishing the captaincy, Luyt was furious. Yet with Jannie reinstated as captain, 'the team found new momentum' and were unlucky to lose to Natal in that year's Currie Cup final when they pushed past them for a 14–13 win. When both the coach and captain resigned from Transvaal following the defeat, Luyt took over as caretaker coach and put Pienaar back in as captain for the knockout Lion Cup. 'I genuinely liked Louis Luyt, respected him for his wisdom and business acumen. He appeared to like me as well, showing real compassion for me as a young captain whom he desperately hoped would succeed where others would fail. I left his room hugely encouraged for the future. He was backing me.'

The team went on to win the Lion Cup under their new coach, Kitch Christie, who became a real inspiration to Pienaar. He was a hard taskmaster who insisted on discipline and hard work, which included a merciless exercise regime, yet the players respected and trusted him. Pienaar and Christie became extremely close, with the captain learning many lessons from his coach. One that was to stand him in good stead was that belief in the players, as well as trust, support and pride, were critical to ensuring that each team member felt valued and gave of their best. 'Everything I became in the game arose from his early, absolute vote of confidence.'

Towards the end of 1992, the Springboks set off to Europe for their first away Test – again without Pienaar – which prompted him to contemplate why he was yet to be included in the squad. 'I asked myself why I was not good enough to play Springbok rugby, which weaknesses I would have to address, and set down my goals and ambitions. The idea of representing my country on the rugby field had always excited me, but from that afternoon it became an obsession.'

Super Rugby debuted in 1993, with the advent of the Super-10 tournament. This brought the players' season forward to January, just three weeks after their return from a tour of Europe. Pienaar was concerned that the team was being treated like professional athletes while being paid like amateurs, but although he could have pursued a career in law at this stage by completing his articles, he decided to focus on rugby. He set about creating a Players' Trust to supplement the paltry R800 match fees they were being paid, which saw him approaching each of the Ellis Park box-holders to persuade them to sponsor R50 for every try. In return, the players would visit the boxes after home matches. He also proposed that, for R5 000, a company could book two appearances by the whole team.

The team were fully behind Pienaar's proposal, which included him earning a 20 per cent commission on all earnings. Although there were problems with some players not pulling their weight, the money began to fill the Trust's coffers, aided by Pienaar's negotiations with Luyt, which saw him agree to bonuses for wins. Other endeavours included buying wine from a bankrupt wine estate, adding Transvaal labels to it and selling it at a premium.

When the time came for the Trust to pay out at the end of the year, however, Pienaar was 'shocked and amazed' when the team announced that he should not earn 20 per cent on the bonuses he had negotiated with Luyt. 'I understood the logic of their view, but it did not match our original agreement.' At a second meeting the difference of opinion started to turn into a dispute. 'The atmosphere was turning distinctly unpleasant; the discussions became emotional and damaging to team spirit. In the end I told the players I would relinquish the 20 per cent commission, but I said that I felt this was unfair and asked to be released from any responsibility for the Trust in the future ... The saga taught me two lessons. The first was that the smell of money affects rugby players like everyone else. The second was that where players are involved, issues of money and playing should always be kept apart. With the benefit of hindsight, the seed of the conflict was my dual role as the players' agent on one hand, taking my commission, and on the other hand their team captain, striving to build team spirit. It was ultimately impossible to perform both roles properly.'

Despite this setback, team spirit continued to be an imperative for Pienaar, as it was to Christie; the coach pushed the team hard, but they bonded well as a result. 'This was the secret of our success: we were a family. That may sound trite and superficial, but I have played in many rugby teams and very few can have claimed to be family.' Christie also went about improving the conditions under which the team played, including building a new training complex. This approach was something Pienaar would use later in his career. Transvaal went on to win that year's Currie Cup, despite the fact that Pienaar was taken off the field with concussion during the final.

It was on a trip to Australia for the Super-10 that Pienaar decided to try a new team-building exercise, which saw him calling out players' names and their team members shouting out what they thought of their abilities. 'My goal was to boost the team's confidence. Daily routines often leave very little time for any praise to be given, and people are rarely told how much they are appreciated and admired by their teammates. I was determined that our players should know their standing, and that they would carry the sense of confidence forward into the game. As the praise flowed I could sense players starting to sit up in their seats. The session was having its desired effect.' Pienaar credits the team's confidence for their success in winning that year's Super-10 final. 'As a captain, I had learned to be sensitive to the moods and vibes of the team at all times. It was a fine balance to say the right things and act in the right way while keeping us on edge for the game.'

This was to stand him in good stead in 1993, when he was finally named for the Springbok squad to play against France in June. 'I can only recall an enormous sense of relief. I had realised what seemed to be the overriding ambition of my life: to be a Springbok. The nerves, the concern and the fear that I would never achieve that goal, that my life would somehow be a failure, literally seemed to melt away.' The telephone rang all weekend and his parents visited him, 'bursting with pride and excitement'.

Although he was thrilled to have reached his goal, Pienaar soon realised that the team had a mountain to climb. The first setback was that there had been no trials or training camp, which meant that many of the team members did not know one another and had not played Test rugby before. Then it was only at the first training session that the coach, Ian McIntosh, announced his selection of Pienaar as captain, which was a concern for him as not only was this to be his debut, but he worried that the older players in the team would resent him for it. After the training session Pienaar was called in for media interviews and at that moment he realised that his life had changed forever. 'Strangers shook my hand like old friends. I felt as though part of me, part of my life, had been claimed as public property.' One of the first things Pienaar learned was that 'as captain, I needed to project a confident and happy mood, and the most effective means of achieving this aim was to smile. I smiled, and smiled, and smiled again.'

There were perks, however, one of which was being able to fly his parents to Durban for the match – their first trip on an aeroplane. In addition, to his 'poorly concealed delight', a Mercedes was allocated to him for the weekend.

'That excited Thursday, I dressed in my new Springbok tracksuit and drove the Mercedes to my parents. In my mind there could have been no more powerful symbols of success.'

Pienaar's first cap was earned against France, which saw the Boks eke out a 20–20 draw. The second Test against France was played under a cloud, when news reached the team that two Transvaal players who were due to play in the curtain raiser had been killed in a car accident. The Boks went on to lose the game by one point. 'I was disappointed, but not shattered. The news earlier in the day had set everything in perspective.'

The French Tests were followed by a tour of Australia, in which Pienaar, the coach – Ian McIntosh – and the team reached the 'ideal mental state'. 'In less than three weeks I had quickly developed a profound respect for Ian McIntosh, not least because his coaching was based on a passionate love for the game. He was evidently a student of rugby not because he thought it could make him rich or famous, but because he truly loved the game.' After winning their first overseas Test, Pienaar was extremely satisfied not only with the win, but with 'the manner in which those squad members who had not been on the field so obviously shared in our delight. We had worked hard at breaking down the barriers of provincialism and I was starting to feel that we could blend as a national team, united in thought and deed.'

The morning after the first Test, Pienaar enjoyed a first-hand encounter with a 'complete international rugby captain', when he met the Wallaby captain, Nick Farr-Jones, before a television interview. 'Setting aside the disappointment of the previous night, he congratulated me warmly. As the show ran on, Nick could not have been more kind and eloquent in conceding we had deserved to win. He had offered me an impeccable lesson in how any captain should behave in defeat. It was a lesson which I hoped I would not require too often, but it was one which I would not forget.'

A follow-up tour to Argentina saw the team really bond. Pienaar knew that to build a great team the players needed to 'grow together as a group of people who genuinely care about each other and enjoy each other's company'. This passion for the game and his teammates was borne out by Pienaar's selection as South African Rugby Player of the Year.

The only problem on the horizon, felt Pienaar, was that because there were no national Tests between the tour to Argentina in November 1993 and a tour to England in June 1994, the team would not only not be playing together, but in fact they would be playing against each other in local tournaments. 'This is the eternal challenge of creating spirit in a national side – the long stretches of complete inactivity.' This problem surfaced in the first Test match of 1994 when the team failed to 'gel' and lost dismally. The next Test saw an intense resolve develop among the team members, and even though Pienaar had broken his nose in a training session, the Boks trounced England 27–9. 'We were cross, bloody-minded, angry, grumpy. We would not be denied, and a broken nose seemed simply irrelevant.' Team spirit and a winning attitude could never be underestimated, knew Pienaar.

The next hurdle for the Boks was an away tour to New Zealand, where again Pienaar was injured – this time with a concussion against Wellington before the Tests had even begun. After sitting out the first Test, which the Boks lost, Pienaar looked to inspire his team, and not for the first time he turned to music. With some help, he created a montage of the players to the song, 'Something Inside So Strong', and could immediately see the effect it had on the team – so much so that he arranged for a television to be placed in the changing room before the second Test so that they could watch it again before kick-off. 'I was amazed by the reaction of the players. I could see they were moved, in fact psyched out of their minds. I have always believed in the power of music, and that team was incredibly motivated when they took the field.'

Unfortunately, the tactic did not work as well as he had hoped – in fact, he believed that the team may have been too hyped up and had used up too much nervous energy in the changing room – and they lost 13–9. Further trouble followed when Johan le Roux bit the All Black captain, Sean Fitzpatrick, on the ear. The team management knew that they had to act, and it was decided that Le Roux would be sent home. 'I did not agree with the decision and, to my eternal regret, I did not disagree with the decision either. With hindsight, I can clearly see we should not have been pressurised into taking any action at that time. The disciplinary process should have been allowed to take its course, but I was still disappointed by the Test defeat, still distracted, not thinking clearly.' It was the only time during his career when, under similar circumstances, Pienaar did not support a player in his team. 'At a time when what seemed like the entire world was against him, I should have backed Johan. It was not so much a matter of right and wrong, as a matter of loyalty.' The next day saw the entire squad go on a scheduled boat trip, with Le Roux being left behind at the hotel. 'It was by far the worst decision I have ever made as a captain on tour. Others told him to stay, but I should have insisted that he join the rest of the squad. The atmosphere on the boat quickly turned sour and morose. The issue was destroying team spirit and ruining the tour. Players felt that one of their number had been sold out by a team management running at the beck and call of the media. In effect, we had left Johan to the wolves. The New Zealand disciplinary tribunal went on to ban him from rugby for 17 months – a punishment that was ridiculously out of proportion to any offence he had committed.'

A further setback rocked the team when Luyt suggested in an interview that both the team manager and coach were 'history'. 'All spirit and morale appeared to evaporate. Everyone became more concerned with their own survival in the wreckage of the tour than what happened with the team.' A team meeting was called in which emotions were laid bare about the treatment of Le Roux, and it was decided that the team should pull together for one last effort in the final Test. The result was a draw, and upon their return home, the coach was fired. Despite the controversies, however, Pienaar was named International Rugby Player of the Year.

As far as Pienaar's Transvaal career was concerned, although 1993 finished with the team winning four trophies, 1994 did not start well. Their first game of the Super-10 saw a furious Christie take Pienaar to task for not playing as a captain should, accusing him of playing for himself and in the process making poor decisions. Pienaar realised that Christie was right and that his problem was complacency. After such a successful year in 1993, the team were resting on their laurels instead of coming out swinging. After addressing the problem, Transvaal went on to win three trophies that year.

Further Springbok Tests bonded the team running up to what was undoubtedly the most coveted trophy in the rugby world – the World Cup. Pienaar believes that for some ex-players and journalists it was seen as an opportunity to muddy the waters with criticism and gossip. 'It had become clear to me that, as the World Cup drew near, such people were resolved to criticise me and the team whenever and wherever possible. We suspected this was motivated by jealousy among former players who had not had the opportunity to play in a World Cup.' But this, combined with some 'venomous' media coverage, only served to sharpen the resolve of the coach and the team. The management also took it upon themselves to organise every aspect of the team's preparations, and 'matters were discussed openly, decided by consensus, finalised and communicated'. Pienaar believes that 'such clear and sensitive leadership served not only to reassure the players and insulate them from outside criticism, but also to give them true confidence in a happy, professional and decent management team'.

The World Cup competition started out well for the Boks, but the final game of the first stage was fraught with electricity blackouts and a fight that saw two Springbok players suspended for the remainder of the tournament. This was followed by miscommunication between Pienaar and the team manager, Morné du Plessis, when Du Plessis was led to believe that Pienaar was ignoring his phonecalls. This led to significant tension in the squad. 'I had become sullen and silent, making no contribution to the team at all.' Christie attempted to talk Pienaar through his emotions, but it was only at a team meeting the following morning that Pienaar was able to admit to the team that he was angry at how he had handled the situation and his emotions. 'With a cracking voice, I pledged myself to the squad and to winning the World Cup.' The result was a team that was focused on their goal and strived for total control on the field. On the way to Ellis Park for the final game, Pienaar again used music to motivate his team, and the rest, as they say, is history. The Springbok team went on to win the 1995 World Cup in Johannesburg, defeating the favourites, New Zealand, 15–12.

MONEY IS THE ROOT OF ALL EVIL

Just eight days later the team became mired in a contractual and financial dispute that lasted over a month. It was inevitable that the game was going to turn professional, and the Australian media mogul, Kerry Packer, was the first to try to take the three dominant teams – Australia, New Zealand and South Africa – down this path. While the Springboks, with the exception of Chester Williams whose lawyer advised him against it, signed contracts joining Packer's The Rugby World Championship (TWRC), it was agreed that Pienaar would hold onto them until they were certain that TWRC was going ahead. It had been decided by the team that they would negotiate together, and that any agreements would have to be reached by all members of the squad. But what followed was a descent into a financial and power struggle. The Transvaal team was also beset with financial wrangling at the same time, with players trying to negotiate for higher salaries only to find four of them being fired by Luyt.

The negotiations on both fronts continued for weeks, with Pienaar trying to manage people's expectations and being accused of selling out South African rugby. Pienaar's perspective was that he was simply trying to negotiate the best deal for the team. Ultimately Luyt agreed to match Packer's terms, which saw the team signing with SARFU. The deal meant the collapse of TWRC, which had signed the trans-Tasman teams as well as over 100 provincial players in South Africa. This in turn led to further accusations that the Springboks – and Pienaar, in particular – were only looking after their own interests. Looking back, Pienaar understands the reaction, but questions whether if the situation where reversed, if those who were critical of them would have sacrificed their own interests for others.

The team went on to win their end-of-year tour and Pienaar was voted Rugby Personality of the Year by the British Rugby Union Writers' Club, Newsmaker of the Year in South Africa, and International Rugby Captain of the Year. The year 1996 looked set to be another good one, beginning as it did with Pienaar's marriage to his university sweetheart, Nerine Winter, and his nomination by the top 20 rugby writers in Britain as Rugby Personality of the Year. Things did not turn out as hoped, however, when André Markgraaff took over the position as Bok coach due to Christie's ongoing battle with cancer. When fabricated stories about Pienaar began to emerge, fracturing his relationships with other players and administrators, they could be traced back to Markgraaff. One such example was when Markgraaff told Luyt, who then told the assistant coach Ray Mordt, that Pienaar had said that he had no respect for Ray – either as a coach or as a person. The situation worsened when Pienaar did not agree with the coach's game plans and then received yet another concussion – his fourth – during a game against New Zealand. When neither Markgraaff nor Luyt checked on Pienaar after his injury, he realised that trouble was brewing. His premonition was realised when Markgraaff accused him of faking his injury, and when the next squad was named, Pienaar's name was not on the list. Despite the support that poured in from around the country, Pienaar was never to play for the Springboks again, and after long discussions with his family, he finally decided to take up the challenge to leave the country to play for Saracens, a London-based club.

A WHOLE NEW BALL GAME

Playing in London was a steep learning curve for Pienaar. The weather, searching for a home and the conditions at Saracens were tough, yet he felt up to the challenge. The other foreign players at Saracens as well as the club owner, Nigel Wray, went out of their way to make him feel at home, but the rest of the team were not as welcoming, and at the first training session they let Pienaar know that they were not going to make things easy for him. The training facilities were terrible, with Pienaar injuring his shoulder by stumbling into a pothole at one training session. He went on to play the next match with his injury, but in trying to protect it, tore a hamstring. He immediately realised his error and was furious with himself. Pienaar knew that the divisions in the club meant that their win rate would not improve; at times the atmosphere at the club was so bad he considered returning to South Africa, but he knew that giving up was not in his DNA and resolved to stay on.

Nigel Wray also realised that something needed to be done and asked Pienaar to take over as captain of the side. With help from weekly telephone calls with Christie, Saracens went on to win the last three games of the season, bringing a new optimism to the players. During the off-season Pienaar and Wray revamped the club's facilities, reasoning that if they wanted the players to perform as professionals, then they needed a professional facility. With a budget of £30,000, which amounted to a once-off 10 per cent increase in costs on the annual bill, the players attitudes increased 120 per cent. When the team returned for the new season they were thrilled with their new facilities, but eyebrows were raised when Pienaar told them that going forward, losing was not an option. At that stage the club's longest winning streak had been five games. This meant overcoming an attitude that losing was inevitable – as evidenced by the club's bookkeeper who only budgeted for winning bonuses for 20 of the 30 matches to be played.

One of the first things the players did was to set team and individual goals; Pienaar was keen to instil a sense of determination and hunger among the team, which included some of them targeting a place in the England squad. During seminars Pienaar would emphasise the four Ds – desire, determination, dedication and discipline – which he had read about in a book given to him by Harry Viljoen. He also set up a disciplinary committee to ensure that everybody stayed on track. When it came to the training, Pienaar again took Christie's advice and for the first three weeks the players only worked on their fitness. This served to bond the team even further, as did the suggestion from Pienaar that during team talks, the players stand in a tight circle with their arms around each other.

Lessons were also learned during that time. One was that while he and Wray did not have a contract, Pienaar soon realised that not everyone sets such stock on their word. Getting signatures to paper became necessary when he twice reached a verbal agreement with another Springbok to join Saracens, only for him to join Northampton.

Being a player coach was not an easy task, but Pienaar felt he was up to the challenge. He continued to look to Christie for advice, so when the coach succumbed to the cancer he had been battling for over 17 years, it was a terrible blow. Pienaar had lost his mentor, friend, advisor and father figure.

Back in London, though, Saracens was growing in leaps and bounds. A marketing strategy was put in place to grow the club's brand, which resulted in numbers through the gates rising from 1 000 to 10 000 in just two seasons. The team began to win, and as a result their morale improved, leading to even more wins. Yet there were still some cracks in the relationships between the English and the foreign players, and these Pienaar was determined to overcome. One relationship in particular that needed to improve was that between Pienaar and the captain, Tony Diprose, but Pienaar decided that at that late stage in the season it was best to focus on the final games of the Tetley's Cup and the League.

When Saracens advanced to the final of the Tetley's Cup, part of Pienaar's strategy was for the team to dress in bespoke suits, believing that if they looked professional, they would feel professional. He also arranged for a video montage of the season to be played to music from the film, *Les Visiteurs*. Winning the Tetley's Cup was a massive boost for the club, and to top that off, five Saracens players were selected for the English squad.

The following year, Pienaar and the club's leadership made a crucial error by not assessing the squad. Pienaar now considers his behaviour to have been 'lazy and unprofessional'; he was so keen to foster the sense of unity that was growing that he did not make the difficult decisions and let people go. And after winning the first few matches, the wheels began to come off. Pienaar was not decisive about game plans, which caused unhappiness and insecurity in the team. He soon realised that he had taken his eye off the ball by not focusing enough on the players, their personalities and their needs. Being a Rugby World Cup year, Pienaar had also been busy with his role as an ITV commentator and an ambassador for Guinness and Visa – both Rugby World Cup sponsors.

Successive losses at Saracens saw Pienaar add to his load by taking over as captain from Diprose, and the team only just managed to secure a spot in the following season's European Cup.

Pienaar knew that things had to change. He had been struggling with injuries and was obsessing about his own poor form as well as the club's, and it was now time to make some tough decisions. One of the first hurdles to face was that the club owners decided to cap the players' total salary bill, which meant that they would be facing a 15 per cent reduction in their salaries. This was difficult for Pienaar, who was a player, captain and coach, as he had to think like a player as well as an administrator. This clash in values and priorities placed considerable strain on him, leading to his decision to focus only on being a player during the 1999/2000 season.

Unfortunately, the team wasted opportunities that season, seeing them lose games they should have won. The pressure on Pienaar was immense – most notably from himself. Disappointment in the European Cup as well as the league and club competitions, compounded by a shoulder injury, was the legacy of Pienaar's farewell season. One of the few positives to come out of that year was being awarded an honorary doctorate by the University of Hertfordshire. Although Pienaar retired as a player at the end of 2000 he stayed on with Saracens as their CEO and coach, but the following two seasons were not a success and Pienaar stepped down in 2002.

HOMEWARD BOUND

Upon returning to South Africa and setting up a home with Nerine and his two sons in Cape Town, Pienaar joined the FirstRand Group as Head of Sponsorships and Strategic Business Development. At a lunch with friends he also decided to start a charitable venture, creating the Make a Difference (MAD) Foundation. He was well-aware that if it were not for his scholarship he would in all likelihood not have seen the success he did, which is why the idea behind MAD was to provide needs-based bursaries and mentorship to academically gifted young South Africans. By 2014 the programme had spread across five provinces with over 3 000 children having received bursaries – one of whom went from the Cape Flats to Harvard where he graduated with an Engineering degree. Among others, MAD is supported by all seven World Cup winning captains. When Pienaar talks to the MAD recipients he gives them advice gleaned from Don Quixote that he has lived by: 'Ultimately all roads lead nowhere so pick one with a heart and follow it with a passion.'

In addition, he focused his passion for children by assisting Sargent Cancer Care for Children, as well as the Reach for a Dream Foundation, while remaining an ambassador for Visa and Guinness for the 2004 Rugby World Cup. He also continued commentating for ITV's rugby coverage, earning himself two nominations from the Royal Television Society for best sports pundit – the only amateur ever to be nominated.

In 2005, Pienaar was inducted into the International Rugby Hall of Fame, and in the same year was seconded by First National Bank to be CEO for the 2011 Rugby World Cup bid, which South Africa ultimately lost to New Zealand. He then became Provincial Chairman of FNB for the Western Cape, a position he held until 2009. Pienaar professes to having great respect for Michael Jordaan, who at that time was CEO of FNB. 'I admire his enthusiasm and vision. He knew that innovation could be a game changer in the financial services sector and was a visionary leader – just look at what the bank has done; to be named the most innovative bank in the world is incredible. Being part of that vision and following through and delivering on that was, for me, wonderful to watch and be part of in a small way.'

When he was approached by the Indian Premier League to lead their marketing campaign in South Africa, he decided to do this by branching out on his own and set up a branding and event company focusing on 'sportainment'. Advent Sport Entertainment and Media (ASEM) launched in 2009 and soon claimed FirstRand Bank as a shareholder. Now the people who inspire Pienaar are to be found in his team. 'When I left the corporate world to invest in the sports and entertainment industry, I couldn't know what a fantastic team we would end up building. We are doing something quite unique; one of our businesses that really excites me is based on the American college sport model, while IMG (similar to IMG College Sport) has us owning all the media rights for all sports at the universities in South Africa, which is groundbreaking. We have rolled out quite a number of initiatives and are seeing so much talent come through. Obviously there is a commercial aspect to it, but South African sport needs the high-performance platform post school, which is what we are providing.'

Leadership is something Pienaar has focused on over the years, and believes his own leadership style would be best described as energetic and 'can do' – he likes to lead from the front. In addition, he likes to 'do things that people say are impossible'. He believes that the biggest challenge facing leaders today is a lack of moral compass, which he says manifests as greed in the business world. In his time captaining and coaching, he came to believe that 'every leader needs a moral compass and a vision. If you are a leader there has got to be a road map of sorts that you aspire to, and with enthusiasm, brains and a strategy, you can bring people along to make the world a better place.'

Pienaar – inducted into the IRB Hall of Fame in 2011 – can now be found going for long walks or playing on the beach with Nerine and the boys, or congregating in the kitchen with extended family and friends. He is also inspired by his sons, who he says give him energy. He remains close to his parents and brothers, and has never stopped being grateful for the support they provided him over his lifetime. The family also go on leadership camps with the MAD team and ski whenever possible.

Looking back, Pienaar wonders at the luck he has had. 'I have been very fortunate when it comes to timing in life, sport and business. Part of that "luck" comes from the values instilled in me by my parents and by my determination to improve my situation through sport and education.' He is, however, also well-aware of his flaws – which he lists as being sensitive, vain, caring too much about what people think of him and overanalysing – but is not one to dwell on those, preferring to focus on his strengths. These he lists as being an activator, strategic, futuristic, and an achiever with a passion for his work and the people he works with. 'I like happy people,' he says. 'I like people who enjoy their circumstances and what they are doing. I think it is very much part of my DNA and my family, friends and colleagues can read me like a book when it comes to my energy levels and mood swings. It is important for me to motivate people, and I like to plan five years at a time, as this helps me to take on new challenges and risks.'

Pienaar is now entering a new five-year cycle, which he hopes will see ASEM opening offices in the UK and the East and the family spending an extended period in Paris. 'Part of my DNA is French Huguenot and I want to learn to speak the language, understand the culture – do the art, wine and food thing. I need to live there to understand it.' He also feels he is a work in progress, and would like to see himself being a better human being who can impact society – and in particular South Africans – in a positive way; to be 'a role model of sorts'.

As far as South Africa's next five years are concerned, Pienaar believes the country will continue to be at a crossroads until its leadership issues are sorted out. 'If we get the right leaders in the right positions, South Africa will thrive; if we don't we will have issues. We have so much potential. I think in five years' time we can still impress the world.'

And what would Pienaar like to have on his tombstone?

'6.'

FRANCOIS PIENAAR is best known as the World Cup winning captain of the 1995 Springbok team, but he is also an entrepreneur, a businessman and a family man. One of South Africa's most respected sporting heroes, he will forever be remembered for the role he played alongside Nelson Mandela in bringing the nation together following the Rugby World Cup final, inspiring South Africans across the world.

INVESTING IN THE THINGS THAT MATTER

MARIA RAMOS

HARD LANDINGS

Life in Portugal in the early 1960s was not easy. As one of the poorest countries in Europe, Portugal saw many citizens emigrating in search of better opportunities, which was further exacerbated when the country waged war against their African colonies in an attempt to retain them. One such citizen was a certain Mr Ramos, who with his wife decided to leave their home in Portugal in 1965 and take their three young daughters to South Africa in search of greener pastures. The oldest of these, Maria, was just six when they began their new life. 'My mother's parents moved to Mozambique to escape the oppression and the economic problems of the time. My grandfather was political and I think he felt unsafe in Portugal. My parents then decided to move so that my mother could be closer to her father and for economic reasons, but they chose to come to South Africa as they believed that the opportunities would be better here.'

As an immigrant, Maria Ramos remembers the hardship of moving to Vereeniging, where discrimination against foreigners was rife. 'There were strata and as a Portuguese immigrant in a town like Vereeniging, you weren't treated very well. I certainly had a sense growing up of a very divided society where discrimination crossed race and class, and people were very unforgiving of those of us who didn't speak the language. If you weren't a white Afrikaner and if you were working class, you were right at the bottom of the pile. My father was a bricklayer so we kept a very low profile.'

Times were tough in those early days; Ramos' mother did not work and there was an extra mouth to feed when a fourth daughter was born. To make matters worse, construction workers in those days had very few rights and her father would be laid off every December so that he did not have to be paid over the holiday period. 'I remember from a very young age growing up without a lot. We didn't even have money for a proper school uniform. But the one thing that had a very high premium placed on it in my house was education, education and education. And reading! To this day I have a very deep love for reading; it's my way of relaxing.'

The girls were taught that they should never be dependent on a man for anything, and instead of being defined by being in a relationship, they should rather be defined by being independent. They were also encouraged by their parents to learn English as quickly as possible, with the sisters speaking English to each other at home to accelerate their learning. Ramos' memories of school are not happy. 'School was something you "got through". Our teachers didn't help us because we were considered outsiders. We didn't speak English when we arrived so we had to find our own way. In fact most of my memories of school are of being in the library. I loved reading but it was also one of those places you could go to and have a space of your own.'

High school was a political awakening for Ramos, thanks in part to a maths teacher who was politically active. 'It was 1976 and the Soweto uprising took place – I remember when it began to dawn on me that Soweto had political meaning.'

Ramos matriculated the following year, but with no money for university she went to work for Barclays in Vereeniging. 'I started as a waste clerk, which basically involved collecting all the paperwork, such as deposit slips and cheques, from behind the tellers, and you punched them in and processed them. The processes then were very, very manual. There were no computers; there weren't even any fax machines. It's hard to believe really! After a month or two I was bored out of my mind. I thought there must be something more – I knew that this was not where I was going to get stuck for the rest of my life.'

FIGHTING THE GOOD FIGHT

Imagining that a bank would have some form of scholarship available, Ramos started reading the Personnel Manual and discovered that they had a great scholarship scheme where they sent employees to university to do a Commerce degree. Upon applying, she was horrified to discover that it was only open to men. A long battle ensued, with Ramos surmounting various obstacles in her attempt to get the rules changed; eventually she was told that if she sat the basic exams and passed, they would consider her. So she duly drove from Vereeniging to Johannesburg three nights a week after work – in the days before the highway was built – to evening classes held by the Institute of Bankers, and duly passed the exam in record time, earning herself a Banker's Diploma.

'I phoned them up and said, "Okay, well, I'm done now – what are you going to do about it?" They then told me that they had a new scholarship scheme, but I would have to study through Unisa, so I said that that wasn't the deal. Chris Ball took over at the bank around that time and that led to a big change as he was very progressive. He wanted to transform the bank in terms of its views on both gender and race. So between that and them thinking that they could not put up with me any more, after six years I finally started studying at Wits in 1984!'

In the interim, Ramos had left branch banking to work in the training department in Johannesburg, but she left her job to study full-time. Initially she wanted to study law but the scholarship would only allow her to study a BCom. 'Fortuitously, I ended up becoming really interested in Economics and, in fact, I did quite well and the bank decided that they would pay for me to do Economics Honours.'

A strong work ethic is something Ramos credits her parents for instilling in her from a young age. 'I always saw them work really, really hard and so I've always worked hard. I always say every time I talk to young people that it doesn't matter how you climb up that corporate ladder, what I've worked out is that you have more to learn, you have more responsibility and you work harder all the time. I'm lucky that I learned my values from my parents at a young age, but throughout my life I've been very fortunate to have been inspired by many people. I still cannot read the accounts of the people who got together to draft the Freedom Charter without getting a big lump in my throat. So many ordinary people across the length and breadth of this country got together, with a deep sense of humility, courage and belief in what was right, in a country that was so divided and where people were being so brutally discriminated against, and still put basic rights and basic dignity above everything else. It says something about what's good about South Africa and our people.'

The values Ramos cherishes most are integrity and respect for others. The traits of being determined as well as willing to fight for something she believes in have also been attributes that have stood her in good stead throughout her life. Humility is another important aspect; having been a waste clerk she learned not to judge until she knew what it felt like to 'walk in someone else's shoes'. Her motto in life is to do everything with passion and commitment; 'I just don't think you can do things you don't believe in and you're not passionate about.'

It was during her years at Wits that Ramos became involved in politics, returning to campus to teach full-time in 1991 while working covertly for the ANC in their Department of Economic Planning. Teaching was a role that Ramos relished. 'I enjoyed the intellectual challenge as well as the research and the stimulation. It was great to be in a classroom with students and to be challenged intellectually.'

The dawning of a new dispensation in South Africa saw her relocate to London to gain more experience, which she gained while studying for her Masters in Economics at the London School of Economics. (She was later to receive honorary doctorates from Stellenbosch University and the University of the Free State.)

This led to her being selected for the position of Director-General of Finance in Nelson Mandela's government in 1996, a position she held until 2003. Working with Mandela made a striking impression on Ramos. 'Everybody talks about being inspired by Madiba, but over the many years that I got to know him, I mean you couldn't be in his presence and not be inspired by him. He had unbelievable humility and generosity and love. Working with him taught me to stay grounded.'

Ramos' tenure as DG of Finance saw her working with the then Finance Minister, Trevor Manuel, to create a fit-for-purpose department. This included introducing new systems, structures and capabilities to ensure that the country's finances were managed efficiently and transparently. One of the priorities was to reduce the country's massive debt burden – experience she would be glad of when she took on the role as CEO of Transnet in 2004.

A loss-making parastatal, Transnet had over 80 000 employees and was a far cry from what Ramos was used to, but her experience at the Treasury meant that she was able to focus on balancing the books. She began by selling off all peripheral businesses, but this was met with fierce resistance from employee unions. Ongoing strikes and dissent led to some of her plans being thwarted, but sufficient progress was made to allow the company to switch from a turnaround strategy to a growth strategy in 2008. That year was not only a successful one for Ramos professionally, but also personally as she married her long-time partner, Trevor Manuel.

Looking back on her time at Transnet, Ramos remembers it as an exciting place to work, given the challenges that she faced. 'It was certainly far out of my technical comfort zone; it was a highly industrial job. It made me realise that if I had been exposed to different things at school, I probably would have chosen Engineering. Being an analytical person, that aspect of the job really spoke to me.'

COMING FULL CIRCLE

In 2009, Ramos found herself back at Barclays, although this time it was not as a waste clerk, but as the CEO of Absa Bank. At the time of her joining the bank, the world was in a financial mess and Ramos had a mountain to climb.

'I remember thinking when I joined Absa that there was a reason that people were angry with banks, and we were going to have to work really, really hard to change people's perceptions of what banks are about.' Coming into the top job at Absa, Ramos knew that although the South African financial system had been protected from the worst of the recession, some pain was going to be felt locally. 'We didn't feel the same strain because the local banking sector was better capitalised and much more regulated than internationally; we didn't have the same toxic assets on our balance sheets and, to a certain extent, the economy was protected by some of the exchange controls in place. As a public official, I had lived through a couple of crises on the other side, and I knew that it was going to take some time to get through this one. I remember an analyst asking me just after I'd joined how long I thought it was going to take for the global economy to recover. When I told him five to seven years he looked at me as if I'd completely lost my mind!

'Now I think it's going to take even longer because financial crises of that depth have significant structural and economic consequences, and history tells us that as well. It was always going to be difficult and I was very conscious of the fact that, irrespective of what I thought needed to change – and there were lots of things, it wasn't always going to be a new broom sweeps clean. It never really is in any case like that. But I certainly couldn't be adventurous in the middle of a crisis. It was always going to be measured and we were always going to have to think about things more carefully and in a deliberate and focused way. In a way, that engendered sustainability and confidence and kept everybody on the same page.'

Some of the people Ramos admires in her field and who she believes are good role models when it comes to finance and economics include Gill Marcus and Pravin Gordhan, both of whom also came on board at a difficult time. An international role model is Ben Bernanke, due to his management of the Federal Reserve Bank in difficult circumstances. 'He had a very difficult task in trying to keep not just the US, but also the global economy from slipping into a global depression, rather than just a massive, deep recession.' If she could host a dinner party with the sky as her guest list limit, Ramos has an eclectic group of people she would invite. 'One would definitely be John Maynard Keynes. There hasn't been another economist who has had the same kind of theoretical and policy impact that he has. We keep going back to solutions that he pulled together at the time.' Another guest would be Amartya Sen, the Nobel Prize winner in Economics, as well as Ben Bernanke and the economists, Stan Fischer and Janet Yellen. Moving away from economics, Ramos would also like to have met the late Steve Jobs, who she thinks 'put together some of the most unbelievable solutions and innovations and built an incredible company'.

Fortunately the dinner conversation would not be all business, however. Ramos remembers, while living in London, going on a trip to Switzerland with Kader Asmal and catching a taxi into town to listen to Etta James and Miles Davis who were playing at the Montreux Jazz Festival. 'We had to walk back to the hotel because there were no taxis around, but it was the most incredible evening. I would love to invite Etta James and Miles Davis to dinner!'

An issue that has concerned Ramos since her days of battling discrimination as a young clerk at Barclays is the role of women in finance. 'I wish I could say categorically that women don't still face challenges in financial services, but I've seen it in both the private and public sector and it's been particularly hard in banking.'

This is something that frustrates her, a firm believer in equality all round. 'It would be so much easier if people just looked at the results. Are they there or not? It's more than annoying – it's actually ridiculous when the first thing out of somebody's mouth is, "Oh well, what do you expect when a woman is running the organisation?" A correlation is made between results and gender. It's a little silly and, frankly, I think immature. It's been a learning curve for me.' She feels an 'enormous sense of responsibility' at the idea of being an icon for women, but it is a responsibility she takes seriously.

Ramos sometimes wonders if she has got to the age where she should be thinking about slowing down, but is also aware that her personality is such that she needs to be on the go. 'I honestly don't know what I'm going to be doing next; I just know that there's a lot more to do be done. We've just done this phenomenal transaction across Africa that is great, and we've got to consolidate this and deliver from here. Ten years from now – who knows?'

She also makes time for charity, explaining that while it's easy to give financially, it's as important to set aside time to give back. 'It's about giving your time and being available. We've got a lot of citizenship work going on at the bank; we encourage everyone to be involved in their personal capacity as well as through work.'

Despite sometimes feeling despair about the country, she generally remains optimistic about the future. 'It feels like a lot longer than 24 years since Madiba was released from jail, but it's not a long time if you think about where we've come from. We're fortunate to have a National Development Plan that gives us a long-term plan for where we want to go. I'm also optimistic about the fact that South Africans can argue and have massive public debates, sometimes pulling each other apart, but we pull back from the brink and agree that there's more to this country than petty differences. I think we'll make the right decisions and the right investments in the things that matter, like our education system and our health system. And we have a business sector that is committed and wants to be here.

'We also have a solid team that knows what it's talking about in the Treasury and the Central Bank and we still have a pretty sound fiscal position. I believe that the overwhelming majority of people in this country want to succeed. There is still too much crime, so we need to keep officials on their toes about what needs to be done. There should not be an excuse for bad service. We need a proper return on the investment we're making into education or water, and we need a much more active citizenry to ensure we get those returns. I'm disturbed that, 24 years on, people feel they need to get out onto the streets and riot in order to have their voices heard. Young people around the world feel disenfranchised.'

Ramos believes that both public- and private-sector leaders face a challenge when it comes to staying current. 'This is a very fast-changing world; the idea that you plan at regular intervals is a thing of the long-distant past. You have to be agile and resilient. It's also about being in touch and knowing what your strengths are, and keeping people with you as you move. Being able to influence people rather than command and control is important. I think that the biggest thing leaders need to avoid is the myth that you yourself alone are in control, because if you believe that then you've already lost the plot. That's not how you lead; you have to lead by influencing and understanding that you've got a team around you and that you're listening to them. It's easy to get out of touch.'

Given her schedule, it's fortunate that Ramos needs very little sleep. She is also not the type of person to lie awake at night 'sweating the small stuff'. 'I'm really a big-picture kind of person. I don't sit around and think, "Well, I should have done this two years ago." Life doesn't work like that; it's too short to worry about things you can't change and there are very few things you can change … you've got to look at things and work out what you need to do – get through it, understand it really well and get on and do it and move onto the next thing. And when things go wrong, you have to go back sometimes and ask yourself, "Okay, what did we get right, what did we get wrong, what are the lessons we can learn?" and then move on. If you're constantly trying to go back you can get caught up in things you haven't got right in the past. I think it becomes counterproductive. I make mistakes all the time – it's human. I am too hard on myself and on others sometimes, though.'

What really energises her is the 'excitement of doing things. I feel deeply privileged that I've got a great job and opportunities, I'm in a great relationship and I've got a wonderful family. I'm also privileged enough to live in a great place and in a great country, and I feel a deep sense of commitment to what we do here. There are times when I feel a deep sense of frustration as well, but there's an opportunity for me to come in and do things – to work with great people and to learn from them. Just getting up and knowing that you're going to work with some phenomenally smart people – they're all smarter than I am! – and I'm going to learn something from them. And maybe drive them crazy! I can't imagine anything more disturbing than thinking you've got nothing more to learn.'

One thing that Ramos is sure of is where her allegiance lies when it comes to home. 'I think of myself as being South African and being rooted here. I can't imagine at this point doing something else somewhere else, but if I did this would still be where I would come home to; this is where my soul is.'

When it comes to the end, Ramos is not worried about a tombstone. 'You know, you live and that's it; I'm hoping I'll get cremated! In fact, I'm going to put that in my will!'

MARIA RAMOS arrived in South Africa from Portugal at the age of six, not speaking a word of English or Afrikaans. Her meteoric rise has been in large part due to the fortitude and determination she has shown throughout her life. Starting her career as a waste clerk at Barclays Bank in Vereeniging, Ramos has come full circle and is now the CEO of Barclays Africa. Ramos was also involved in the anti-apartheid struggle and played a key role as Director General of the National Treasury in building a high-performance team and fit-for-purpose department. As CEO of Transnet she was instrumental in turning around the parastatal's fortunes.

SPIRIT OF YOUTH

NIZENANDE MACHI

The idea of speaking on behalf of South Africa's youth is overwhelming, but it is also an honour that requires bold action. When I look through history, men and women who have spoken on behalf of many bravely executed their causes despite great trials. Anthony Benezet, a French-born American who fought for the abolition of slavery during the 1700s, witnessed a number of his family members being hanged for his 'radical' beliefs. During the 1800s, Florence Nightingale promoted nursing as a respectable profession for women in a time when only marriage and childbearing was seen as a fitting vocation for upper-class women. The 1900s boasted people such as Martin Luther King Jr, Giovanni Falcone, Mahatma Gandhi and Nelson Mandela, among many others, who fought against oppression, often resulting in persecution and death. Each of these displayed great resilience in using the voices entrusted to them to the benefit of the people they represented.

With that said, I write these words in full knowledge of the responsibility I have, and have been given, to detail the excitements, thoughts, doubts and anxieties of young South Africans today. I tell you not only so that you are aware of what our deepest passions and fears are, but also to bear testament to the responsibility I have taken to help advance my peers towards a common future: that of an empowered, visionary and inspired youth.

My journey of youth leadership began in 2007, my twelfth grade of high school, when I was elected to participate in the Gordon Institute of Business Science's (GIBS) Spirit of Youth Programme. Spirit of Youth is a platform for Grade 11 and 12 learners to define and voice their vision for South Africa. Through workshops, historical and cultural immersions, and facilitated dialogue, the programme challenges young leaders to critically engage around the relevant social, political and economic issues that may better define and create a South Africa in which we would like to live.

I learned a lot during my time as a Spirit of Youth participant. I learned about my country and its turbulent history; I met and listened to the stories of people who were making great strides in achieving their goals and personal successes; and I learned that leadership is not for the chosen few who have the courage to advance their own causes, but that it is about creating an enabling environment for others to flourish. But most importantly, Spirit of Youth taught me about myself. It helped me to develop a better, more contextual narrative about what my desires for South Africa are. I was challenged to see myself honestly, and lay bare some of the egocentric motives behind my calling myself a young leader. I was taught that to be a young leader I had to be in service to my peers. Spirit of Youth showed me that today was the best day to actuate the South Africa in which I would like to live, and I was inspired to do so.

One story I remember quite clearly from my time as a Spirit of Youth delegate was that of Nonhlanhla Noni Gasa. At one of the sessions, Noni Gasa gave a talk about overcoming your fears to achieve personal success. She started the story of her life by telling us how she was bullied in school because she was a Zulu girl with freckles. She had been the butt of many jokes because she looked too 'different' to the rest of her black peers. The bullying escalated when her friends discovered that she wanted to be a model. 'How can you be a model with a dirty face?' was an example she gave of some of the criticism she heard in response to her dream.

Of course, we know what the end of her story is, because Noni Gasa has gone on to become an award-winning style icon. She ranks among South Africa's most recognisable TV personalities, working as a runway model and fashion journalist, even launching her own clothing range in 2006. One thing that struck me the day Noni Gasa gave her presentation was her honesty about her poor self-esteem and insecurities borne from years of bullying. She understood that her poor self-image was the greatest challenge to overcome if she was to realise her dream of becoming a media personality. At the time she spoke to us she had already made a name for herself in the fashion industry, so it was overwhelming to hear her talk about such a personal experience.

I have never forgotten her story, because it was not elaborate; it was personal, it was true and it was hers. What Noni Gasa showed us that day is that leadership journeys, more often than not, will entail us overcoming our insecurities and framing our 'shortcomings' so that we can use them to fulfil our dreams. Noni Gasa has become famous *because* of her freckles, not despite them; she used them as a tool to challenge modelling norms and standards, and redefined beauty in the industry.

DRAWING INSPIRATION

From the time I became a Spirit of Youth delegate to my role today as one of its facilitators, the things that inspire us young people have not changed. In a South Africa plagued by poverty, high youth unemployment and widespread hopelessness, we draw inspiration from hearing the stories of people who have beaten the odds and realised their dreams. The stories of Nelson Mandela and Steve Biko, while ultimately tales of triumph and hope over brutality and despair, are also intimidating and at times demoralising. What they did can seem outside of our reach – so big to attain that they immobilise us into inaction. So we find the story of the layman inspiring. It tells me that even I, just an ordinary South African girl, must challenge myself to work towards a future I envision; I must overcome my impossible. The reason the success stories of people resonate with young people today is that they light a flame of hope in our hearts and create a spirit of agency. They embed the understanding that change begins with you; it's a process that moves from the inside out.

South Africa's youth is also inspired by the idea of creating a common vision for our country. Because we bear the brunt of a high unemployment rate and other such 'afflictions', we realise that we know our plight better than anybody else does, so we're encouraged to collaborate in solving our challenges. Youth-led organisations and movements inspire us to celebrate young people's achievements, and spur others on to do the same in their own fields of interest. As young people, we inspire one another!

YOUNG, GIFTED AND FREE

Young South Africans are excited and excitable! The thing that motivates us the most is the shift in paradigm that is taking place the world over, because it is finally accommodating our thinking. The world is moving away from a transactional and needs-focused model, towards one of relationships and an outcomes-based focus; it's about caring less about jobs and more about vocations. The youth lives in a world of co-creation, co-initiation and co-evolution. The words 'innovate' and 'collaborate' are our daily mantras, and it seems as if the generations older than ours are finally responding to our call. This is exciting because it means there are more opportunities for us to seize which are better aligned to our gifts and interests.

We are excited that the country is fostering and supporting entrepreneurship, as it makes it easier for us to challenge our parents' thinking of a 'stable income in the short term' with 'financial independence in the long term' as a response. Having entrepreneurship at the forefront of the national dialogue has given us the freedom to start businesses as conduits for our passions. We have the advantage of being able to access a large repertoire of entrepreneurs, both locally and internationally, who have shown resilience and dedication even in the face of failure. So we are not very afraid of failing, rather we're willing to embrace it if it is part and parcel of realising our dreams for the future. We're starting businesses, even in the townships, because we have 'the-first-world-is-our-saviour' fatigue. We're tired of applying external solutions to internal problems. As agents of change in our own societies, we believe that because we understand the context of our challenges well, we are fully equipped to solve them.

We as South Africa's youth are also excited about our futures. We are thrilled that more programmes are geared towards developing us to take over the reins from our current leaders in the future. We're excited that we're being groomed to lead our nation tomorrow by leading each other today. Because we believe that our future began yesterday, on the day that we decided to make a change in our societies, we are in fact running late. So to try to catch up, we hustle, we move, we push forward; working towards a common vision for our nation. This is what gets us up in the morning, and keeps us going throughout the day.

WHEN DOUBTS CREEP IN

Because there is a lot that South Africa's youth is excited about, a number of anxieties are always at play within our enthusiasm. As radicals and misfits – maybe even rebels – one thing that scares us is having to one day pack away our dreams and go downstream. In a nation filled with possibility, to have to settle into a humdrum life and be bogged down by repetitive daily challenges would not be a life for us. We have witnessed our parents working long, tiring hours to earn a living, often in jobs they did not enjoy. Although we did and still do appreciate the labour and heart that went into their sacrifice for their families, we saw the difficulty it caused our mothers and fathers. We each made a silent vow never to go through it in our own lives. For this reason, to not follow the desires of our hearts would feel like we were giving up on our dreams for a better future to revert to the past we came from.

This is not to say that young South Africans are not anxious about venturing into the unknown. We have big visions and even greater plans, but we do not act on these without fear. We have heard many success stories from people who have paved the way before us, but we understand that there is no guarantee that our journeys will be exactly like theirs. There is no blueprint that we can follow to ensure a more secure future; we are fearful of not knowing what the future holds. We hold steadfast to the belief that our forging a different path and leaving a new trail for those to come is what we need to do in mentorship to the next generation, but this path is accompanied by uncertainty and we don't like uncertainty. It makes us unsure and doubtful. We are fearful of what we cannot perceive, and trying to decipher it has the potential to distract us from our goals. 'Do not be distracted by the distraction' is a message my mentor used to drum into my head and heart whilst I was under his tutelage, but as a person who wants to secure everything, it has been a difficult concept to internalise. And I know my struggle resonates with many of my peers.

Something that makes young people most anxious is humility. We spend every day of our lives set apart in our various contexts, because we have dreams different to the generations before us; dreams that extend beyond the walls of our backyards and the borders of our country. But because we ourselves are works in progress as we pursue our various causes, we often need guidance from those who have gone before us. All this does is lay bare our need to be humble, and acknowledge that there is so much we do not know and have yet to learn. It is a difficult thing for us to work towards where we want to be while being fully aware of where we are … and are not. To bridge this gap often requires re-engagement and to move forward humbly. So we learn, albeit begrudgingly, to progress through the discomfort of humility.

BUT THE FUTURE IS OURS

The future that South Africa's youth envisions is one free of poverty, with bountiful resources and ample employment. We envision a nation where every child receives a level of education that enables him or her to earn a dignified living. We dream of a world where no child below the age of 21, who is the head of her household, is not in receipt of government support; a world where the opportunities in the marketplace are readily taken advantage of by active jobseekers. We envision a nation completely freed from the mental chains of racial prejudices; a place where we filter peer-to-peer engagements first according to interest, then ability, and hopefully never on race. We dream of a South Africa that continuously develops its youth; not only their self-actualisation, but also as part of a leadership succession plan.

With this vision in mind, we understand our various roles in the futures that we are trying to build. We understand that not all of us will be leaders of the nation. Some will be doctors, others nurses, some engineers and others teachers, but we are many parts of the one body of South Africa. We know that the functioning of each part is crucial to the performance of the whole.

One thing that makes me feel even more secure in the future I am trying to build is having a few people to inspire me. The story of Noni Gasa helped me decide from whom I should draw inspiration, and made me build certain criteria around who I should consider my role models to be. I don't choose role models because they are famous or well-known, I measure them against their own criteria: what did the person in question say he/she wanted to achieve, what did he/she do to achieve it, and how did he/she empower others to realise their own dreams.

One person I respect and admire most is Strive Masiyiwa, the founder and Chairman of Econet Wireless, a global telecommunications group. Mr Masiyiwa gained prominence when he fought a five-year constitutional legal battle in Zimbabwe, the ruling of which led to the removal of the state's monopoly in telecommunications and opened the African telecommunications sector to private capital. Mr Masiyiwa is now a prominent global business leader, having grown Econet Wireless into a global telecommunications group.

At the beginning of his entrepreneurial endeavours, Mr Masiyiwa identified a gap in the telecommunications market. He realised that the state holding a monopoly in this sector made it inaccessible to the masses because the state had control over both prices and distribution, which made life difficult for the communities at large. He identified that he wanted to shift this imbalance of power and make telecommunications accessible to many. The five-year legal battle drained him not only of his financial resources, but also put strain on his personal life and family as they were exposed to threats and intimidation. Yet he continued to fight for his cause even in the face of immense challenges. And through it all, he remained true to himself. He is a pious man, with his values rooted deeply in his faith, and like Noni Gasa and her freckles, he has managed to build his business identity around his faith, which the world has come to accept and admire. Apart from being a mentor, he sits on the boards of organisations that focus on poverty alleviation and education, enabling more Africans to advance past their dreadful circumstances and hope for a better future.

I also have a deep admiration for former President Thabo Mbeki. I have a secret desire to one day have an eight-hour tea date with him, just so I can gather as much information as he is willing to give me about African politics, leadership in Africa and his personal experiences! I believe he has a wealth of knowledge and wisdom, and would love to know how he developed such a pragmatic understanding of what South Africa and Africa at large needs. Stepping into Nelson Mandela's shoes must have been a great honour, but it came with immense national pressure and criticism, and I would like to know how he kept his eye on the prize of leading a nation with such a turbulent history, towards the goal of national prosperity. I can almost imagine such a date; I hope I would be awarded a qualification of sorts after it!

AN OPEN LETTER TO OUR INFLUENCERS

There are many current South African leaders in business, politics and the social sector who inspire me; who encourage me to continue on my journey towards actuating the South Africa in which I would like to live. So I, on behalf of the nation's youth, have a message to give them:

Dear South African Leaders

I am a young South African leader, who aspires to one day achieve the many great things that you have achieved in your lifetime. You have shown me that it is not impossible to pursue the desires of my heart, even if it may not be without struggle. Your stories have shown me that I have the capacity to achieve, and because of this, I must challenge myself to do so.

But there is something that's been on my heart that I want to alert you to. Although your story of success and accomplishment is wonderful, not enough of us have heard it. You are somewhat inaccessible, maybe even invisible. When I want to ask you a few more questions about your journey, or refer my peers to your story, I don't exactly know where to find you. Please try to be a little more within reach, not just to a chosen few, but to those of us from under-resourced communities where your story may be our only encouragement to get up in the morning.

Apart from your visibility, we request your sincerity. There are a number of leaders, the world over, whose message is concerned less with integrity, and more with public relations and marketing. This fatigues us; being used as pawns in a strategy towards accumulating fame and fortune. If there is anything you want us to know, or participate in, say or do it genuinely, with few affectations and great honesty. Be earnest in your message to us and be clear about the lesson you would like to teach us. Whether it is a message about perseverance, purpose, entrepreneurship or career planning, make sure that it is relevant and applicable to us. Learn about our contexts and circumstances before wanting to teach us, because then we will be better able to receive it in the authentic manner in which it was given. If you do this, you will also enrich our morality and forge responsible value systems.

When it comes to teaching, please be patient with us. I know, embarrassingly so, that your apprehension about us young people is that we have become 'know-it-alls' who do not take well to teaching, criticism and advice. This isn't true. Rather, advice makes us feel vulnerable and exposed to our shortcomings. We didn't grow up thinking that there was much wrong with us, because our parents told us that we could do anything we put our minds to. Unfortunately we are now realising, rather slowly, that what they said wasn't completely true. Some things we will need to be taught by those more knowledgeable than we are, so this is quite an adjustment. Guide us through our arrogance and enlighten us about where our values should lie. One day you will need to hand over your power to our generation and it will be no good to any of us if we cannot administer this power well on behalf of future generations. So teach us gently, with a constant reminder of the goal that we are working towards.

I want and need you to be my role model. Please be the example against which I model my cause and journey. Show yourself to be a candidate worthy of my sincere admiration and praise, and encourage me, albeit unknown to you, to be a responsible leader, who has a clear identity and awareness of myself; who will focus on empowering myself and others, regardless of my field of interest. Most importantly, press on towards your goal. I, along with many other young South Africans, am watching and following closely behind you, ready to have the baton passed on. We have your big shoes to fill, but if you teach and show us well, we will take this nation to greater heights for the next generation.

Yours sincerely,

NIZENANDE MACHI is the South Africa Programme Manager for Emzingo Group LLC, a people development and community building organisation. As a young woman passionate about the development of South African youth, she has committed her life to addressing the challenges that plague young people, by reinforcing the value of education as a powerful tool to overcome poverty. Her dream is to build low-fee paying charter schools that encourage non-conventional learning practices.

SELECT REFERENCES

Bloomberg Businessweek. (23 June 2014). *Executive Profile: Brian Molefe.* Retrieved from http://investing.businessweek.com/research/stocks/private/person.asp?personId=30439482 (accessed on 4 August 2014).

Imaralu, D. (29 September 2013). Africa's Most Innovative Banker – FNB CEO, Michael Jordaan. *Ventures Africa.* Retrieved from http://www.ventures-africa.com/2013/09/mr-innovator-fnb-ceo-michael-jordaan/ (accessed on 4 August 2014).

Luhabe, W. (2002). *Defining Moments.* Pietermaritzburg: University of Natal Press.

Makura, M. (2010). *South Africa's Greatest Entrepreneurs.* Johannesburg: MME Media.

Mashaba, H. (2012). *Black Like You.* Johannesburg: MME Media.

Pienaar, F. (1999). *Rainbow Warrior.* London: CollinsWillow.

Solsten, E. (Ed.). (1993). *Portugal: A Country Study.* Retrieved from http://countrystudies.us/portugal/ (accessed on 24 April 2014).

Thomas White International. (April 2011). *Emerging Leaders: Maria Ramos, CEO, ABSA Bank.* Retrieved from http://www.thomaswhite.com/global-perspectives/maria-ramos-ceo-absa-bank/ (accessed on 4 August 2014).

ABOUT THE AUTHOR

After having spent two decades working in the communications arena both locally and globally, **Jennifer Lindsey-Renton** broke away from corporate life to focus on her passion for writing. A visit to the Maboneng precinct in Johannesburg planted the seed for *Inspired*, at which time she decided to uncover some of the stories of South Africans who have overcome incredible odds to make a real impact on this country and its people.

To Finn, Scout and Jamie

You inspire me every day. Never stop living, loving, sharing, hugging, working, playing, laughing, dreaming, dancing and singing.

Love always,
Mum

ABOUT THE GORDON INSTITUTE OF BUSINESS SCIENCE

Founded in 2000, the University of Pretoria's Gordon Institute of Business Science (GIBS) is an internationally accredited business school, based in Johannesburg, South Africa's economic hub. As the business school for business, we focus on general management in dynamic markets to significantly improve individual and organisational performance, primarily in the South African environment, through the provision of high quality business and management education. In May 2014 the annual UK *Financial Times* Executive Education rankings, a global benchmark for providers of executive education, once again ranked GIBS as the top South African and African business school. This is the eleventh year running that GIBS has been ranked among the top business schools worldwide. In October 2013 the GIBS MBA was ranked among the top 100 business schools globally in the prestigious *Financial Times* Executive MBA Rankings. Ranked in 70th position, GIBS is the only business school in Africa to appear in this ranking.

GIBS is accredited by the Association of MBAs (AMBA), the Council on Higher Education (CHE) and is a member of the South African Business Schools Association (SABSA), the Association of African Business Schools (AABS) and the European Academy of Business in Society (EABIS).